LEO on the Cheap
Methods for Achieving Drastic Reductions in Space Launch Costs

John R. London III
Lt Col, USAF

ARI Command-Sponsored Research Fellow
Air Force Materiel Command

Books for Business
New York-Hong Kong

LEO on the Cheap:
Methods for Achieving Drastic Reductions in Space
Launch Cost

by
John R. London III

ISBN: 0-89499-134-5

Copyright © 2002 by Books for Business

Reprinted from the 1994 edition

Books for Business
New York - Hong Kong
http://www.BusinessBooksInternational.com

Disclaimer

This publication was produced in the Department of Defense school environment in the interest of academic freedom and the advancement of national defense-related concepts. The views expressed in this publication are those of the author and do not reflect the official policy or position of the Department of Defense or the United States government.

This publication has been reviewed by security and policy review authorities and is cleared for public release.

Contents

Illustrations

Photographs

Foreword

Military commanders have known for centuries the critical importance of transportation to success in battle. The introduction of the railroad helped make the American Civil War one of the first "modern" wars. Sealift was fundamental to the operation and sustainment of US forces during World War II. And only massive and highly capable airlift and sealift assets allowed the deployment of hundreds of thousands of US troops and their equipment to the sands of Saudi Arabia over a few short months in the fall of 1990.

Military spacelift, although most closely akin to military air transportation, does not begin to approach existing airlift systems from the standpoint of efficiency, responsiveness, or cost-effectiveness. The high cost of space launch, in particular, has been a chronic problem that engineers have been seeking solutions to for decades with little success. As we move further into the fiscally-constrained post–cold war era, the inexpensive deployment and replenishment of force-multiplying space systems will become increasingly important.

Colonel London has developed an extensive and well-documented amount of information on the original causes of high launch costs, the specifics of current costs, and the reasons that these costs continue to be perpetuated. He offers recommendations that buck the popular trend of advanced technology solutions, and he describes how a significant reduction in launch costs would have a broad positive impact on a variety of space systems and activities. His research is thorough and his command of the subject is impressive. I commend Colonel London's report to the reader as a roadmap through an esoteric subject that is useful and more topical than ever as spending for defense steadily diminishes. This work is worthy of serious consideration.

JOHN M. SPRATT, JR.
Congressman Spratt is a senior member
of the House Armed Services Committee
and represents the 5th District of
South Carolina

About the Author

Lt Col John R. London III

Lt Col John R. London III completed this study as an Air Force Materiel Command 1992–93 command-sponsored research fellow at the Airpower Research Institute, Center for Aerospace Doctrine, Research, and Education, Maxwell Air Force Base, Alabama. In 1975 Colonel London graduated from Clemson University and was commissioned through the Air Force Reserve Officer Training Corps program. He entered active duty in 1976 and was initially stationed at the Oklahoma City Air Logistics Center, Tinker Air Force Base, Oklahoma. While at Tinker, Colonel London served as the Directorate of Materiel Management's Nondestructive Inspection Program Manager.

After attending Squadron Officer School in 1980, Colonel London was assigned to the 6555th Aerospace Test Group, Cape Canaveral Air Force Station, Florida. He initially was detailed to the Kennedy Space Center, working for NASA's Space Shuttle vehicle operations and vehicle engineering organizations. Later, he worked as the launch operations manager for the NAVSTAR Global Positioning System at Cape Canaveral Air Force Station. He earned a Master of Science degree from Florida Institute of Technology in 1983. In 1984 Colonel London was assigned to the Secretary of the Air Force Special Projects Office.

Colonel London was a member of the 1989–90 class of the Air Command and Staff College (ACSC) at Maxwell Air Force Base. After ACSC, he was stationed at Los Angeles Air Force Base, California, working at Space Systems Division (SSD). While at SSD, he was the systems integration and operations division chief for the Starlab program, a Shuttle-borne laser experiment for the Strategic Defense Initiative Organization (SDIO). He subsequently became the concepts and analysis division chief for the Brilliant Eyes program, an SDIO-sponsored, space-based sensor system for tracking ballistic missile warheads.

After the one-year command-sponsored research effort at Maxwell, Colonel London was assigned to the Pentagon in 1993 to work for the Ballistic Missile Defense Organization. He, his wife Joyce, and their children Betsy and Joshua, live in Herndon, Virginia.

xvii

Preface

While assigned to the Kennedy Space Center as a young captain in the early 1980s, I worked a variety of Space Shuttle launch processing jobs as this revolutionary reusable vehicle began its operational life. I also had the chance to serve at Cape Canaveral Air Force Station as a payload integration engineer for satellites that were flying on Titan 34D, Atlas Centaur, and Delta launch vehicles. Consequently, I became familiar with all of the United States' large launch vehicles and their ground processing requirements. Although these boosters were highly capable machines that would set any engineer's pulse to racing, it became increasingly evident to me that cost-effectiveness was not their long suit. In many cases, it seemed that managers chose the most complicated and costly design solutions imaginable to provide new capabilities or solve problems. Inspired by a handful of "radical" thinkers who worked at the eastern launch site in those days, I began to develop a belief that design simplicity (and not increasingly elegant applications of advanced technology) was the key to lowering launch costs.

As I left my Florida assignment and progressed through a string of space-related jobs, my convictions deepened about the need for inexpensive boosters and the methods to develop them. I volunteered for this research fellowship because I felt it represented an outstanding opportunity for me to describe some practical methods for dramatically reducing space launch costs. Over the years, I had collected a wealth of evidence that would help to substantiate my position. When Air Force Systems Command initially selected me to perform this research project, I was excited that I would be able to finally put into writing what I had been saying for so long.

The subject of space launch is diverse and highly dynamic. I have sought to include an appropriate amount of current information so that the proposals offered by this study could be considered in the proper context, recognizing that some of this information will become dated very quickly. However, the basic principles that are set forth in the study should be applicable for many years to come.

It is my hope that the ideas and information contained in this report will stimulate some of the people at the center of the debate on future launch vehicles to consider simple solutions as a complement or alternative to technological leaps or business-as-usual approaches. The fundamentals of these ideas are not new, but for a variety of reasons they have never been seriously applied to the problem of reducing the high price of launch. The extent of our ability as a nation to economically expand our military, civil, and commercial exploitation of space is directly dependent on the amount we are able to shrink launch costs.

The concepts described in the following pages could go a long way toward achieving the drastic reductions in the cost of space access that are necessary to bring about a dramatic expansion in US space activities.

JOHN R. LONDON III, Lt Col, USAF
Research Fellow
Airpower Research Institute

Acknowledgments

My year at Maxwell has been extremely rewarding, and I have thoroughly enjoyed immersing myself in this issue for such an extended period. I would like to recognize the many people who have contributed to the content and development of this study. I could not have accomplished this effort without their help.

I would first like to thank Bob Truax, Arthur Schnitt, Jerry Elverum, and Paul Dergarabedian. Over a period of many years, these four individuals have faithfully and consistently supported the idea that simple, low-cost, launch vehicles are practical and achievable. They have been an inspiration to me, and have provided invaluable guidance, insight, and information.

In addition to the individuals mentioned above, a number of other people have given of their time to review drafts of this study and provide valuable comments and inputs. These individuals are: Jim French, Col Chuck Banta, Maj Lee Carrick, Jim Wertz, Bob Conger, Pete Wilhelm, Wilson Lundy, Cargill Hall, Dave Crisalli, Ken Mason, and B. J. Humphreys.

Many people have provided notable assistance and inputs that have contributed significantly to the content of this study. They are: Denny Plunkett, Ron Lash, Elliott Katz, Chet Whitehair, Jim Whittier, Heather Williams, Barry Moss, Dom Scrooc, Mike Asato, Joe Dodd, George James, Maj Jess Sponable, Bob Wong, Stephen Rast, Frank Stoddard, Jack Hardgrove, Larry Mattson, Montye Male, Susan Brough, Rick Fleeter, Gary Hudson, Capt Jim Ramsey, Bill Claybaugh, Jack Chapman, Shannon Hammonds, Ed Keith, Dave Harris, Charliene McGlothin, George Dosa, George Morgan, Richard Ryan, Lt Col Jack Robbins, Lt Col Jay Melin, Capt Ron Marx, Andrejs Vanags, Tom Mueller, John McIver, Pat Buddington, Sandy Noah, Pat Lowden, Laura Ayers, Evelyn Smith, Don Arabian, Joe Angelo, Capt Curtis McNeil, and Ron Lerdal.

While I was still at Los Angeles Air Force Base, Lt Col Joe Rouge, a former research fellow, strongly recommended the program to me. Col Brent Collins and Col Ralph Gajewski deserve a thank-you for supporting my efforts to volunteer to be the Systems Command representative for the program.

I owe a tremendous debt of gratitude to my editor, Preston Bryant, and to my research advisor, Rich Muller. They read through many drafts of my work, and provided expert correction and advice that significantly improved the quality of my written product. They were always positive and upbeat, and offered plenty of help and encouragement.

Col Glenn Easterly, the Air Force Materiel Command (AFMC) Chair at the Air War College, has been an available and helpful supervisor who has provided much practical guidance for the study as well as for my career. I am also indebted to Col Ken Walsh, the Air Force Space Command Chair, for his support and guidance.

Norma Raiff at AFMC Headquarters, Wright-Patterson Air Force Base, was patient and helpful with all of my TDY requests and other administrative support requirements.

Lt Col Tom Nowak, the coordinator of the command-sponsored research program at Air University, was always responsive to my requests, inquiries, and problems. He served in a largely thankless position, but always maintained a high level of dedication to the program.

Col Bob Johnston, the director of the Airpower Research Institute, has been very supportive of the research fellows program and was helpful in finding solutions to my problems and concerns.

Lt Col Bill Furr and Lt Col Orv Lind were our resident computer gurus who never failed to patiently give of their time and energy to help me.

Dot McCluskie helped me out a number of times when I was in a pinch and needed some quick graphics support.

Lt Col Dan Leaf and Lt Col Kevin Smith were two research fellows who provided a lot of leadership and unit identity for all of us. They deserve a great amount of credit for efforts above and beyond the call. Maj Steve Webb was another research fellow who was a helpful and considerate office mate.

My family and I owe a great deal of appreciation to Pastor Ryan Dexter and the church family at Trinity Evangelical Methodist Church in Pike Road, Alabama. They were a joy to be associated with and were a spiritual anchor throughout our year in Montgomery.

Finally, and most significantly, I want to thank my wife Joyce, and my children Betsy and Joshua. Joyce tirelessly took care of the kids all year long, and it was always comforting to know they were in such good hands. They all had unlimited patience for the time I spent on my work, and never failed to raise my spirits whenever I was with them. This was a special and enjoyable 12 months for us in the South, and we will never forget it.

This nation should commit itself to achieving the goal, before this decade is out, of landing a man on the Moon, and returning him safely to the Earth.

—President John F. Kennedy
25 May 1961

We should work to reduce substantially the cost of space operations. Our present rocket technology will provide a reliable launch capability for some time. But as we build for longer range future, we must devise less costly and less complicated ways of transporting payloads into space. Such a capability—designed so that it will be suitable for a wide range of scientific, defense and commercial uses—can help us realize important economies in all aspects of our space program.

—President Richard M. Nixon
7 March 1970

Introduction

President Kennedy's call for a manned lunar landing within the decade galvanized our country for a massive and challenging undertaking. Neil Armstrong stepped onto the Moon a little more than eight years after the President's May 1961 speech before Congress—an accomplishment that stands as one of the great scientific, technical, and management achievements in human history. Viewed within the context of today's typical large aerospace programs, the rapidity of the Apollo Program's development is particularly impressive. Apollo succeeded despite the tragic January 1967 fire that prompted a major redesign of the manned capsule as well as significant personnel and management changes within NASA. As the 1960s drew to a close with the US basking in the limelight of its space successes, some space managers were already developing plans for space initiatives that would follow the Apollo Program.

Despite the breathtaking success of Apollo, American public and Congressional opinion did not support funding large new space missions at the level and priority enjoyed by the manned lunar landing program. President Nixon's March 1970 statement reflected the sentiment within the US government at the time. The US needed a cheaper, simpler means of achieving access to space. The strong desire for economical space transportation may have been partially motivated by an image of wastefulness associated with the Apollo launch vehicle.

The Saturn V Moon rocket was an enormous space launch vehicle that stood 110.6 meters (363 feet) tall. Designed to support the manned lunar exploration effort, the Apollo/Saturn V launch system was focused on mission expediency and not economic efficiency. The vehicle accommodated the concept of lunar orbital rendezvous, developed by Langley Research Center engineer John Houbolt, by steadily shedding hardware as the mission progressed.[1] When an Apollo mission left the pad, it was a massive tower of machinery and fire; when it returned to Earth, all that remained was a tiny three-man capsule that could not be reused. This approach may have been appropriate for Apollo because the ends justified the means, but follow-on launch systems would clearly have to be dramatically different in order to achieve significant cost reductions.

In the late 1960s, two completely different approaches emerged as potential means of reducing the cost of putting payloads into space. One proposed using simplified expendable boosters, the other a winged, fully reusable, manned launch system.[2] In 1972 the US government officially came down on the side of a winged, fully reusable system. The Space Shuttle was established as America's future launch vehicle and the solution to high costs. Although the ultimate Shuttle configuration would be only partially reusable, cost analysts at that time nevertheless predicted launch costs would be at least an order of magnitude lower (around $365 per pound) than those of existing expendable systems. The Shuttle proved to be an engineering marvel with a broad range of orbital capabilities, but as a launch system it has been an economic failure. The Space Shuttle is the most expensive large launch vehicle in the US inventory, whether based on cost per launch or on dollars per pound to orbit.

In 1987 the DOD began a cooperative effort with NASA to develop a new simplified booster called the Advanced Launch System (ALS). Once again, the goal was to

The Saturn V launch vehicle.

achieve order-of-magnitude launch cost reductions. Congress specified in November 1987 that any ALS request for proposal would include the target of $370 or less per pound of payload to low earth orbit.[3] The National Launch System (NLS), which represented a family of simplified expendable boosters for future US space launch needs, evolved out of the ALS development effort. By 1992, however, the nonrecurring development cost projections for the NLS were in excess of ten billion dollars and Congress cancelled the program.[4] Today the problem of high space launch costs still begs a solution, and a solution is critical to our continued use and exploitation of space. This research study addresses the key issues and provides some practical approaches to finally achieving the elusive goal of inexpensive space transportation.

Study Boundaries

The high cost of space transportation can be attacked on several broad fronts, including launch vehicle design and manufacturing, launch operations, procurement streamlining, and program management. This study will touch on each of these areas, but the emphasis will be on launch vehicle design and manufacturing. It is the author's belief that cost savings begin with how a launch vehicle is designed and how it will be manufactured. Further research in all four areas is appropriate, but a detailed treatment of launch operations, procurement streamlining, and program management is beyond the scope of this study.

Air Force Space Command specifies four basic characteristics of any launch system: capability, reliability, affordability, and responsiveness.[5] Once again, a comprehensive analysis of all of these areas would be beyond this study's scope. However, improving each of these characteristics starts with the vehicle design, and the concepts proposed by this study to drastically reduce launch costs will have a positive collateral benefit to all four.

Foreign launch systems, operations, and management will not be addressed directly. Some comparisons will be made with Soviet/Russian design, manufacturing, and launch operations practices, but the research will focus on existing and future US launch systems. Potential cooperation with foreign launch programs and manufacturing agencies is not addressed.

Only systems or concepts capable of providing transportation to orbit will be considered. Suborbital sounding rockets deserve a dedicated cost evaluation that is outside this study's scope. Interorbital and interplanetary space transportation will not be discussed.

Some Definitions

The study will use the terms *space launch* and *space transportation* interchangeably. Specifically, the study will address the high cost of launching payloads from the surface of the earth to low earth orbit (LEO). This study will define LEO as circular orbits with altitudes in the range of 185 kilometers (100 nautical miles) to 460 kilometers (250 nautical miles).

Certain terms will be routinely and interchangeably used. The vehicles used to launch payloads into space will be referred to as launch vehicles, space launch vehicles, launch systems, launchers, and boosters. Launch services will be used to describe the total package of launch support, range support, launch vehicle hardware, software, propellants, personnel, documentation, payload integration, and other items required to achieve orbit. The vehicles and equipment launched into space will be described as space vehicles, space systems, spacecraft, satellites, cargo, and payloads. The act of launching a vehicle will be called launch, flight, lift, and mission.

All dollar values quoted in this study have been adjusted to reflect constant 1993 dollars.[6]

Notes

1. Roger E. Bilstein, *Stages to Saturn* (Washington, D.C.: National Aeronautics and Space Administration, 1980), 63, 405.

2. Paul Dergarabedian, "Comments on National Space Transportation" (Position paper, The Aerospace Corporation, El Segundo, Calif., 1988), 2–3.

3. Scott Pace, "US Space Transportation Policy," *Space Policy,* November 1988, 321.

4. Jeffrey M. Lenorovitz, "Congress Cancels NLS Launcher Family," *Aviation Week & Space Technology,* 12 October 1992, 20.

5. Lt Col Timothy K. Roberts, "The Need for New Spacelift Vehicles," *Space Trace,* June 1993, 2.

6. Escalation factors are based on Office of the Secretary of Defense procurement rates revised in 1992.

Chapter 1

The Problem

On 19 October 1992, vice presidential candidate Al Gore delivered a campaign speech at the Goddard Space Flight Center in Maryland. In the speech, he said, "One of the most critical issues facing the US space program is the need to reduce the cost of launching payloads, whether they be military, scientific, or commercial satellites."[1]

The expense of launching payloads into space today is very high. Launch vehicles and their operation—whether expendable or reusable, whether small or large—cost millions to hundreds of millions of dollars per flight. And this expense is in addition to the usually very expensive payload the launch vehicle is carrying. A payload budget planner must allocate such a significant portion of the budget to launch services that these considerations have a powerful ripple effect on all aspects of the space mission. The cost of space vehicles has become almost inextricably linked to the cost of launch, and reducing the cost of space systems and missions is largely dependent on achieving lower space transportation prices.

Expensive Transportation with Broad Impacts

Launch costs consume a large percentage of the average space system's life cycle cost. In the case of NASA's space station *Freedom* design, one estimate based on National Research Council projections and NASA estimates indicated that 37.5 percent of the station's entire life cycle cost would have been attributable to the cost of Shuttle launches.[2] A space-based tracking system called Brilliant Eyes, which is being developed for the Ballistic Missile Defense Organization, is projecting launch costs using expendable launch vehicles of around 25 percent of total life cycle cost.[3] This percentage is highly dependent on the program's achieving its goal of launching at least four space vehicles on each booster. Attaining this goal is having a major design influence on the Brilliant Eyes space vehicle. If growth in satellite weight or volume causes the number of spacecraft per booster to drop from four to three, there will be significant increases in launch costs and a serious effect on the system's orbital deployment strategy and constellation architecture.[4]

Current Launch Vehicle Cost Range

Although most space planners have come to accept the current price of space launch and to routinely factor it into overall program costs, these high transportation expenses are without precedent. Using today's large launch vehicles, it costs from $45 million to over $500 million to orbit five to 25 tons of cargo several hundred kilometers above the earth. These stiff launch tariffs provide the customer a one-time, and usually one-way, transportation service.

Unique Transportation Requirements

The major unique characteristic of this transportation service is that it imparts to its cargo the velocity necessary for orbital flight—about 9,150 meters (30,000 feet) per second.[5] This and other unique characteristics make space launch significantly different from more conventional forms of transportation. However, this study will show that these differences do not justify space transportation costs being 100 to 10,000 times higher than their terrestrial counterparts.

Establishing the Cost per Launch of Expendables

Establishing the actual cost per launch of expendable launch vehicles operating today can be a challenging task. Launch expenses are strongly influenced by the "options" each vehicle manufacturer makes available to prospective customers.

One example of these options is the various sizes (and prices) of payload fairings that booster manufacturers offer.[6] Another example of an option with a big cost impact is the payload customer's choice of an upper stage configuration. Despite this research study's focus on the cost of transportation to low earth orbit (LEO), many launch vehicle price quotes include the cost of an upper stage that may or may not be required to achieve LEO. This can have an especially big impact when the upper stage is the costly Inertial Upper Stage or Centaur.[7]

Because of the plethora of options available, launch vehicle manufacturers use different designations to identify the various versions of their boosters.[8] It is therefore important to remember that launch vehicles cannot simply be referenced by name, such as "Atlas" or "Titan" for example, when comparing their respective costs.

A number of other factors can influence an expendable launch vehicle's cost. Launch insurance coverage may or may not be included in a launch cost quote.[9] The amortized nonrecurring cost to develop the booster may or may not be included, and it is often not easy to discern whether this very significant cost constitutes part of a particular launch cost calculation. Government-furnished support for government-sponsored launches can be from 10 to 20 percent of the total expense, and it is not usually accounted for.[10] And finally, the launch (and therefore launch vehicle production) rate per year has a strong influence on a given vehicle's cost per mission.[11]

Establishing the Cost per Launch of the Shuttle

The preceding discussion provides some idea as to the complicated nature of establishing reliable prices for expendable launchers. Establishing the ac-

The Space Shuttle on the pad at Launch Complex 39, Kennedy Space Center, Florida.

tual cost per launch of the Space Shuttle can be even more daunting. Many circumstances and system design characteristics influence the price of a Shuttle launch. For example, it is difficult to pin down the actual nonrecurring cost of the Shuttle's development and how it is (or if it has been) amortized. The partially reusable and partially expendable nature of the Shuttle complicates

3

the establishment of per-flight costs. The budgetary impact of the two-and-one-half-year Shuttle hiatus in the wake of the *Challenger* loss is not clear. One must somehow account for the cost of maintaining for 30 months the large team of ground processing, flight operations, and support personnel; the cost of storing and maintaining spacecraft awaiting Shuttle flights; and the cost of the replacement orbiter, *Endeavour*.[12] The cost of product improvements such as the advanced solid rocket motor program must also be considered. These factors have contributed to the development of wide-ranging estimates for the Shuttle's cost per flight.

Representative Vehicle Costs

Taking into consideration the costing complications covered in the previous paragraphs, this study will discuss approximate launch service prices for four expendable US launch vehicles and the Space Shuttle (see table 1). These launch costs will include the unit cost of a particular vehicle as well as other required launch services. Government-furnished support will not be included in the expendable launch vehicle quotes.

Pegasus

The winged, air-launched, solid-propellant Pegasus launch vehicle is representative of the class of boosters designed to launch small satellites. The price for Pegasus launch services ranges from $10.5 to $13.4 million.[13]

Delta II 7920

Moving up the launch vehicle performance scale, we find the Delta II 7920, a much larger booster than Pegasus. It has a liquid-propellant core stage that uses liquid oxygen and RP-1, and it employs nine solid-propellant strap-on motors with graphite epoxy cases. The Delta II 7920 does not use an upper (third) stage. The particular configuration example we are considering employs a 2.9-meter-(9.5-foot-) diameter payload fairing. The price for Delta II 7920 launch services is in the $45–$50 million range.[14]

Atlas IIA

The Atlas IIA is a more powerful launch vehicle than the Delta II 7920. The configuration selected uses a 3.4-meter-(11-foot-) diameter payload fairing. Launch services cost between $80 and $90 million.[15]

Titan IV

Still more powerful is the Titan IV, the largest expendable US booster. The configuration chosen for comparison, which uses no upper stage, has a 5.1-meter-(16.7-foot-) diameter payload fairing. Launch services cost between $170 and $230 million per mission.[16]

Space Shuttle

For the Space Shuttle, the cost comparison assumes a configuration using no upper stage. Estimates of the cost for Shuttle launch services vary widely, but are, at a minimum, between $350 and $500 million.[17] Estimates range as high as $750 million per flight, and NASA Shuttle program director Thomas Utsman said it was "fair enough" to include the costs of ongoing Shuttle upgrades like the advanced solid rocket motor when calculating per-mission prices. By doing this, the cost of a single Shuttle flight in 1993 is $547 million.

Table 1

Existing Launch Vehicle Comparison

VEHICLE	COST RANGE ("M, Per Launch)*	PAYLOAD CAPACITY (LEO)	PAYLOAD LAUNCH EFFICIENCY (Cost per kg to LEO)*	EFFICIENCY RATIO	NORMALIZED EFFICIENCY RATIO
Pegasus	$10.5–$13.4	369 kg. (814 lb.)	$32,366/kg. ($14,681/lb.)	3 4	N/C
Delta II 7920	$45.0–$50.0	5,040 kg. (11,110 lb.)	$9,426/kg. ($4,275/lb.)	1.0	1.0
Atlas IIA	$80.0–$90.0	7,122 kg. (15,700 lb.)	$11,935/kg. (5,414/lb.)	1.3	1.6
Titan IV	$170.0–$230.0	17,690 kg. (39,000 lb.)	$11,306/kg. ($5,128/lb.)	1.2	2 1
Space Shuttle	$350.0–$547.0	24,358 kg (53,700 lb.)	$18,413/kg. (8.352/lb.)	2.0	3 9

*Costs are in 1993 Dollars

Launch Vehicle Cost Fraction

It is instructive to examine the percentage of the total cost of an entire booster stack, including the payload, that is attributable to the launch vehicle and associated launch services. This approach is different from the previously discussed comparison between a space system's life cycle launch services cost and its overall life cycle cost. By comparing the cost of the entire booster stack with the cost of the payload on top of the stack, one can gain an appreciation for the significant percentage of an individual mission's cost that is consumed by the launch vehicle and related services. Two DOD space systems will be considered: the Defense Support Program (DSP) and the Global Positioning System (GPS) (see table 2).

DSP Launch Cost Fraction

DSP provides a ballistic missile early warning capability. DSP Block IV units 18–22 have a single space vehicle unit cost of $254 million. The launch vehicle is normally a Titan IV with an Inertial Upper Stage. Launch services usually cost $203 million, or 44.4 percent of the entire booster stack's cost. If the expense of government-furnished support for launch is added in, the per-

Table 2

Launch Vehicle Cost Fraction

DSP		GPS	
Spacecraft Cost ($M)*	$254.0	Spacecraft Cost ($M)*	$53.0
Launch Services Costs ($M)*		Launch Services Costs ($M)*	
Titan IV	$203.0	Delta II 7925	$49.0
Titan IV w/government furnished support	$251.0	Delta II 7925 w/government furnished support	$59.8
Space Shuttle	$350.0	Launch Vehicle Cost Fraction	
Launch Vehicle Cost Fraction		Delta II 7925	48.0%
Titan IV	44.4%	Delta II 7925 w/government furnished support	53.0%
Titan IV w/government furnished support	49.7%		
Space Shuttle	57.9%		

*Costs are in 1993 Dollars

centage of launch costs to overall costs increases to 49.7 percent. When the Space Shuttle was used as the DSP launch system, launch services absorbed 57.9 percent of overall costs.[18] This calculation assumes the lower-end cost estimate for Shuttle launch services ($350 million) and ignores the expense of special payload integration hardware and documentation required for the Shuttle. Of course, NASA charged DOD much less than $350 million to fly the DSP satellite on the Shuttle.

GPS Launch Cost Fraction

The second space system to be considered is the Global Positioning System (GPS), which provides constant and precise navigational information world-wide through a constellation of satellites. The GPS Block II space vehicle's average unit cost is $53 million.[19] GPS is launched on a Delta II 7925, which uses a PAM-D upper stage. Cost of the 7925 launch vehicle and services is $49 million.[20] The percentage of the entire booster stack's cost attributable to the launch vehicle and services is 48 percent. Adding government-furnished support increases the launch services percentage to 53 percent.[21] Whether launch cost is considered as a percentage of total life cycle costs or as the percentage of an individual booster stack's total cost, it is clear that the expense of launch is a significant portion of the overall cost of US space programs.

Vehicle Performance Values

The launch vehicles discussed in this chapter vary widely in cost, and this variance is related, at least to some extent, to each vehicle's performance. But establishing a vehicle's specific performance for the purpose of comparison can be as difficult as nailing down its cost. A number of variables can affect performance values, and any performance survey of different boosters must account for as many of these variables as possible.

Key variables include latitude of the launch site, available launch azimuths, altitude of the desired orbit, inclination of the desired orbit, and eccentricity of the desired orbit.[22] This study will establish approximate performance figures for the previously discussed expendable launch vehicles and the Space Shuttle. Assumed values for the key performance variables are as follows: a launch site latitude of 28.5 degrees (Cape Canaveral),[23] a launch azimuth due east, and a 100-nautical-mile circular orbit with an inclination of 28.5 degrees. These values are not applicable to the Pegasus, however, since its air launch capability provides launch site flexibility. Pegasus performance figures will be based on a due east launch from a zero-degree latitude launch point and a 100-nautical-mile circular orbit with zero-degree inclination.

Based on these assumed values and the manufacturer's options selected earlier, the Pegasus has a payload capacity of 369 kilograms (814 pounds). The capacity of the Delta II 7920 is 5,040 kilograms (11,110 pounds). The Atlas IIA can boost 7,122 kilograms (15,700 pounds), and the Titan IV has a payload capacity of 17,690 kilograms (39,000 pounds).[24] The Space Shuttle has a capability to low earth orbit of 24,358 kilograms (53,700 pounds) (see table 1).

Payload Launch Efficiency Values

By relating launch vehicle and launch services cost to launch vehicle performance, one can establish a measure of a booster's overall payload launch "efficiency." Launch cost for a particular vehicle is divided by the amount of kilograms (or pounds) of its performance, resulting in a value for the number of dollars required to place one kilogram (or pound) into low earth orbit. This payload launch efficiency rating can be a helpful tool for evaluating various boosters.

Some caution should be exercised in using this efficiency rating method for comparing one launch vehicle with another. The rating provides the most valid comparison values when various vehicle concepts *that have the same payload lift capacity are considered.* The efficiency ratings of various boosters with different payload lift capacities are somewhat skewed in favor of larger boosters because of the efficiency advantage that larger vehicles have over smaller vehicles.[25]

The cost and performance values already established can be used to derive measures of efficiency for each of the expendable launch vehicles and the Shuttle. This study will assume median cost values based on the cost range stated for each vehicle. It will also assume that each vehicle is loaded to its maximum payload capacity.

The Pegasus has an efficiency rating of $32,366 per kilogram ($14,681 per pound) of payload placed into low earth orbit. This effectively means that the payload owner, or customer, must pay $32,366 for every single kilogram, or $14,681 for every single pound, of cargo transported into space. The Delta II 7920 has an efficiency rating of $9,426 per kilogram ($4,275 per pound) to low earth orbit. For the Atlas IIA, the efficiency rating is $11,935 per kilogram ($5,414 per pound), while the Titan IV has a rating of $11,306 per kilogram

($5,128 per pound). The Space Shuttle's efficiency is $18,413 per kilogram ($8,352 per pound) (see table 1).

Expected Efficiency Trends

Generally, payload launch efficiencies should improve as vehicle performance increases.[26]

This is because there are many costs associated with a launch vehicle and its operation that are essentially independent of size.[27] Also, nonrecurring development costs do not increase as fast as launch vehicle size.[28] However, even if we throw out the Space Shuttle rating because of the Shuttle's many unique features and processing requirements, the efficiencies for existing expendable launch vehicles still do not correspond exactly to this expected trend. The Pegasus does have the least efficient rating, as would be expected; but it is the Delta II 7920, and not the Titan IV, that turns out to be the most efficient. The higher frequency of Delta launches relative to Titan launches is probably one of the reasons for this disparity.

Vehicle Development Cost and Scaling Effects

By establishing the Delta II 7920 efficiency rating to be a value of 1.0, we can derive relative efficiency rating ratios for each of the launch systems considered. This gives the following ratios: Pegasus—3.4, Atlas IIA—1.3, Titan IV—1.2, and Space Shuttle—2.0 (see table 1).

To make some comparison between vehicle efficiency ratings and at the same time account for the fact that all the vehicles being considered have different payload capacities, each vehicle can be plotted against a curve of a scaled Delta II 7920. The two curves shown in Figure 1 represent different efficiency ratings for notional Delta II 7920 boosters with varying payload capacities up to 79,800 kilograms (176,000 pounds) to low earth orbit. The lower curve plots the efficiency ratings of these imaginary Deltas based on recurring costs only. The upper curve adds in the predicted nonrecurring development costs for the different imaginary Deltas, amortized at 10 percent of capital over 100 flights in 10 years. The curve assumes that the nonrecurring cost of the existing Delta II 7920 booster, if it were developed today using the technologies extant on the current vehicle, would be $1 billion. Using the stated amortization calculations, the per-mission nonrecurring costs would be $16 million, or $3,200 per kilogram (1,450 per pound), to low earth orbit. The curve projects the nonrecurring development costs of the largest notional Delta vehicle (79,800-kilogram capacity), using current Delta technologies, to be $5.6 billion.[29]

Using the lower curve, which does not include amortized nonrecurring development costs, we can compute for the various existing launch vehicles *normalized* efficiency rating ratios that are calculated against notional Delta vehicles with the same relative payload capacities. This method gives the following ratios (assuming a Delta II 7920 value of 1.0): Atlas IIA—1.6, Titan IV—2.1, and Space Shuttle—3.9 (see table 1).

Figure 1 illustrates several important points. It shows the major impact that nonrecurring development costs can have on the cost-per-kilogram to orbit, emphasizing that any new launch vehicle development program must have low nonrecurring costs and deliver a low-recurring-cost booster that can be flown often for an affordable price. This figure also highlights the influence of any given vehicle's size (and payload capacity) on its payload launch efficiency rating. Finally, the figure indicates that the efficiency ratings of the Atlas IIA, the Titan IV, and the Space Shuttle, when compared to notional vehicles in their same respective lift classes that use Delta-like technologies, are poorer than their raw efficiency ratings. This illustrates the progressively higher cost of progressively less efficient design concepts.[30]

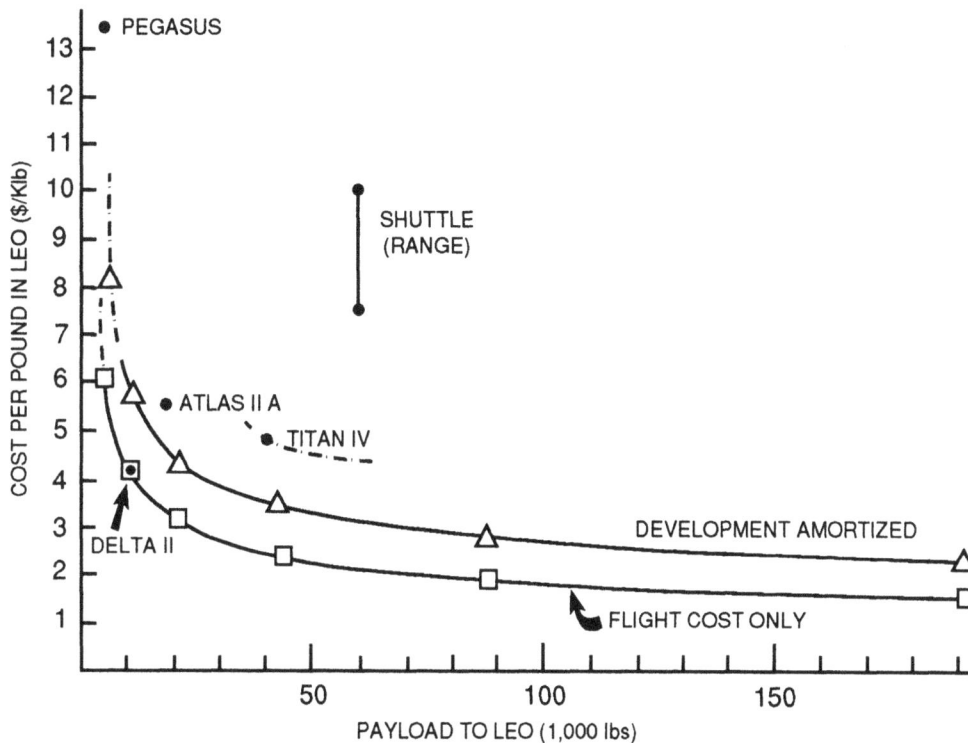

Figure 1. Effect of scale on cost per pound in LEO

Limited Launch Capacity

Most payload customers do not have the flexibility to select the launch vehicle with the best payload efficiency. The satellite owner will usually select the lowest performance booster that will accommodate the payload to be launched, independent of that booster's payload efficiency rating. For example, a customer wanting to launch a 6,350-kilogram (14,000 pound) satellite would be forced to select the Atlas IIA launch vehicle. The customer would not

9

select the Delta II 7920, despite its better efficiency rating, since it does not have sufficient performance to lift 6,350 kilograms. The Titan IV is more efficient than the Atlas IIA and more than capable of lifting 6,350 kilograms, but it would be a poor choice since its per vehicle cost is much higher than the Atlas IIA. The only other solution available in this case (assuming choices are limited to US launch vehicles) would be to share a ride to orbit with one or more other payloads on a Titan IV or the Shuttle—and orbital ride-sharing brings its own set of complicating factors that must be carefully considered.

Satellite designers, in an effort to maximize payload launch efficiency for their particular mission, will seek to utilize every kilogram of launch capacity available and will design the space vehicle to do so. This practice necessarily establishes the spacecraft's target weight and volume early, but it may end up requiring a very expensive redesign to shave grams (ounces) off the spacecraft so it will fit on the chosen launch vehicle.

The satellite designers' usually costly efforts to squeeze their spacecraft on board the lowest performance (and presumably least expensive) booster possible could be ameliorated somewhat by more flexible launch vehicle designs. Specifically, launch vehicle performance should be customizable to individual spacecraft lift requirements, and boosters should be able to accommodate a wider range of satellite designs. The French have been somewhat successful in achieving this capability with their Ariane family of launch vehicles. The Ariane launcher can be readily configured for a variety of performance levels through the use of different mixes of solid-propellant and liquid-propellant strap-on boosters, and it can accommodate single or multiple payloads. Some US launch vehicle manufacturers are now moving in this direction.

Cost Goals and Cost Realities

The introduction to this study described how the Space Shuttle was originally intended to provide payload efficiencies of $800 per kilogram ($365 per pound) to low earth orbit. Achievement of this goal probably would have allowed the Shuttle to realize its advance billing as the vehicle that would revolutionize space transportation. It is in fact a highly capable, manned heavy lifter with tremendous mission flexibility and an orbital retrieval and return capacity. However, it has (by far) the poorest payload efficiency and the highest cost of all large boosters operating today.

The Advanced Launch System (ALS), originally proposed in 1987, was envisioned to succeed where the Shuttle had failed; that is, to provide economical access to space. The US Congress directed that the ALS would have a payload efficiency goal of $815 per kilogram ($370 per pound) to low earth orbit.

Budgetary and political pressures caused the original ALS initiative to be eventually transformed into a follow-on program called the National Launch System (NLS). NLS depended on Shuttle-derived hardware for some key components and was touted as holding great promise for reliable, responsive space transportation. The NLS program deemphasized the goal of $815 per kilogram to low earth orbit.[31] Program planners emphasized a simpler design approach to keep manufacturing and operating costs down, but development cost projections for the new launch vehicle were high. Congress canceled the NLS program in October 1992 because it offered too little for too much.

Commercial Launch Industry Considerations

Today the only near-term solution for acquiring launch systems with payload efficiencies of less than $1,760 per kilogram ($800 per pound) to low earth orbit appears to be a Russian solution.[32] Choosing this solution, however, could be hazardous to the health of the existing US launch industry and its fleet of expendable rockets. Also, once Western satellite customers had committed to use Russian boosters and the Russians were faced with the typical launch services demands of the Western payload community, their launch prices would likely increase significantly.[33]

Foreign Competition

Over the last 10 years, the US share of the international space transportation business has gone from 100 percent down to 25 percent. This is largely due to the emergence of the French Ariane onto the commercial launch scene. The US Commerce Department projects the US share will drop as low as 21 percent in the decade of the 1990s.[34] However, the more recent threat posed by potentially very low cost Russian and Chinese boosters could eventually drive this percentage so low that US launch vehicle companies could no longer compete commercially. If this happened, the US government would be placed in the position of either totally subsidizing the US launch industry or seeking slots on foreign boosters for launch of its military and civil spacecraft.

US booster manufacturers have asked the US government to provide protection from the anticipated onslaught of cut-rate foreign rockets, especially those from Russia. Fears that Russia would price its large, diverse, and capable inventory of boosters as low as required to win launch contracts may be well founded. The Inmarsat organization has selected a Russian Proton vehicle to launch its Inmarsat 3 spacecraft in late 1995. Russia's DB Salyut bid a launch price of $36 million, which is about 40 percent less than US and European competitors.[35]

Lockheed is joining with Russian companies Khrunichev Enterprises and NPO Energia to form a new company called Lockheed-Khrunichev-Energia International to market Russian Proton launch vehicles. Lockheed feels its experience in marketing, launch insurance, and payload integration will bring considerable expertise and credibility to the joint venture.[36]

The United States and Europe have reached a tentative accord with Russia on limitations to Russian participation in commercial launch activities.[37] The accord limits Russia to signing only eight contracts for launches to geosynchronous earth orbit or geosynchronous transfer orbit between 1993 and 2000. Contracts for launches to other orbits will be reviewed on a case-by-case basis.

11

Foreign competition: the Chinese LM-2E launch vehicle on the pad at Xichang

Russian launch prices must not fall more than 7.5 percent below the lowest Western bid, or special consultations will be called.[38]

Possible US Responses

Protectionism is one solution that will help preserve existing US booster companies and their respective launch vehicles (and launch services prices). Another solution, of course, is to develop less expensive domestic launchers that can compete internationally with all comers. The report, "The Future of the United States' Space Launch Capability," issued by the White House on 19 November 1992 stated that "there is little hope for the United States to be price competitive in this [commercial launch] market without major reductions in launch vehicle costs and mutual agreements on pricing guidelines and enforcement provisions." The report further stated, "If the United States is to remain competitive, it must reduce its cost (and price) to launch payloads by a *factor-of-two. . . .*"[39]

Surplus strategic missiles made available by recent arms treaties offer the potential for inexpensive space access for small payload customers. The government has already contracted with Martin Marietta Corporation to modify Minuteman II intercontinental ballistic missiles (ICBM) for use as suborbital launchers.[40] Missiles such as the Minuteman, Poseidon, and Trident could also be used to launch payloads ranging from 360 to 680 kilograms (800 to 1,500 pounds) to low earth orbit.[41] Because these missiles were designed to carry nuclear warheads and not spacecraft, they generally would provide a "hard ride" with high acceleration, vibration, and acoustic conditions. This would require some "hardening" and acoustic protection for spacecraft before they were suitable for flight on one of the surplus missiles.[42]

Use of surplus missiles has the potential of damaging the US commercial launch industry, particularly entrepreneurial companies seeking a niche in the small payload launch market. US companies have therefore sought and received, at least temporarily, protection from the "dumping" of surplus missiles into the marketplace.[43] However, the November 1992 report on the future of the US launch capability called for limited use of decommissioned missiles for government-sponsored orbital research in a controlled manner. One of the authors of the report, Paul Coleman of the University of California at Los Angeles, said the surplus missiles offer particular benefits " by breaking the hammerlock on high [launch] costs."[44] The DOD has recommended that proposals for the use of surplus missiles for orbital launches be subjected to case-by-case reviews and be restricted to noncommercial applications. Use of the missiles for non-orbital missions would be much less restrictive.[45] In any case, old strategic missiles could offer at best only a partial, short-term solution to the problem of high-cost space access.

Commercial Transportation Cost Comparisons

To better appreciate the cost of placing payloads into orbit, we will compare it with the cost of more conventional means of transportation (see table 3). Payload launch efficiencies range from about $9,400 per kilogram ($4,300 per pound) to

$32,400 per kilogram ($14,700 per pound). The cost of transporting an average passenger with luggage, coach class, on a round-trip domestic US airline flight is around $2 per kilogram ($1 per pound). The Concorde, a much more sophisticated form of air transport, can move people intercontinental distances at twice the speed of sound for about $60 per kilogram ($30 per pound).[46] These commercial aviation costs are for the transportation of people and their cargo on vehicles that are fully "man-rated." Of course, there are dramatic differences between traveling from New York to Los Angeles and traveling from Cape Canaveral to low earth orbit. However, these differences may not be dramatic enough to justify the very high cost of space launch; and large reductions are possible.

Table 3

Commercial Transportation Cost* Comparison

MODE	COST (per kg)
Launch Vehicles (to LEO)	$9,400–$32,400
Domestic Airline Flight	$2
Concorde Aircraft Flight	$60

*Costs are in 1993 Dollars

Impacts of High Launch Costs

The expensive nature of space launch has wide-ranging and pervasive impacts on the design and operation of spacecraft. Launch costs make up such a large portion of space system life cycle cost that launch considerations heavily influence satellite capability, weight, volume, and complexity, as well as mean mission duration, deployment options, constellation quantities, and cost. A retired TRW executive stated that because launch systems cost so much, satellite designers always pick the smallest and least expensive launch system possible and spend large amounts of effort and money trying to get their space vehicle to meet booster weight and volume constraints. He cited instances where designers spent up to $400,000 per kilogram ($185,000 per pound) in taking the last few kilograms out of a satellite so it could meet the selected launch vehicle's lift weight-to-orbit capability.[47]

National Space Policy Impacts

High launch costs also have a broad impact on national space policy decisions. The US space station program continues to be vulnerable to cancellation largely due to its price tag; and this price is strongly influenced by the station's launch, deployment, and sustainment being tied to the expensive Shuttle. The cost and responsiveness of large boosters like the Titan IV drive the launch timing and deployment sequencing of a variety of large DOD space systems, and the expense of these launch systems reinforces the need for a less expensive US launch capability like the National Launch System was promised to be. But Congress canceled the NLS program primarily because of

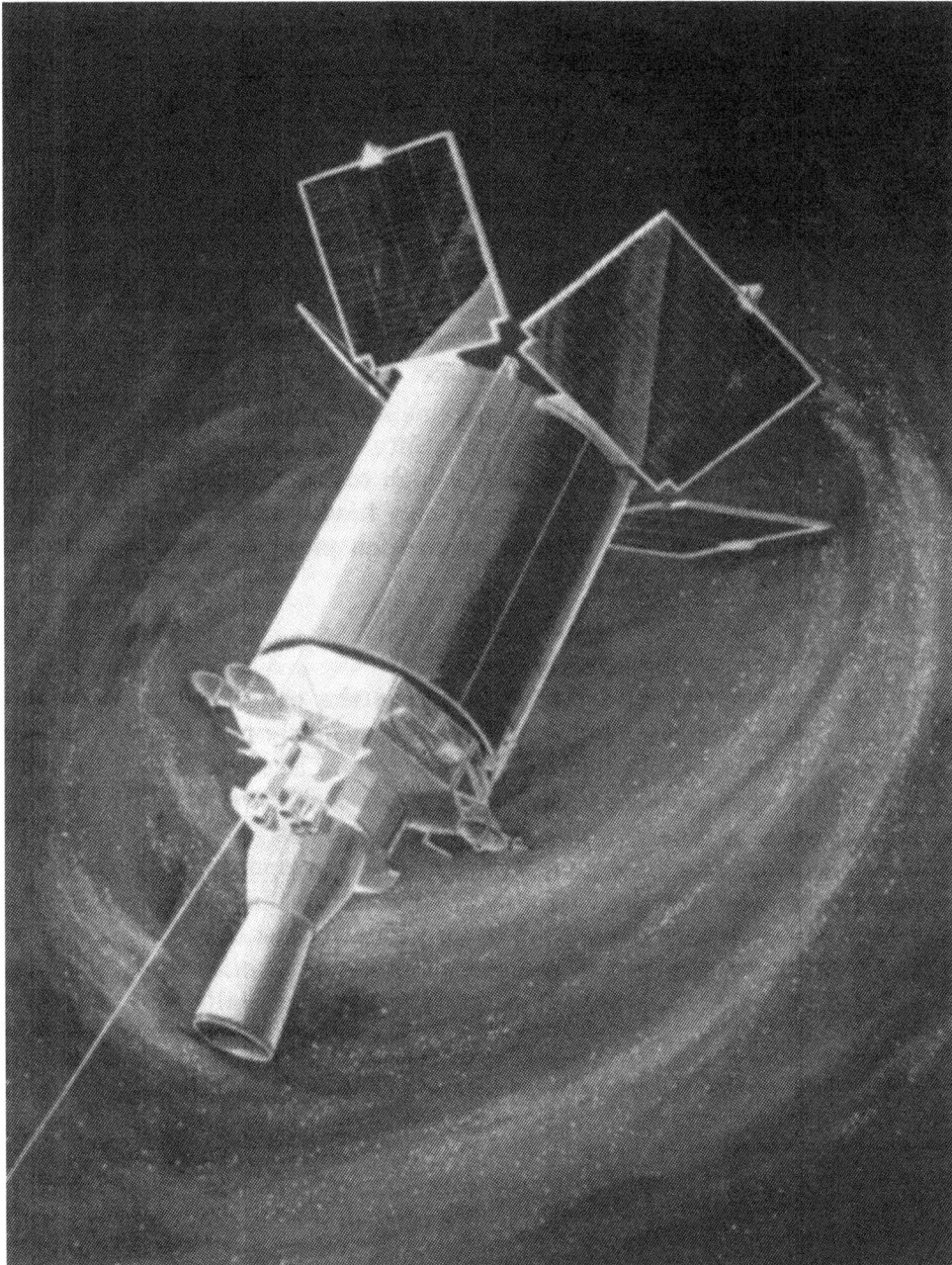

The Defense Support Program spacecraft.

anticipated large development costs, thus underlining the importance of reducing not only recurring launch costs, but launch system development expenses as well. Reductions in space launch prices would have a dramatic influence on many aspects of space policy decisions.

15

New Initiatives

Perhaps the most profound impact of high cost is on the quantity and scope of new space initiatives. The influence of launch cost has its ultimate expression in this area. Assuming that US defense and civil space budgets remain flat or have only modest growth in the coming years, they will be largely consumed by currently operational programs or programs already well under way in the development cycle. Making room for any significant new space initiative will require major reallocations of funding, thus cutting back on or eliminating existing programs. If military and civil space budgets decline in the coming years, as many predict, the impacts caused by expensive space transportation will become even more acute.

Many military space systems have become key components of force application planning and operations, and their utility cuts across the different military services. Without some relief to the high cost of launch, just the cost of continuing to replenish existing systems may have a negative impact on the services' (especially the Air Force's) acquisition plans for new weapon systems.

Launch Failure

The high cost of space transportation and the expensive payloads they carry have helped to make launch failures particularly painful. This is especially true in the case of a reusable launch system like the Shuttle, where a single failure can eliminate a large percentage of the available launch fleet. The high price of launch failure affects booster design practices, satellite design practices, and launch operations. The Aerospace Corporation estimated that the total cost of a Delta II 7925 failure, including replacement hardware and downtime, is $338 million; while the cost of a Titan IV failure would be $2.124 billion.[48] The monetary cost of the *Challenger* accident has never been officially established, but it was clearly many billions of dollars.

The Means for Expanded Space Activities

If the cost of launch could be reduced to one-tenth of present levels, the lift capacity available for an equivalent national space launch budget could be increased 10 times over. Having 10 times the launch capability currently available at no additional cost would open up tremendous opportunities for the DOD and NASA. If only half of the newly expanded launch capacity were used, the DOD and NASA would still have five times the current lift capability; and half of the current DOD and NASA launch budgets would be available for new program starts or other budget requirements. Additionally, a tenfold reduction in space launch costs should stimulate a revolution in satellite design. It would allow for larger numbers of less expensive, but not less capable, space vehicles. Lower priced space systems will multiply the positive

The Space Shuttle lifts off on STS mission 51-L.

effect of decreased launch costs, paving the way for a greatly expanded exploitation of space for defense, civil, and, perhaps most of all, commercial users.

Many government-sponsored studies have unequivocally stated the importance of a capable space transportation capability to the future of the US space program. The Advisory Committee on the Future of the U.S. Space Program said, "The most fundamental building block without which there can be no future space program is the transportation system which provides our access to space."[49] The Vice President's Space Policy Advisory Board declared, "The space launch capability of the United States is the most critical aspect of our overall space program, for without the ability to reliably deliver payloads to orbital velocities, the U.S. space program would not exist."[50] The President's National Commission on Space stated:

> The two most significant contributions the U.S. Government can make to opening the space frontier are to ensure continuity of launch services and to reduce drastically transportation costs. . . . Reliable, economical launch vehicles will be needed to provide flexible, routine access to orbit for cargo and passengers at reduced costs. . . . For cargo transport, we propose that a new vehicle be put into operation by the year 2000 with a goal of achieving operation costs of [$254] per pound delivered into orbit.[51]

A number of noted authorities in the space business have forcefully stated the importance of lowering the cost of launch. Roy Gibson, former director-general of the British National Space Center, stated that "it is now really time to understand that the key to space utilization in the future is cheaper launch capability."[52] Gordon Woodcock of the Boeing Company said that "the basic physics of space flight allows costs 100 times cheaper [than] we now have. . . . The nation that first cracks the technological secrets of low-cost [space] transportation will lead an economic revolution dwarfing the one created by the commercial passenger jet."[53] Retired Lt Gen James Abrahamson, first director of the Strategic Defense Initiative Organization, recognized the criticality of lower launch costs: "We need to bring down launch cost by at least two orders of magnitude!"[54] Mr. Gibson's, Mr. Woodcock's, and General Abrahamson's comments capture the strong desire for, and potential impact of, significantly lowering space launch costs.

Summary

It is difficult to imagine an expansive defense, civil, or commercial space endeavor when the cost of placing a kilogram into low earth orbit today exceeds the purchase cost of a kilogram of gold. Manned exploration initiatives will be difficult to afford when transporting a single meal to the US space station will cost $15,000.[55] Space launch is too expensive, and the US will be handicapped in accomplishing its national space policy objectives until drastic reductions can be achieved.

Notes

1. Albert Gore, "A New Approach to Civil Space," *Space News,* 9–15 November 1993, 15.
2. Steven J. Hoeser, "The Cost Impacts of True Spaceships," *The Journal of Practical Applications in Space,* Summer 1990, 1.
3. Memorandum, Barry Moss, The Aerospace Corporation, to Lt Col John Vuksich, Strategic Defense Initiative Organization, subject: Launch Costs, 13 December 1990; John R. London III, Jack R. Weissman, and R. Curtis McNeil, "Brill Eyes—Developing Small Space Systems in a New Environment" (Paper, World Space Congress, Washington, D.C., 4 September 1992), 6.
4. Ibid., 3, 6–7.
5. Edward L. Keith, "Low Cost Space Transportation: The Search for the Lowest Cost" (Paper presented at the AAS/AIAA Spaceflight Mechanic Meeting, Johnson Space Center, Houston, Tex., 13 February 1991).

6. Edward H. Kolcum, "NASA, Pentagon Charts Ambitious Unmanned Launch Vehicle Program," *Aviation Week & Space Technology,* 16 March 1992, 131.

7. Hoeser, 6.

8. Kolcum.

9. Hoeser.

10. The Aerospace Corporation, "Cost of Space and Launch Systems" (briefing presented at the Space Systems Division Commanders' Offsite, Fort MacArthur, San Pedro, Calif., 3 January 1990), chart BB-2793.

11. Ibid.

12. Hoeser, 7–8.

13. Kolcum.

14. Ibid.

15. Ibid.

16. Ibid; The Aerospace Corporation; Col Chuck Banta to Lt Col John London, letter, 11 January 1993.

17. Hoeser, 6–8.

18. The Aerospace Corporation, charts BB-2793 and AA-3380.

19. Ibid., chart AA-517.

20. Ibid., chart BB-2793; Kolcum; Steven J. Isakowitz, *International Reference Guide to Space Launch Systems* (Washington, D.C.: The American Institute of Astronautics, 1991), 205.

21. The Aerospace Corporation.

22. 6555th Aerospace Test Group, "Astrodynamics for Titan Managers" (Guide produced by the Launch Vehicles Division, Cape Canaveral AF Station, Fla., January 1983).

23. This is the latitude of Cape Canaveral Air Force Station and Kennedy Space Center, Fla.

24. Kolcum; Hoeser, 6.

25. Gerard Elverum to John London, letter, 2 January 1993.

26. R. C. Truax, "Cheap Transportation for Cheap Satellites" (Paper presented at the AIAA/DARPA meeting on Lightweight Satellite System, Monterey, Calif., 10 May 1990), 1.

27. James R. French, "Paperwork is a Launch-Vehicle Roadblock," *Aerospace America,* April 1988, 18.

28. Elverum to London, letter.

29. Ibid.

30. Ibid.

31. "There and Back Again," *The Economist,* 15 June 1991, 10.

32. Edward L. Keith, "For the Smart Space Shopper," *Newsweek,* 17 August 1987, 50.

33. Elverum to London, letter.

34. Daniel J. Marcus, "Commercial Space Sees Growth, Problems," *Space News,* 14–20 December 1992, 8.

35. Peter B. de Selding, "Low Cost Proton Purchase Confirms Competition Fears," *Space News,* 16–22 November 1992, 3.

36. Peter B. de Selding, "NPO Energia Joins Lockheed, Khrunichev to Market Protons," *Space News,* 19–25 April 1993, 1, 28.

37. Peter B. de Selding, "Russians Say Launch Accords Still in Flux," *Space News,* 14–20 June 1993, 4.

38. Jeffrey M. Lenorovitz, "Russia Nears Entry Into Launch Market," *Aviation Week & Space Technology,* 24 May 1993, 26.

39. Vice President's Space Policy Advisory Board, *The Future of the United States' Space Launch Capability* (Washington, D.C.: National Space Council, November 1992), 5, 21.

40. Andrew Lawler, "Missiles Tapped for Post–Cold War Launchers," *Space News,* 30 November–6 December 1992, 27.

41. "Old Missiles Could Hurt Business," *Military Space,* 21 September 1992, 6.

42. Paul Dergarabedian, The Aerospace Corporation, telephone conversation with author, 6 January 1993, 27.

43. Michael Potter, "Swords into Ploughshares—Missiles as Commercial Launchers," *Space Policy,* May 1991, 148–49.

19

44. Lawler.

45. Ben Iannotta, "DoD Recommends Tight Restrictions for Use of Missile Launchers," *Space News,* 10–16 May 1993, 1.

46. Hoeser, 1.

47. G. W. Elverum, Jr., "Boosters" (Transcript of a talk presented at Aerospace Productivity Conference, The Aerospace Corporation, El Segundo, Calif., 1987).

48. "Launch System Costs" (Briefing prepared by the Aerospace Corporation, El Segundo, Calif., 23 May 1991).

49. Advisory Committee on the Future of the U.S. Space Program (Washington, D.C.: November 1990) in *The Future of the U.S. Space Launch Capability* (Washington, D.C.: National Space Council, November 1992).

50. Vice President's Space Policy Advisory Board, 3.

51. The National Commission on Space, *Pioneering the Space Frontier* (New York: Bantam Books, 1986), 12–13.

52. "Criteria for Determining a Valid UK Space Programme," *Spaceflight,* December 1992, 375.

53. Hoeser, 2–3.

54. Ibid., 3.

55. Edward L. Keith, "System Analysis and Description of an Ultra-Low Ground to Low Earth Orbit Cargo Delivery System" (Paper presented at the World Space Congress, Washington, D.C., 31 August 1992), 10.

Chapter 2

Existing Launch Systems

The existing fleet of US launch systems is capable, but expensive. There have been a number of recent proposals for new systems that promise lower launch costs. However, with the exception of some small commercial booster programs, none of these initiatives have entered into full-scale development. This chapter will provide a brief technical survey of existing US boosters and an introduction to the better known new booster concepts. No direct comparisons between the different launchers will be made, but a later chapter will provide general comparisons of some key design choices that are applicable to these systems.

The Space Shuttle

The Space Transportation System (STS), better known as the Space Shuttle, is the most capable of all US launch systems in terms of lift capacity to orbit. It is also the most costly to operate. The Shuttle is mostly reusable, with only the large external propellant tank being expended each flight. In the specific case of the Shuttle, however, reusability has not proven to be the answer to high launch costs. Malcolm A. LeCompte said of the Shuttle, "it became a temperamental thoroughbred requiring constant attention and enormous expense to sustain—a spacecraft with inadequate payload capacity and inordinate operational costs that have inhibited commercial space development."[1]

The Space Shuttle absorbed more than a third of NASA's FY 1992 budget and will use a similar percentage in FY 1993.[2] The Shuttle's annual costs are relatively insensitive to the number of flights conducted each year, a testimony to the expensive nature of the so-called standing army that currently supports Shuttle operations. This large team of support personnel is located at the launch site, at other NASA centers, and at various contractor facilities around the country.

In the aftermath of the *Challenger* loss in January 1986, all commercial payloads were deleted from the Shuttle manifest. Since that time, the DOD has removed virtually all future military payloads; and the Bush administration's national launch policy required the Shuttle to be used only when a particular mission needed its unique capabilities or astronaut support.[3] With the slip in the scheduled deployment of the US space station by the STS and the elimination of commercial and military cargo launch opportunities, flight planners may have to scramble to fill Shuttle payload bays. Some analysts noted that the very modest payload carried on the STS-52 mission in October 1992 was an indication of poor payload planning and the relative dearth of Shuttle cargo.[4]

Titan Launch Vehicles

The Titan class of launch vehicles includes the most powerful expendable booster in the US fleet. The Titan IV is the nation's workhorse for launching the heaviest DOD payloads, and it will continue to serve in this capacity for a number of years. It can be configured with no upper stage, a liquid propellant Centaur upper stage, or a solid propellant Inertial Upper Stage.[5] The Titan IV is a direct result of the vision and dedication of then-Under Secretary of the Air Force Edward C. Aldridge, Jr., who in 1984 recognized the criticality of having a "complementary" alternative to the Shuttle for access to space. Prior to the *Challenger* accident, he met stiff opposition in Congress and from NASA for proposing to buy a limited quantity of Titan IVs to act as a hedge against potential future Shuttle problems.[6]

The Titan IV program suffered its first failure on 2 August 1993, but this loss has not been the only problem the program has experienced. These vehicles have a propensity for lengthy and costly delays in launch processing, resulting in long pad dwell times—in some cases more than a year. General Charles Horner, commander in chief of US Space Command, stated on 29 October 1992 that the Titan IV delays are damaging the military's readiness and costing between $1 million and $7 million a day.[7] General Horner has been critical of the high cost and poor performance (in meeting launch schedules) of the US military space launch capability in general, and the Titan IV in particular. Speaking of the lengthy schedule delays common with many launches, he said, "We may have spent over $3 billion of the taxpayers' money because of our inability to make take-off times."[8] The White House's November 1992 report on the future of the US space launch capability puts the cost of Titan IV delays at a staggering $8 million per day.[9]

The Titan III is similar to, but less powerful than, the Titan IV. It was developed primarily as a commercial launch vehicle. The Titan II launch vehicle is a decommissioned Titan II intercontinental ballistic missile (ICBM) that has been overhauled and configured for space booster duty. A total of 56 deactivated Titan II ICBMs were placed in storage at Norton Air Force Base (AFB), California, for possible use in the future.[10] A contract is in place to convert 15 of these Titan IIs to space launch vehicles.[11] The Titan II, which provides the least capacity to orbit of the current Titan family, does not use solid-propellant strap-on boosters (although Martin Marietta has proposed various configurations of the Titan II that do employ solid-propellant strap-ons).[12]

A Titan II ICBM is launched from Vandenberg AFB, California.

Atlas Launch Vehicles

The Atlas launch vehicle has undergone a significant evolution in recent years, resulting in a set of boosters with a spectrum of capability. The Atlas E space launch vehicle is a modified, decommissioned ICBM that has operated from Vandenberg AFB, California, for many years. Only a few Atlas Es, which represent the low end of performance within the Atlas family, are left in the inventory.[13] The Atlas I, II, and IIA, which are increasingly powerful versions of the same vehicle, provide some performance selection flexibility to the prospective user. The most powerful Atlas launch vehicle is the Atlas IIAS. It will employ four solid propellant Castor IVA strap-on boosters.[14] Two Atlas missions failed (1991 and 1992) because of identical start-up problems with the Centaur upper stage. The source of the failure was associated with the Centaur's RL-10A-3-3A engine turbomachinery.[15] A third Atlas failed in March 1993 due to a loss of thrust in the booster engine.[16]

23

An Atlas E booster launches a Defense Meteorological Satellite from Vandenberg AFB.

A Delta II 7925 booster launches from Cape Canaveral Air Force Station, Florida.

Delta Launch Vehicles

The Delta launch system has steadily evolved over the years, developing into increasingly capable boosters. Originally derived from the Thor intermediate range ballistic missile (IRBM), the Delta has become a popular vehicle for missions to geosynchronous orbit and other high altitude orbits. The Delta II 7925 has become the vehicle of choice for many of these missions, including NAVSTAR Global Positioning System Block II space vehicles, which were originally intended for launch on the Space Shuttle.[17]

Pegasus

Pegasus is a highly innovative, air-launched, expendable launch system. Targeted at the small satellite market, this winged vehicle uses a carrier aircraft, aerodynamic lift, and solid-propellant rocket power to place payloads into low earth orbit. Being air launched, the Pegasus offers the important capability of launch point flexibility. Pegasus can be launched due east from the equator, taking full advantage of the earth's rotational velocity to maximize payload capability to orbit. Early missions have been accomplished employing a B-52 "first stage." The particular B-52 used was the venerable NB-52B serial number 008 that supported the X-15 experimental rocket plane program.[18] The Pegasus transitioned from a development effort to an operational launch system with its fourth launch on 25 April 1993. Initial Pegasus launches have not been without incident, however. The second mission placed seven microsats in an elliptical orbit that was lower than intended.[19] The 25 April launch of the Los Alamos National Laboratory Alexis satellite resulted in the spacecraft being placed in the proper orbit, but ground personnel were not able to communicate with it.[20] Video imagery from a camera system on the second stage of the Pegasus appears to have exonerated the launch vehicle from any blame. A Lockheed L-1011 aircraft will replace the B-52 and serve as carrier for future Pegasus missions.[21]

The Pegasus air-launched booster and its B-52 carrier aircraft.

SCOUT

The SCOUT launch vehicle has been flying since 1960, providing a low earth orbit capability for small satellites of the same class that Pegasus launches. The booster, a four-stage, solid-propellant vehicle, has operated from four different launch sites. In addition to Cape Canaveral and Vandenberg AFB, the SCOUT has flown from the San Marco platform off the coast of

A four-stage SCOUT launches from Vandenberg AFB.

Kenya and from the Wallops Flight Facility on Wallops Island, Virginia.[22] Only a very few SCOUTs are left in the inventory, and the vehicle is no longer in production.[23] Production by Loral Vaught Systems could resume, however, if a plan by the University of Rome goes forward to produce an enhanced version of the SCOUT. This San Marco SCOUT would use Italian-built, solid-propellant strap-ons based on Ariane technology, and would operate from the San Marco range.[24]

Summary

This chapter has briefly summarized major existing US launch systems. Current US launch systems continue to provide a fairly robust, albeit expensive, space transportation capability. However, dark clouds of foreign competition loom ever larger on the horizon, particularly from Russia and China.

Notes

1. Malcolm A. LeCompte, "SSTO Vehicle: Low-Cost Alternative," *Aviation Week & Space Technology,* 8 March 1993, 57.

2. Andrew Lawler, "New Programs Fare Poorly in '93 Budget," *Space News,* 5–11 October 1992, 10.

3. William J. Broad, "Question on Eve of a Shuttle Flight: Is it Worth It?," *The New York Times,* 22 October 1992, 1.

4. Ibid.; David A. Brown, "Columbia Mission Pioneers Remote Science Operation," *Aviation Week & Space Technology,* 2 September 1991, 70.

5. Edward H. Kolcum, "Reduced Military Budgets Revamp Titan 4 Product and Launch Program," *Aviation Week & Space Technology,* 2 September 1991, 70.

6. Victor W. Whitehead, "The Complementary Expendable Launch Vehicle" (Paper presented at the AIAA Space Programs and Technologies Conference, Huntsville, Ala., 25–28 September 1990), 1.

7. William Boyer, "U.S. Space Command Chief Blasts Titan 4 Program," *Space News,* 2–8 November 1992, 13.

8. William Harwood, "Horner Calls Launch Record a 'Horror Story'," *Space News,* 3–9 May 1993, 1.

9. Vice President's Space Policy Advisory Board, *The Future of the United States' Space Launch Capability* (Washington, D.C.: National Space Council), March 1983, 2.

10. Bruce French, "Innovative Concepts for the Titan II Space Launch Vehicle" (Paper presented at the AIAA/SAE/ASME 27th Joint Propuls Conference, Sacramento, California, 24–26 June 1991), 2.

11. Vice President's Space Policy Advisory Board, 7.

12. Andrew Wilson, "Titan Grows Stronger," *Space,* September–October 1987, 9–10.

13. United States Air Force Fact Sheet, "Atlas Space Boosters," Headquarters Space Division, Los Angeles Air Force Station, Calif., March 1983, 2.

14. Atlas marketing brochure, General Dynamics Commercial Launch Services, San Diego, California, 1992.

15. James T. McKenna, "Centaur Loss Slows GD's Efforts to Win Contract," *Aviation Week & Space Technology,* 31 August 1992, 22; "Atlas AC-71 Failure Probed," *Aviation Week & Space Technology,* September 1992, 38.

16. Jeffrey M. Lenorovitz, "Atlas Failure Highlights Need for Improved U.S. ELVs," *Aviation Week & Space Technology,* 5 April 1993, 57.

17. J. F. Meyers, "Delta for the 1990s" (Paper presented at the World Space Congress, Washington, D.C., 31 August 1992), 3–4.

18. "Spacesaver," *Aviation Week & Space Technology,* 3 September 1990.

19. "Second Pegasus Launched Successfully; Small Satellites in Elliptical Orbit," *Aviation Week & Space Technology,* 22 July 1991, 24.

20. Bruce A. Smith, "Alexis Launched, But Not Communicating," *Aviation Week & Space Technology,* 3 May 1993, 59.

21. "Launchers," *Military Space,* 27 January 1992, 4.

22. Steven J. Isakowitz, *International Reference Guide to Space Launch Systems* (Washington, D.C.: The American Institute of Aeronautics and Astronautics, 1991), 239; The San Marco platform is close to the equator, at 2.9 degrees south latitude.

23. Isakowitz, 232.

24. Robina Riccitiello, "ASI Pays First Installment, Scout's Future Still Uncertain," *Space News,* 8–14 March 1993, 9.

Chapter 3

Proposed Launch Systems

Primarily because of the recognized need to lower the cost of transportation to low earth orbit, different government agencies and aerospace companies have proposed a number of new booster system concepts. These concepts differ radically, and proponents of each system believe their particular approach is the correct one to achieve launch cost reductions.

National Launch System

The National Launch System (NLS) was a joint DOD/NASA program to develop a new family of expendable boosters that would improve reliability and lower manufacturing and operating costs. It was canceled by Congress in 1992, but the Air Force and NASA are hopeful they can structure a new program that captures the best elements of NLS and has a lower development cost.[1]

The heart of the NLS program was the development of a new main propulsion system called the Space Transportation Main Engine (STME). The three major US rocket engine manufacturers formed a partnership in 1991 to develop the oxygen/hydrogen-powered STME.[2] The engine design emphasized larger design margins and simpler manufacturing techniques than the Space Shuttle Main Engine (SSME). This approach translated into a design with lower performance numbers and higher weight than the current SSME, but the benefits of higher reliability and lower cost more than compensated for the performance losses and weight gains. To illustrate how much simpler the STME manufacturing process was, program managers routinely compared the STME to the high-performance, extremely complex, very expensive SSME. The part count and the number of welds, processes, and inspections for each major STME component were much lower than for comparable SSME components.[3]

The NLS family of launchers consisted of three vehicles. NLS 1 was the heavy lifter, with a capability of placing 61,250 kilograms (135,000 pounds) into low earth orbit. NLS 2 could carry 22,700 kilograms (50,000 pounds) to low earth orbit. The smallest vehicle in the NLS family, NLS 3, had a 9,100-kilogram (20,000-pound) capacity.[4] The NLS had a modular design, providing a large amount of subsystem and component commonality among the three vehicles, including the common use of the STME. In 1992 a National Research Council panel recommended that the NLS 3 vehicle be developed first. The

US needed a booster that could compete effectively in the international launch market, and they saw no urgent near-term need for the two heavier launchers.[5] Subsequently, NASA dropped support for NLS 1 and planned an even larger booster to support Moon and Mars exploration. The Air Force's new emphasis was on a booster in the lift class of NLS 3.[6]

Reasons cited for the demise of the NLS program include its high development cost, a lack of support by Congress and the aerospace industry, the joint Air Force/NASA program management approach, and a lack of specifics for future NLS missions.[7] For example, NASA Administrator Daniel Goldin said much needed to be done on the NLS program to streamline management. When the program was terminated, over 1,000 government and contractor personnel were supporting NLS from eight Air Force and NASA centers.[8] And despite the fact that seven major aerospace contractors were involved in the program, there was a perception that most aerospace companies provided inadequate advocacy for the new booster. There were even reports that some companies lobbied against the new booster because it was a perceived threat to existing launch programs.[9] The study on the future of US launch capabilities accomplished for the National Space Council in the fall of 1992 said:

> The current contractors for Titan, Atlas, Delta, and upgrades to these systems are worried about their current business base and are reluctant to abandon near-term business for an uncertain future program. Also, they are worried about the potential "winner-take-all" aspects of a future vehicle competition and the lack of Congressional support for the program.[10]

Spacelifter

In November 1992, a working group chaired by Pete Aldridge and sponsored by the Bush administration's National Space Council recommended that a new launch system called Spacelifter be developed. The Spacelifter concept differed from NLS because it concentrated on initially developing an expendable core launch vehicle with a payload capacity to low earth orbit of 9,070 kilograms (20,000 pounds). Through modular performance improvements, the vehicle's capacity would be expandable to 22,700 kilograms (50,000 pounds). The working group's report called for the Air Force to manage the program (as opposed to the joint Air Force/NASA NLS program). The vehicle was to be man-ratable, with the ability to carry a piloted spacecraft like the Langley Research Center's Personnel Launch System. The Spacelifter was to be designed to decrease launch costs by a factor of two, relative to existing US launch vehicle costs. This amount of reduction was deemed essential if the US launch industry was to remain competitive with foreign commercial launchers.[11]

Since the November 1992 report, the Air Force has broadened the definition of "Spacelifter" to mean the next generation of Air Force launch vehicles, with a target payload capacity range of 5,440 to 11,340 kilograms (12,000 to 25,000 pounds) to low earth orbit.[12] The service has opened the competition for virtually all concepts, including single- and two-stage-to-orbit reusable proposals, upgrades to existing launch vehicles, and new launch vehicle designs based on existing technology. The intent is to let the aerospace industry lead the effort to define the best answer for the next US booster.[13]

Single-Stage Rocket Technology

The Ballistic Missile Defense Organization (BMDO) has been developing technologies that could lead to a fully reusable vertical takeoff/vertical landing single-stage-to-orbit (SSTO) launch system. The program called for suborbital flight tests of a one-third scale demonstrator vehicle in mid-1993 at White Sands Missile Range, New Mexico. Three successful tests were conducted in August–September 1993. BMDO managers used these tests to evaluate flight characteristics as well as to demonstrate airline-like operations such as small support crews and rapid turnaround. The ground and flight operations crew, which consists of only a handful of people, is extremely modest when compared to personnel requirements for existing systems.[14] Since the vehicle cannot fly far enough to leave the confines of the range, there is no range safety destruct package on board the test vehicle. This is a significant departure from previous launch system range safety requirements, and a positive step toward achieving routine access to space.

The demonstrator vehicle for the SSTO program is called the DC-X. Using liquid oxygen and liquid hydrogen as propellants, it is powered by four Pratt & Whitney RL-10A-5 rocket engines modified for throttling and sea-level op-

Artist's concept of a McDonnell Douglas DC-Y SSTO vehicle.

31

eration.[15] The DC-X is a precursor to a more advanced suborbital vehicle called the DC-X2, which would have an altitude capability of 160 kilometers (100 miles).[16] After the DC-X2 would come the full-scale DC-Y demonstration vehicle and the DC-1 operational launch vehicle, both of which will have orbital capability. (It is no coincidence that the operational SSTO system bears a designation that is similar to the designation of the aircraft that opened the era of commercial air transportation, the DC-3.) Payload capacity for the DC-1 is targeted at around 9,100 kilograms (20,000 pounds).[17] McDonnell Douglas estimates the operational system can ultimately reduce costs down to $1 million per flight, which equates to $100 per kilogram ($50 per pound) to low earth orbit.[18] However, the interest costs on a $2 billion development program for the DC-Y/DC-1 could be $200 million a year, and launch insurance costs for the payload could be $2 to $3 million per flight.[19]

Little funding has been established for SSTO development beyond the DC-X flight tests. The flight tests themselves have come under criticism by some members of Congress as inadequately demonstrating key technologies that would be required by a DC-Y vehicle.[20] Nevertheless, limited funding has been provided to pressure the option for additional DC-X flights. The future prospects for an operational vertical takeoff and vertical landing SSTO system, however, are not clear.

National Aerospace Plane

The National Aerospace Plane (NASP) program is a joint DOD/NASA effort to develop and demonstrate the technologies necessary for both single-stage-to-orbit flight and hypersonic atmospheric cruise by fully reusable aerospace vehicles. The program originally planned to build a flight test vehicle, designated the X-30, that would exercise horizontal takeoff and horizontal landing and demonstrate an SSTO capability.[21] Program engineers envisioned vehicles, derived from the NASP effort, that would significantly reduce the cost of space transportation through routine, airline-like operations.

The X-30 and the follow-on NASP-derived vehicles would require major advances in a number of technology areas. NASP vehicles would achieve orbit by using the atmosphere for both aerodynamic lift and the oxygen necessary for propulsion. The aerospace plane must therefore follow an air-breathing trajectory and must linger in the atmosphere much longer than a more conventional launch vehicle. Under these conditions, a NASP-type vehicle would experience severe boundary-layer conditions and thermal loading due to atmospheric friction, a fact that creates big development challenges in the area of structural design and materials. Air-breathing propulsion would also require new scramjet propulsion development. Drag losses caused by the lengthy flight through the atmosphere induce large inefficiencies in the vehicle's actual attainable velocities, compared to the velocities that are theoretically attainable. Because the vehicle carries every gram of its entire dry weight through the atmosphere and into orbit, structural weight and volume

The NASP as it might have looked as an SSTO vehicle.

must be minimized. This creates additional requirements for materials development. The ramjet-scramjet propulsion system would use hydrogen as a fuel. Because of the low density of hydrogen, however, exotic hydrogen slush may be required (to reduce propellant tank size).[22] These and other technical hurdles made the NASP concept a very high-risk, but possibly high-payoff, program.

DOD and NASA have not articulated a compelling near-term operational need for a vehicle like the NASP. In fact, former Air Force Secretary Donald Rice said about the NASP program, "The focus should be on technology. . . . It's so far out into the future, we're doing a disservice to talk about [operational] activities."[23] The Air Force announced on 7 December 1992 it would reduce the NASP budget by 66 percent.[24] The program has consequently been restructured to concentrate on hypersonics research and development. In an effort to avoid cancellation, the NASP Joint Program Office formulated an approach that reduces the scope of the program. The near-term program goal would be to reach speeds in the region of Mach 12–15, not the originally planned Mach 25. The new plan calls for conducting a set of boundary transition and scramjet experiments called Hyflte 1 and 2 by flying them on surplus Minuteman II ICBMs, although weight growth of the test articles may force the use of surplus Peacekeeper ICBMs. Tests of a small (30 percent scale) unmanned hypersonics test vehicle would follow. This test would be called Hyflte 3 and would use a surplus Titan II booster to carry the vehicle to hypersonic speeds.[25] Program managers believe this plan will be affordable and that it will provide sufficient validation of critical technologies to allow future development of an operational air-breathing SSTO vehicle.[26]

SEALAR

The Naval Research Laboratory's (NRL) Naval Center for Space Technology initiated a program in 1987 to develop a new space launch capability called the Sea Launch and Recovery (SEALAR) launch system. The intent of the program is to provide less-expensive, yet more flexible, space transportation through the use of simple, reusable boosters launched and recovered at sea.[27] Launching from a sea-mobile platform or directly out of the ocean itself, SEALAR boosters would enjoy flexible launch points and be able to fly direct-ascent trajectories into any orbital inclination. SEALAR would eliminate the need for fixed launch sites, which are expensive to build and maintain, expensive to refurbish after launch, and militarily vulnerable. Launching at sea would avoid some environmental entanglements (although it could create others), and range safety concerns caused by the potential overflight of populated areas could be minimized or eliminated.[28]

The SEALAR launch concept drew on a proposal developed in the late 1950s and early 1960s by Aerojet General to build an enormous launch vehicle capable of putting 544,000 kilograms (1,200,000 pounds) into low earth orbit. The booster, called Sea Dragon, was so large it would have required fabrication in a shipyard.[29] Aerojet designed Sea Dragon for launch directly out of the ocean. It was to be big, simple, and reusable because Aerojet believed this was the best way to achieve economical space access.[30] The SEALAR system did not embrace the large size of Sea Dragon, but it did incorporate the concepts of sea launch and recovery, simplicity, and reusability. NRL also applied design criteria developed by The Aerospace Corporation in the 1960s called "Design For Minimum Cost." Aerospace developed the criteria for ballistic missiles and space launch vehicles, but it had seen little application beyond the paper study phase.[31] The SEALAR booster that was derived from the Sea Dragon concept and the minimum cost criteria was the SubCalibur, a vehicle with an all pressure-fed propulsion system designed to launch 4,500 kilograms (10,000 pounds) to LEO from the sea (or land).[32]

NRL contracted with Truax Engineering (TEI) for development and flight test of near-scale test articles of the SubCalibur's first stage, called the X-3, X-3A, and X-3B.[33] TEI conducted a number of static propulsion tests and drop tests into water.[34] By late 1991, NRL had fabricated a suborbital flight test vehicle and was only a few months away from launch when funding was terminated by the Navy.[35]

Since that time, the vehicle has evolved into a new design that uses a two-stage approach with hybrid (solid fuel and liquid oxidizer) boosters comprising the first stage. The portion of the vehicle's first stage structure containing the solid fuel is expendable, but the rest of the first stage is recovered via a ram air-inflated wing and a reciprocating engine-driven propeller. The new SEALAR design is launched from an ocean-going dry dock staging out of Hawaii, and the first stage is recovered by a catch net on board the dry dock. This recovery technique is similar to those used by some unmanned aerial vehicles. The second stage carries the payload into orbit and, after payload deployment, performs a deorbit maneuver and glides back to the recovery site via a ram air-inflated wing.[36]

NRL announced on 8 January 1993 a joint venture with a private company called Sealar Corporation to commercialize the SEALAR booster. The laboratory and Sealar Corporation signed a cooperative research and development agreement that gives the company access to government technical data and expertise relating to sea launch and recovery technologies.[37]

Taurus

The Advanced Research Projects Agency (ARPA) is developing a new solid propellant expendable booster that will provide simple, inexpensive, and responsive access to low earth orbit. Called Taurus, the vehicle is based on components derived from ARPA's Pegasus program. The system was designed by Orbital Sciences Corporation, the same company that developed the Pegasus. Taurus is a four-stage launcher whose upper three stages are essentially a modified Pegasus vehicle. ARPA's new launch vehicle uses a modified Peacekeeper ICBM first stage as a stage zero. (The Pegasus uses a launch assist from the B-52 carrier aircraft for its initial thrust into space.)[38] Payload capacity is 1,360 kilograms (3,000 pounds) to low earth orbit, and Orbital Sciences is already planning to offer enhanced versions with greater capacities.[39] The Taurus vehicle was launched successfully on its first mission, 13 March 1994.

The Taurus represents a serious attack on traditional techniques for launching payloads. Key requirements for Taurus include the ability to set up for a launch on a bare-base concrete pad within five days, and to launch no more than 72 hours after receipt of a payload.[40] These timelines are revolutionary when compared to current launch vehicle schedules, and the entire on-site ground crew is composed of only 20 people. The Taurus approach promises realization of true launch-on-demand, a capability long sought by many within the military space community. A fleet of Taurus-type boosters could rapidly deploy, or reconstitute, large numbers of small military satellites. Military space operators would have great flexibility in launch site selection and launch scheduling.[41] The tough ground processing timeline requirements levied by the DOD will provide major benefits when the Taurus is used for commercial launches, since these launches will have less demanding processing schedules. Taurus program manager Joseph Padavano stated that the challenging DOD ground schedule forced Orbital Sciences to design-in simplified interfaces and procedures that required a minimum number of people. Because of these design steps, "your costs come down; your reliability goes up because the system has been simplified quite a bit."[42]

Despite the promise the Taurus system holds, program managers face several technical and programmatic issues. Technical issues include the rapid deployment requirement, which precludes the use of a fixed launch pad. The proximity of the Peacekeeper first stage to the ground, the lack of a flame bucket, and the lack of sound-suppression water have created conditions for high ignition overpressures and acoustic conditions. This has required extra efforts to elevate the launch vehicle off the pad surface and to protect Taurus payloads during the first few seconds of launch.[43] Also, solid propellants cause higher acceleration loads than those generated by liquid propellant-powered boosters, which places additional constraints on spacecraft designers.[44]

Programmatic issues include the cost per kilogram to orbit for the Taurus, which is at least as high as existing US launch systems—and it could be even higher. Additionally, with production of the Peacekeeper first stage ceasing for the ICBM program in July 1993, and with potential long-term constraints on the commercial use of surplus ICBM components, procurement costs for the Taurus stage zero would likely become prohibitive.[45] Orbital Sciences has therefore chosen to use the new Thiokol Castor 120 solid propellant motor for the stage zero of future Taurus vehicles.[46] The Castor 120 design draws on the heritage of the Peacekeeper first stage motor but employs simplified design features and manufacturing processes in order to be better suited for commercial applications.[47] It also will provide a more "payload friendly" ride than the Peacekeeper first stage.[48] One other programmatic issue is the recent dramatic changes in the military threat to the US, which should prompt a review of the necessity for the requirement to have a quick launch response capability from bare pad environments. These requirements have driven the Taurus design.

Proposed Commercial Systems

A number of other commercial launch companies are marketing launch vehicles that have not yet flown. This study will briefly discuss some companies and their products that are representative of entrepreneurial launch initiatives in the US.

EER Systems Conestoga

EER Systems is offering the Conestoga booster for payloads in the same class as those proposed for Pegasus/Taurus. EER Systems acquired Space Services, Incorporated, which had conducted a commercial suborbital launch of the Conestoga I vehicle from Matagorda Island, Texas, in 1982.[49] The Conestoga uses solid-propellant Castor IVA/B motors in a modular fashion in order to provide a level of customization for prospective payload customers.[50] EER Systems has been selected to launch the COMET space vehicle on a Conestoga booster from the Wallops Flight Facility, Virginia.[51]

AMROC Aquila

The American Rocket Company (AMROC) is developing the Aquila family of launch vehicles for boosting payloads in the Pegasus/Taurus and Conestoga classes. The four-stage Aquila clusters three H-1800 hybrid propulsion systems to form the first and second stages. The hybrid system offers several advantages over solid-propellant systems, including the ability to throttle and terminate thrust, to have clean exhaust effluent, and to have safe ground-handling of propulsion elements. To accommodate the polar orbit market, launches are planned from Vandenberg Air Force Base, California.[52]

E' Prime Eagle

E' Prime Aerospace Corporation is proposing a family of launchers based on the Peacekeeper ICBM design. Their Eagle S-Series launch vehicles will provide a LEO capability ranging from 1,360 to 4,540 kilograms (3,000 to 10,000 pounds). However, E' Prime may face the same procurement limitations (relative to Peacekeeper) as those mentioned for Taurus. Primary launch site for the Eagles is Ascension Island in the South Atlantic Ocean, with Cape Canaveral Air Force Station serving as an alternate launch base.[53]

Lockheed Launch Vehicle

Lockheed Missiles and Space Company is developing a family of solid propellant launch vehicles that are targeted at placing payloads in the 1,045 to 4,080-kilogram (2,300 to 9,000-pound) weight range into low earth orbit. The vehicle has three basic configurations and uses the Thiokol Castor 120 motor, along with Castor 4 strap-ons for the largest vehicle version. The vehicle is being designed to require a launch operations crew of about 20–25 people. First flight is planned for November 1994.[54]

Sea Launch Services Surf

Initial agreements have been reached for a US-Russian joint venture, called Sea Launch Services, to develop a new commercial launch vehicle based on Russian submarine-launched ballistic missile components. The vehicle, called Surf, would employ both solid and liquid propellant stages in its five-stage configuration. Surf's lift capacity is estimated to be 2,400 kilograms (5,280 pounds) to low earth orbit. The vehicle would be launched directly out of the water, taking advantage of the launch site selection and operational benefits of sea launch.[55]

Summary

This chapter has briefly summarized major proposed US launch systems. A variety of new launch system proposals are on the table, but there is no firm consensus as to which of these initiatives can best provide an inexpensive means of space transportation for the US over the long haul. The high cost of launch continues to be a daunting obstacle to space progress. To solve the problem of high cost, we must understand its root causes.

Notes

1. "Air Force Could Take Lead Role in New Expendable Launcher," *Aviation Week & Space Technology,* 2 November 1992, 26–27.

2. Jerry W. Smelser and Marc T. Constantine, "STME: Streamlining the Engine of Change," *Aerospace America,* July 1992, 23.

3. Ibid., 23, 25.

4. Jerry Grey, "Ups and Downs of the New Space Launcher," *Aerospace America,* June 1992, 28.

5. Patricia A. Gilmartin, "NRC Panel Urges Heavy-Lift Booster Be Dropped in Favor of Smaller Vehicle," *Aviation Week & Space Technology,* March 1992, 24.

6. "NLS Program Slims Down as AF, NASA, Refine Requirements," *Military Space,* 10 August 1992, 5.

7. "Air Force Could Take Lead Role in New Expendable Launcher," 26.

8. Liz Tucci, "NLS Criticized as Bloated, Slow," *Space News,* 12–18 October 1992, 29.

9. Liz Tucci, "Congress Halts NLS Work," *Space News,* 12–18 October 1992, 29.

10. Vice President's Space Policy Advisory Board, 9.

11. Ibid., 31–32.

12. Ben Iannotta and Barbara Opall, "Air Force, NASA Diverge on Space Launch," *Defense News,* 24–30 May 1993, 22.

13. W. A. Gaubatz, P. O. Klevatt, and J. A. Cooper, "Single Stage Rocket Technology" (Paper presented at the World Space Congress, Washington, D.C., 28 August–5 September 1992), 5–6.

14. Lt Col Pat Ladner and Maj Jess Sponable, "Single Stage Rocket Technology: Program Status and Opportunities" (Paper presented at AIAA Space Programs and Technologies Conference, Huntsville, Ala., 24–27 March 1992), 3.

15. Edward H. Kolcum, "Delta Clipper Partners Set Goal For Single-Stage-to-Orbit Vehicle," *Aviation Week & Space Technology,* 3 February 1992, 55; Otis Port, John Carey, and Seth Payne, "Is Buck Rogers' Ship Coming In?" *Business Week,* 21 June 1993, 118.

16. Gaubatz, Klevatt, and Cooper, 2.

17. J. R. Wilson, "Designing the DC-3 of Space?" *Interavia Aerospace Review,* January 1992, 41.

18. Gerard Elverum to John London, letter, 2 January 1993.

19. "Struggle Continues Over DC-X Flights," *Military Space,* 7 September 1992, 7.

20. V. L. Rausch and C. E. K. Morris, "Technologies for the National Aero-Space Plane" (Paper presented at the World Space Congress, Washington, D.C., 28 August–5 September 1992), 1.

21. Thomas Powell and W. Powell, "The NASP Program: A Status Report" (Paper presented at the AIAA Space Programs and Technologies Conference, Huntsville, Ala., 24–27 March 1992), 1.

22. Rausch and Morris, 5.

23. "Mission Control," *Military Space,* 16 November 1992, 1.

24. "Space Plane Budget Reduced," *Early Bird,* 8 December 1992, 2.

25. Stanley W. Kandebo, "NASP Cancelled, Program Redirected," *Aviation Week & Space Technology,* 14 June 1993, 32.

26. Stanley W. Kandebo, "New Direction for X-30 Eyed in Bid to Save Program," *Aviation Week & Space Technology,* 16 November 1992, 21.

27. Naval Center for Space Technology, *Sea Launch and Recovery (SEALAR)—System Concept to Launch Brilliant Pebbles* (Washington, D.C.: Naval Research Laboratory, January 1992), 1.

28. Thomas H. Moorer, "Breaking the Space Launch Bottleneck," *Washington Times,* 2 March 1993, F-1; Layne R. Boone, "A Cost Estimation Model for the Sea Launch and Recovery Space Transportation System" (Masters thesis, Naval Postgraduate School, September 1990), 5.

29. William H. Ganoe, "Rockets from the Sea," *Ad Astra,* July/August 1990, 71.

30. Boone, 6.

31. Naval Center for Space Technology, 18.

32. Boone, 6.

33. Ibid., 7–8.

34. T. J. Frey, Jr., "Sea Launch and Recovery (SEALAR): Responsive and Affordable Access to Space" (Paper presented at the AIAA Space Programs and Technologies Conference, Huntsville, Ala., 24–27 March 1992), 4.

35. Naval Center for Space Technology, 13.

36. Conversation with Peter G. Wilhelm, director of the Naval Center for Space Technology, Naval Research Laboratory, Washington, D.C., 3 September 1992.

37. "Research Lab, Sealar Corp., to Develop New Launcher," *Space News,* 18–24 January 1993, 11.

38. Taurus briefing, Orbital Sciences Corporation Space Systems Division, Chantilly, Va., 1992, chart 90629.03h.

39. James R. Asker, "Quick Response Key to Next U. S. Launcher," *Aviation Week & Space Technology,* 28 September 1992, 44.

40. C. C. Schade, "Pegasus, Taurus and Glimpses of the Future" (Paper presented at the AIAA Space Programs and Technologies Conference, Huntsville, Ala., 25–28 September 1990), 6.

41. Asker, 44, 46.

42. Frank Colucci, "Taurus Technology," *Space,* December 1992–February 1993, 19.

43. Jeffrey M. Lenorovitz, "First Taurus Mission Set for Mid-1993," *Aviation Week & Space Technology,* 8 February 1993, 22.

44. Asker, 44.

45. Ibid., 44, 46; Colucci, 20.

46. "Thiokol Castor 120 solid rocket selected to boost SDI experiment," *Spacewatch,* November 1992, 12.

47. Colucci, 20–21.

48. Capt Jim Ramsey, Peacekeeper Program Office, telephone conversation with author, 8 July 1993.

49. Peter J. Armitage, "Reliable, Low Cost Launch Service" (Paper presented at the Aerospace Technology Conference and Exposition, Anaheim, Calif., 25–28 September 1989), 2.

50. D. K. Slayton and M. H. Daniels, "Reliable, Low Cost Launch Services" (Paper presented at the AIAA/ASME/SAE/ASEE 25th Joint Propulsion Conference, Monterey, Calif., 10–12 July 1989), 8.

51. NASA Office of Commercial Programs brochure, "COMmercial Experiment Transporter," National Aeronautics and Space Administration, Washington, D.C., 1992.

52. R. Jay Kniffen, "The Development Status of the 260,000 lb-Thrust Hybrid Rocket Booster" (Paper presented at the World Space Congress, Washington, D.C., 28 August–5 September 1992), 2.

53. E' Prime Aerospace Corporation marketing brochure, "Launch Services-Commercial Space," E' Prime Aerospace Corporation, Titusville, Fla., 1992.

54. Jeffrey M. Lenorovitz, "Lockheed Develops Low-End Launch Vehicle," *Aviation Week & Space Technology,* 10 May 1993, 29.

55. Jeffrey M. Lenorovitz, "U.S.-Russian SLBM Venture Plans Initial Test for 1994," *Aviation Week & Space Technology,* 3 May 1993, 60.

Chapter 4

Causes of High Launch Costs

The high cost of today's space launch systems cannot be attributed to one particular circumstance or event. Rather, multiple causes have combined over the years to create the present condition of expensive space transportation. Some of the reasons for high launch costs are traceable to the development of the first US ballistic missiles, whose designs provided the foundation for the Delta, Atlas, and Titan families of booster systems. The heritage of the early manned space program of the 1960s is also a contributor to current costs. Design and manufacturing considerations related to present boosters, as well as the very high development costs of new launch systems, continue to have a major impact on launch prices. The demand for increasingly greater vehicle reliability also strongly influences space transportation cost. This chapter discusses these causes of high launch costs in some detail, since a firm understanding of them will establish a solid basis for developing solutions to the problem.

The ICBM Heritage

In the 1950s the Soviet Union posed a potentially devastating military threat to the United States in the form of nuclear-tipped intermediate-range and intercontinental ballistic missiles. In response to this threat, the US embarked upon its own ballistic missile program, despite the fact that this undertaking presented a number of significant technical challenges. Because of unflagging advocacy for the ICBM by Assistant Secretary of the Air Force Trevor Gardner and Air Force General Bernard Schriever, and others, President Eisenhower gave development of a US ballistic missile capability the highest national priority.[1] The emphasis was on achieving an initial operational capability as quickly as possible, and the Air Force turned to the aircraft industry for development of America's first long-range ballistic missiles. Engineers were not concerned about developing low-cost missiles, but about rapidly providing a functioning, capable, weapon system. Also, since ballistic missiles were designed to perform a one-way mission that likely would not occur unless a general nuclear war broke out, no thought was given to making the missiles or any of their components reusable.

The push was on to design the smallest missiles possible that could deliver a thermonuclear warhead with the required accuracy. The missiles needed to be of minimal size so they could be deployed in concrete "coffins" or "silos" and maintained on alert. Although the resulting Atlas, Titan, and Thor missile designs were not "small" by most standards, they were smaller than comparable Soviet ballistic missiles of that day.

Maximum performance and minimum weight were the overriding design drivers for the US ballistic missiles. These design drivers were, and still are, the norm for the aircraft manufacturing industry. Consequently, there were extraordinary efforts to decrease structural weight and increase propulsion performance. Engineers kept design margins low in order to keep weight down. The rocket engines were configured for high combustion chamber pressures and were fed by sophisticated turbopumps. In the case of the Atlas ICBM, designer Charlie Bossart employed an ingenious method for obtaining lightweight structural rigidity. He designed the propellant tanks to be integral pressurized balloon structures that required no internal stiffeners.[2] Therefore, the ballistic missiles developed in the 1950s became effective long-range nuclear weapon carriers. But they did not represent the most inexpensive designs—requirements other than minimizing cost had preeminent priority.

Although there have been numerous product improvements along the way, the United States' large expendable launch vehicles are direct descendents of the liquid-propellant ballistic missiles developed by the US Air Force in the 1950s. The Thor intermediate-range ballistic missile (IRBM) design formed the basis for all Delta central core vehicles. The Atlas ICBM evolved into the family of Atlas launch vehicles of today. Surplus Atlas E ICBMs are still used as space launch vehicles. The Titan II ICBM, taken off alert and deactivated in the 1980s, survives today as a space launcher. The Titan III and Titan IV core vehicles directly evolved from the Titan I and II ICBMs.

Manufacturers of the Thor, Atlas, and Titan missiles took advantage of the development costs already sunk into these systems by the US government and simply derived space launch vehicles from the existing IRBM/ICBM designs. Although the aerospace companies saved some up-front development expenses by using this approach, the resulting space boosters brought along the ballistic missile's maximum performance/minimum weight baggage. And like the ballistic missile, these launch vehicles were not designed to be low cost.

The Manned Space Program Heritage

The early manned space program of the 1960s bore some resemblance to the ballistic missile development effort. It was also focused on achieving certain operational goals, and minimizing cost was not a priority. The Mercury, Gemini, and Apollo programs were designed for mission expediency, not cost-effectiveness. The schedule for placing a US astronaut on the Moon, set by President Kennedy in 1961, was a dominant consideration for each of these programs, especially Apollo.

ICBM turned launch vehicle: an Atlas Agena in the early 1960s.

An Atlas ICBM lifts off in the late 1950s.

The early ballistic missiles were also used by America's Mercury and Gemini manned space programs. Here Gemini astronauts John Young and Gus Grissom leave their Gemini Titan vehicle after completing tests at Launch Complex 19, Cape Kennedy AFS, in March 1965.

The Titan I ICBM (above) and its successor, the Titan II, formed the design basis for the current Titan IV core vehicle.

Simpler days: V-2 firing control at White Sands Proving Ground, New Mexico, in the late 1940s.

Concepts for the control of launch and mission operations that were developed during these early manned programs became institutionalized. Although launch control and monitoring approaches can trace their heritage back to V-2 operations at White Sands Proving Ground in the late 1940s, they reached their manpower zenith during Apollo. The current Space Shuttle launch and mission control system has strong historical links to previous NASA manned programs.

Reasons for the Shuttle's High Cost

Reusable launch systems do not have to be expensive. To the contrary, many launch vehicle designers believe reusability is still the only solution to achieving greatly reduced launch costs, despite the experience with the Shuttle. It is worthwhile, therefore, to examine the reasons that the mostly-reusable Shuttle is the most expensive large launch system in the US inventory.

NASA intended the Space Shuttle to be the solution to the high cost and perceived wastefulness of the Saturn V and other expendable launch vehicles. The keys to the Shuttle's planned economic success were reusability and high usage rates. Reusability was an intuitively cost-effective approach, since "they don't throw away airplanes after one flight." High usage rates were critical to the Shuttle's economy because its huge development costs needed to be amortized in a reasonable amount of time. By taking advantage of the anticipated fast, low-cost refurbishment and turnaround, and by flying often, the Shuttle was expected to provide very low recurring costs per flight. In actuality, however, there never was any real intention to amortize the Shuttle's nonrecurring development costs. All estimates, including those that cited the need for high launch rates, were for recurring costs only.[3]

Making the Shuttle a Manned Vehicle

There is no doubt that human presence has provided a major, if not indispensable, benefit to many of the Space Shuttle missions. Astronauts have conducted a variety of complex operations that were either not feasible or not practical with automated systems. These include on-orbit satellite retrieval and maintenance, satellite pre-deployment troubleshooting and repair, comprehensive and detailed life sciences experiments, and space manufacturing and construction activities. All of these operations depended on human interaction, but few required a piloted, heavy-lift booster to be successful. The reason the Shuttle was used to support many of these missions is that it was, and still is, the only operational space launch system for humans available to the US.

The Space Shuttle was designed to carry both people and payloads. In retrospect, combining these two functions on a single vehicle was probably a mistake. A piloted launch vehicle design incurs a lengthy list of requirements not present in unmanned boosters. The entire system must be "man-rated," requiring additional steps to maximize launch reliability. Reliability objectives are much greater than those for unmanned boosters, although the extremely high cost of unmanned spacecraft has pushed even unmanned reliability requirements to high levels. It is very expensive to raise the target reliability from 98 percent, which would be acceptable for unmanned launch systems, to the 99.8 percent figure, or better, sought for human space flight.[4] Engineers must build extra levels of redundancy, additional design margins, and new safety-oriented subsystems into the design in striving for this increased reliability.

A piloted launch vehicle also requires many subsystems specifically dedicated to supporting the human cargo. The crew compartment, environmental control and life-support subsystems, and related equipment must be boosted into space for each mission. Each of these items takes away from the amount of usable payload capacity that would otherwise be available.

The Cost of Shuttle Recoverability/Reusability

In addition to the overhead required for manned launch systems like the Shuttle, reusability can bring its own set of liabilities. A reusable system is economically dependent on high launch rates, because the refurbishment and turnaround personnel and infrastructure must be maintained continuously, regardless of whether the launch system is operating or not. High launch rates require a large mission model, and NASA sought to establish an appropriately-sized one by lobbying for a US launch policy that declared the Shuttle to be the single launch vehicle for all future civil, military, and commercial payloads.

Reusability does not automatically make a launch system cost more. In fact, it can be the key to cost-effectiveness. The techniques used to achieve reusability are important factors in determining how cost-effective a booster becomes. But by requiring the Shuttle to glide through the atmosphere to a landing on a runway, designers imposed severe performance penalties on the system.[5]

Robert C. Truax is a retired Navy captain who was the Thor ballistic missile program manager for Bernard Schriever in the 1950s; he later worked for Aerojet General. In 1970 Truax stated his feelings about the Shuttle design proposal:

> These [Shuttle design] features, unfortunately, are near and dear to many proponents of reusable vehicles. They make the "aero" part of the aerospace industry feel needed. They even have an appeal to the non-technically minded. But they make about as much sense as requiring airplanes to be able to land at railroad stations. . . . There is no approach for returning a craft to Earth from orbit that is simpler, which costs us less payload, or, I submit, which is either quicker or less costly to develop or operate than the low-L/D [low lift-to-drag ratio], parachute-landed spacecraft using water touchdowns.[6]

Since the Shuttle lands like an airplane, it necessarily requires runways to land, not only at its primary landing site, but also at various secondary, tertiary, and contingency landing sites around the world. Some of these landing sites must be staffed by landing crews during each Shuttle mission, and the weather and lighting conditions at certain landing sites are limiting factors for launch and landing times.[7] For example, a number of Shuttle launch schedules have been negatively affected by the weather at the launch site—not because the weather was too bad to launch in, but because the weather at the Kennedy Space Center's Shuttle landing area (adjacent to the Shuttle launch pads) was not sufficiently good to allow high confidence in a landing there if an abort occurred during the Shuttle's ascent phase.

To glide to the recovery site and land like an airplane, the Space Shuttle Orbiter must have a host of structures and subsystems dedicated solely for this function. These include wing structure, tail structure, landing gear and associated components, control surfaces, extensive thermal protection, hydraulic systems, and flight control avionics. All of these weighty elements must be hauled into orbit every mission even though they are used only during the final minutes of flight.

Weight Penalties of the Shuttle's Design

If all of the structure and subsystems required to make the Orbiter recoverable as a glider were deleted, the dry weight of the Orbiter would decrease by 47 percent.[8] The solid rocket boosters (SRB) used by the Space Shuttle are also reusable, but they use parachutes and ocean splashdown for their recovery mode. The parachutes constitute only 3.4 percent of the SRBs' empty weight.[9]

If all of the structure and subsystems required to make the Shuttle a manned launch vehicle were removed, additional weight reductions could be achieved. If these reductions were combined with those postulated by the deletion of the elements required for an airplane-like recovery, the Orbiter's dry weight would decrease by 68 percent.[10] This figure is validated by the conceptual work done on the Shuttle-C proposal. Shuttle-C was intended to be an unmanned heavy lifter derived from Space Shuttle components. The vehicle would have used the Shuttle's external tank and SRBs, but designers planned to replace the Orbiter with an expendable payload shroud. The rear of this shroud would have contained elements of the Orbiter's aft fuselage, or "boattail" area, including the main engines.[11]

Space Shuttle Payload Fraction

The extra hardware required for the Shuttle's increased reliability, the subsystems needed to make the Shuttle capable of carrying humans, and the structure and components required for the Shuttle Orbiter's airplane-like recovery combine to add significant weight to the overall system. The ratio of the gross lift-off weight of the Space Shuttle (including payload) to the maximum amount of payload it can carry to low earth orbit is about 87:1.[12] In other words, for every 87 kilograms of total vehicle lift-off weight (including propellants), only one of these kilograms is useful payload weight. This payload fraction for the Shuttle compares with a 45:1 payload fraction for the Delta II 7920, a 27:1 fraction for the Atlas IIA, and a 48:1 fraction for the Titan IV (see table 4).[13]

Table 4

Ratios of Vehicle Gross Weight to Payload Weight

VEHICLE	RATIO
Delta II 7920	45 to 1
Atlas IIA	27 to 1
Titan IV	48 to 1
Space Shuttle	87 to 1

It is worth noting that the Orbiter itself, or certain portions of it, could be viewed as payload. The crew compartment provides an orbital work space where astronauts can conduct a variety of experiments and tests. The payload bay and associated airborne support equipment provide additional orbital work support functions for certain missions, including nondeployable payloads. A case can be made to consider the crew (or at least the mission and payload specialists) to be payload, which would cause all subsystems and equipment required to support astronauts in space to become payload as well. If one evaluated the Shuttle in this manner, its overall payload fraction would improve considerably.

Because of the Shuttle's relatively inefficient payload fraction, engineers had to take heroic steps in performance enhancement to obtain a useful amount of payload lift capacity. Propulsion technology had to be pushed to its limits through the use of cryogenic oxygen and hydrogen, very high chamber pressures, high-performance turbomachinery, and individual engine computer control for the main propulsion system. Structural weight had to be shaved to the last kilogram, and the thermal protection system required lightweight, very fragile, labor-intensive ceramic tiles. Since the tiles were so lightweight and fragile, they had to be protected at lift-off from falling ice that would form on a bare cryogenic propellant tank. Consequently, the large External Tank (ET) had to be completely covered with foam insulation, and a large gaseous oxygen vent mechanism had to be installed on the pad to prevent ice from forming on the tank's oxygen vents. Engineers designed the ET to be expendable, making the Space Shuttle only a partially reusable launch system. Even the expendable External Tank, which was originally conceived to be a very simple vehicle component, turned out to have a very sophisticated design.

In a continuing effort to increase the Space Shuttle's payload fraction, NASA is proposing to manufacture the External Tanks out of a new lightweight alloy. If the ETs were built of aluminum lithium instead of the heavier aluminum, the Shuttle would gain an additional 3,600 kilograms (8,000 pounds) of payload capacity. NASA estimates it would take four years and cost $134 million to convert to aluminum lithium ETs, and each tank's recurring cost would increase by $3 million.[14]

High Complexity Equals High Cost

The combination of reliability maximization, a human space flight capability, an airplane-like recovery mode, and overall performance maximization turned the Shuttle into a very complicated launch vehicle. This high complexity meant that launch processing and recovery turnaround operations would be an expensive, time-consuming undertaking that would require an army of people. The paper trail needed for documenting ground processing activities was staggering, and was exacerbated by the Challenger accident. Considering all these factors, it is not surprising that per-mission costs for the Shuttle have risen to as high as $547 million.[15]

The Design Establishes the Cost

Design considerations play a dominant role in establishing launch vehicle costs. For example, the decisions to base the Delta booster on the Thor ballistic missile and to make the Shuttle a piloted launcher that lands like an airplane were top-level design choices. The DOD's Defense Systems Management College teaches that 70 percent of the entire life cycle costs of DOD weapon systems are fixed during the concept exploration phase of development.[16] A NASA study stated that the configuration of a launch vehicle has a dominating influence on launch processing requirements and personnel head count, as well as on life cycle costs. The study found that simplicity was the key to reducing launch costs.[17]

The manufacturing process for a launch vehicle is driven by its design. Design considerations that directly affect manufacturing include the relative complexity of the design, the types of structural material and parts that will be used, and how much the design will push the state-of-the-art. The number of units produced each year has a major impact on manufacturing and cost—and design choices affect component manufacturability, which ultimately influences production rates.

Launch Vehicle Hardware Cost per Kilogram

Launch vehicles are, kilogram-for-kilogram, more expensive than almost any other manufactured product. Their cost, on a dollars-per-kilogram basis, is much higher than the cost of mass-produced commercial products, and is generally higher than the cost of aircraft (see table 5). By dividing the cost of a launch vehicle by its dry weight, you can derive how much, on the average, each kilogram of that particular vehicle costs to procure. A Delta II 7925 booster costs about $2,820 per kilogram ($1,160 per pound); an Atlas IIA costs around $6,530 per kilogram ($2,990 per pound). The Titan IV 401 configuration, which uses a Centaur upper stage, costs about $2,325 per kilogram ($1,050 per pound).[18] The recurring cost of a reusable Space Shuttle Orbiter, not including its external tank, its two solid rocket boosters, or its upper stage, is about $29,280 per kilogram ($13,285 per pound).[19] It should be noted that Delta's and Titan's heavy, relatively simple, and comparatively inexpensive solid-propellant strap-ons tend to skew their cost per kilogram downward. If the empty weight and the total cost of the solid strap-ons were deleted from the Delta and Titan calculations, the Delta's cost per kilogram would be comparable to that of an Atlas, while the Titan's cost per kilogram would be higher. These high per-kilogram costs are directly tied to design decisions and manufacturing processes.

Table 5

Vehicle Hardware Cost*

VEHICLE	COST
Delta II 7925	$2,820/kg. ($1,160/lb.)**
Atlas IIA	$6,530/kg ($2,990/lb)
Titan IV 401	$2,325/kg. ($1,050/lb.)**
Space Shuttle Orbiter***	$29,280/kg. ($13,285/lb.)
F-15 aircraft***	$2,650/kg ($1,200/lb)
Commercial jet***	$880/kg. ($400/lb)
Automobile***	$7/kg. ($3/lb.)

*Costs are in 1993 Dollars
** Heavy solid strap-on cases tend to skew costs downward
*** Reusable vehicle

The cost per kilogram of a high-performance fighter aircraft like the F-15 is about $2,650 ($1,200 per pound). A commercial jet costs approximately $880 per kilogram ($400 per pound), and a new automobile is about $6.50 per kilogram ($3 per pound).[20] Many would argue that a launch vehicle's high costs relative to other manufactured products are justified because of complex designs, unique performance requirements, exotic materials, aerospace-grade parts, government documentation requirements, and very low production rates.[21] These are clearly some of the reasons launch vehicles cost so much, but we can also view these so-called justifications for high launch prices as targets of opportunity to cut the cost of space transportation.

Production Influences

Launch vehicles are produced in extraordinarily small quantities. Consider for example that one of the higher production rates in the entire launch vehicle industry was only six units per month. Hercules vice president Nick Vlahakis said, "On GEMs [the graphite epoxy motors used as strap-ons by the Delta booster], we built six a month. That's a pretty big production rate."[22] Low production rates are usually caused by low launch rates, which are caused by low demand. This is the case with expendable launch vehicles. The reusable Shuttle Orbiter, of course, had such low manufacturing rates (only six were ever built, including *Enterprise*) that economy-of-scale considerations were never applicable. The low demand for expendable launch vehicles is caused by their own high cost, as well as the high cost and low quantity of payloads. The high cost of payloads, as we will discuss in more detail later in this study, is strongly influenced by the high cost of low-production-rate launch vehicles. This situation has created a vicious economic circle that neither the US government nor the aerospace industry has found a way out of.

Another factor contributing to the low production rates (and high costs) of expendable launch vehicles is that they are not designed to accommodate high-, or even modest-, rate production runs.[23] Engineers have a propensity for designing elegant solutions to problems. Unfortunately, rocket engineers do not always consider the manufacturing, operational, or cost implications of their designs. For example, a Titan IV fuel torus requires 186.6 work-hours of direct labor to manufacture. In addition, the process requires 93 indirect, or supervisory work-hours and 143 product assurance work-hours.[24] This totals 422.6 work-hours for the building of a single fuel torus, one of a myriad of components required for the engine alone. Prior to cancellation of the NLS effort, program personnel had worked hard to simplify the manufacture of key booster components and to reduce the number of parts. They recognized these as keys to lower manufacturing costs.

A large percentage of the work-hours used in manufacturing the Titan IV fuel torus is expended in striving for the high reliability needed for today's launch vehicles. The fuel torus will become part of a very expensive booster that is launching a very expensive payload. If the Titan IV had been designed to be man-rated, reliability requirements would have been even higher. The aerospace industry builds components very carefully and deliberately. It uses the very highest quality, most thoroughly tested, and most expensive parts available. It carefully documents every manufacturing process and every test of each component, from its origin as raw material all the way through launch.[25] This documentation process has become an enormous and costly, sometimes even schedule-driving, effort.[26]

The High Cost of Maximum Performance
and Minimum Weight

The quest for maximum performance and minimum weight is deeply ingrained in aerospace industry design approaches. Pilots have traditionally wanted to go faster and farther, and better performing, lighter aircraft have usually been the answer. This is why aluminum, composites, and even cloth, have been widely used as aircraft materials and why steel has not. In the case of a launch vehicle, however, it doesn't really matter how large the ratio of initial vehicle weight to payload weight is, as long as the cost per kilogram to low earth orbit is low. That is, the size (weight) of a booster might not be as critical as we normally assume. It may not be the most cost-effective solution to develop very high performance engines with high-power densities to boost the lightest booster airframes and payloads we can possibly design. Maximum performance and minimum weight designs are fundamental requirements for single-stage-to-orbit vehicles, but not for two- or three-stage vehicles. In fact, the more stages a booster has, the less important high performance and low weight become.[27]

The late George Koopman, cofounder of AMROC, said, "Existing aerospace firms are set up to produce maximum-performance products without regard to cost. They don't know how to think in commercial terms."[28] The result of a maximum performance, minimum weight launch vehicle design is a complex, high-technology booster with low design margins. These low design margins mean that the vehicle will not be rugged, fault-tolerant, or weather-insensitive, and that when failures occur they will tend to be instantaneously catastrophic. To compensate for this fragile, unforgiving vehicle design, engineers have typically added multiple redundant on-board systems, and have specified very deliberate manufacturing procedures using the highest reliability parts and components. The added redundancy and the specialized manufacturing compound the problems of complexity and high cost.

A complex, high-tech, highly redundant launch vehicle will be composed of a large number of parts, each representing a potential failure point. The higher the number of parts, the higher the number of interfaces. The more interfaces that are present (especially external interfaces), the more people that are required, both in the factory and at the launch base. Because of the intense deliberations and scrutiny associated with launch vehicle manufacture and operations, the number of interfaces a booster contains has a major influence on manpower requirements and total cost. Orbital Sciences Corporation's Taurus program manager, Joseph Padavano, said, "From the beginning, Pegasus and then Taurus were designed to minimize interfaces and to enable a small crew to check out the vehicle and integrate and launch it."[29]

The High Development Cost Roadblock

Major aerospace programs usually have very large development (onetime nonrecurring) costs for designing, developing, and prototyping the first copy of the desired system. Launch systems have historically followed this pattern, although the Space Shuttle is the only new large launch system developed by the US in the last 25 years. Big development costs for new launchers create a significant early hurdle for program proponents seeking to justify their system. In the case of new weapon systems, operational necessity is typically the central issue that program supporters must address. This is not the case, however, with new launch system proposals.

New launchers, particularly in the post-cold war environment, must increasingly pass the cost-effectiveness test—and high development costs make this difficult. These large initial outlays must be amortized somehow, and within a reasonable amount of time, so the launch system can start "paying its own way." There is a temptation to construct large, speculative, future mission models to allow projections of a high launch rate and rapid retirement of the development debt. In fact, this is one of the traps the Shuttle fell into. But the Shuttle's projected large mission model and frequent launch rate never materialized.

The high development costs of new launch systems tend to direct decision makers away from new program starts and toward maintaining the status quo. For example, the estimated development cost of the National Launch System, even after removing the NLS-1 heavy lifter, was $10.5 billion. For this money, the US would have gotten an initial NLS capability by the year 2002.[30] For the same amount of dollars, a payload customer could go out today and purchase 221 Delta II 7925 launches. This represents almost as many Delta launches as all the Delta missions flown since the program began in 1960.[31] The existing stable of US launch vehicles is expensive and not very responsive, but these vehicles are currently available at known prices and their development costs have long since been paid for. If Congress is to appropriate dollars for a new launch system, development costs must be significantly lower or proponents must articulate sufficiently compelling justifications for large development expenditures.

One of the reasons development costs are typically very high for large aerospace systems is the considerable amount of new technology, hardware, and software development required to field the system. Further, DOD and NASA program managers have often allowed, or even used, the acquisition of major aerospace systems to serve as a mechanism to advance the state-of-the-art in key technology areas. Although technology advances may be required in many cases in order to achieve program objectives, these new technologies are costly and managers must minimize their development. In the case of launch vehicles, the desire for a new booster that has maximum performance and minimum weight will demand certain technology advances and will require "repackaging" of existing systems and components to minimize weight and volume, all of which are expensive propositions.

The ticket to Orbital Sciences Corporation's successful commercial development of the Pegasus air-launched booster was low development costs. These low costs were enabled by savvy management and engineering, maximum use of off-the-shelf technology, hardware, and software, and a commercial development environment that was free of government involvement.[32]

Large government-funded aerospace programs generally have big development budgets, are staffed with many government employees, and attract large numbers of contractor personnel not directly involved in production. These contractors provide systems engineering technical advice and other analytical services. This government and contractor "oversite" can make development costs spiral upward, not only from labor costs, but also from the prodigious amount of data and studies they produce that require additional work-hours to review. They also develop technical analysis requirements for the contractor building the aerospace system that often are of questionable value but that still require significant work-hours and dollars to respond to. This, of course, is completely contrary to the approach taken by the early Lockheed "Skunkworks" programs, which had minimal government program office personnel and which achieved remarkable success.

It is likely that aerospace programs with big development costs will result in operational systems with big recurring costs.[33] This is particularly true with respect to expendable launch systems. Large development budgets, and the army of people that accompany them, usually build-in costly complexity, non-mandatory capabilities (bells and whistles), over-optimized performance (gold-plating), and excessive oversight and analysis. Reusable launch systems, especially single-stage-to-orbit designs, would likely have higher development costs than expendable vehicles, but they could have lower recurring costs. However, they would still need aggressive management to avoid the pitfalls normally caused by large development budgets.

One final factor in the cost of aerospace system development is the amount of modularity and system commonality in the design. For example, each of the Delta II 7925 vehicle's three stages is a completely separate design with its own unique propulsion system. There is no commonality between engine designs or propellants. The 7925 also employs a completely separate (and different) system of solid-propellant strap-on boosters (i.e., the Delta II 7925 configuration employs a core vehicle first stage using LOX/RP-1 propellants, a second stage using hypergolic propellants, a third stage using solid propellant, and a set of solid propellant strap-ons). If the Delta were designed today from a clean sheet of paper, it would require separate, dedicated development efforts for each of the stages and propulsion systems. The Titan IV with a Centaur upper stage has four unique stages (counting the solid strap-ons and the Centaur), and the Shuttle uses three separate and unique propulsion systems to achieve orbit. Each of these launch vehicles uses three of the major (and different) classes of chemical propellants: cryogenics, hypergolics, and solids.[34] The designers of these vehicles were not trying to maximize system commonality, but commonality can be an enabling technique for holding down the cost of new system development.

A Zero Tolerance for Failure

The demand for increasingly greater launch reliability continues to have a major influence on space transportation costs. This pursuit of high reliability is a manifestation of a larger cultural phenomenon: a zero tolerance for, and fear of, failure. To have a detailed understanding of in-flight performance and to be able to thoroughly troubleshoot problems, designers extensively instrument launch vehicles. Launch systems and their payloads are subjected to exhaustive testing at the factory and at the launch base. Arrays of engineers and managers closely monitor each launch. (In the case of the Shuttle, its entire mission.) Range safety requirements force the inclusion of onboard command destruct systems and the addition of a significant ground infrastructure of people and equipment. Downrange tracking stations provide booster tracking and communications connectivity for telemetry downlinks. Accountability, traceability, and quality assurance requirements have resulted in a gigantic documentation system and a commensurate amount of work-hours to create, update, review, and maintain it. This entire system of detailed oversight is motivated by a general lack of confidence that launch vehicles will perform as planned. Stamatios Krimigis, head of the Applied Physics Laboratory's space department, said, "[NASA] believe[s] reliability means expense. It's a disease that has permeated the NASA system."[35]

NASA Administrator Daniel Goldin, speaking at a NASA town meeting in Tampa, Florida, in December 1992, said that the fear of failure was "a sickness that pervades our society."[36] In government-run programs, government managers will inherently select what appears to be the safest option, with little regard for cost. This is because government employees are not motivated by profit, but by mission success. They are aware that honest cost overruns are much more acceptable, professionally, politically, and culturally, than program failures. And as previously mentioned, in-flight booster failures tend to be catastrophic. The media thrives on failures, and a government employee's worst nightmare is a high-visibility, career-ending aerospace fiasco. Therefore, when confronted with a set of options, managers almost never select those that might hold the promise of reduced cost, greater efficiency, or more capability if the options have a perceived higher risk, however slight.

In the US, the space program in general, and human space flight in particular, has always been a highly visible, public undertaking. Both the accomplishments and the problems of the early manned space program received extraordinary media coverage and public interest. The Shuttle program also received widespread and relatively balanced coverage initially. As Shuttle flights became more and more routine, however, mission successes became less and less newsworthy. The media began to focus on problems, with Shuttle ground maintenance difficulties and the Hubble Space Telescope problems being some examples.

The Apollo capsule fire and the *Challenger* accident brought about intense media scrutiny, political inquiry, and public finger-pointing. Although these losses were indeed tragic, seasoned test pilots questioned why there was so much public hand-wringing, concern, and sympathy when many of their comrades had suffered similar fates in virtual anonymity. They viewed flight testing as a very dangerous profession and accidents as an unfortunate but inevitable part of aerospace progress. This is in no way meant to imply that we should not be sensitive to the loss of human lives. However, there was a time when taking well-considered risks and having occasional accidents were better tolerated in our society. If early aviation pioneering in the US had been subjected to the same amount of oversight, and the failure intolerance afforded today's space program, its astoundingly successful commerical application would have been, at best, severely delayed.

Navy Captain David C. Honhart, former president of the American Astronautical Society, said about the *Challenger* accident:

> My personal thought is that we made a mistake following the *Challenger* accident. After it was determined that the booster joint was the cause of the accident, we should have taken the position that the problem was not an engineering problem, but rather an operational problem, and rather than looking for an engineering fix, we should have looked for an operations fix; that is, we will not operate the shuttle launch system below some temperature and surely not with icicles hanging from the gantry. . . . I think it is important for the American people to realize that space travel is a dangerous business—more so than flying in an airplane or driving in a car—and that other accidents will occur, and all the fancy formal reviews and all the finger pointing and all the 20-some approval signatures required in the future will not alter the statistical fact of accidents to come. There is risk involved. However, when accidents happen we must pick up the ball and start running again without significant delays.[37]

Launch Vehicle Remote Monitoring

Current launch vehicles are complicated systems that can have very complicated failure modes. When vehicle failures occur, they are usually very costly, gut-wrenching experiences. Consequently, engineers have, for years, designed extensive system monitoring instrumentation into launch vehicles for ground testing and in-flight analysis. This instrumentation, and the communications equipment to get its data to the ground, is the rough equivalent of the "black box" voice and data flight recorders carried on today's large aircraft. In contrast to the aircraft recorders, however, data provided by booster monitoring instrumentation can be analyzed in real time by the team of ground personnel tracking the vehicle's progress. Downrange stations are necessary to provide tracking data and communications connectivity, and this capability for remote, instantaneous assessment of space boosters is expensive to develop, install, and staff. Even with this capability, there are no guarantees that all failure modes will be identified.

Despite large amounts of data from an array of sensors, engineers could not directly and immediately ascertain the cause of the two identical Centaur engine failures that occurred in 1991 and 1992. General Dynamics even considered attempting a recovery of Centaur hardware to help identify the source of the failure, despite the fact that the wreckage splashed down into deep water in the Atlantic Ocean. Michael Wynne, president of space systems and commercial launch services at General Dynamics, said "I'm not sure whether we will understand fully why this engine failed."[38] The cause of the failures was ultimately uncovered through intensive analysis and testing.[39]

In the aftermath of failures like the Centaur engine experienced, there is a strong inclination to increase the vehicle's instrumentation to enhance the probability of easier and more direct failure analysis when future failures occur. Such practices tend to put the vehicle into an instrumentation growth spiral, but the complex nature of current booster designs may not allow any other solutions.

One school of thought supports extensive vehicle instrumentation for future expendable launch vehicles so that system downtime can be minimized if a failure occurs.[40] This approach has some merit, but program managers must carefully weigh its benefits with the added complexity, manpower overhead, and cost that such an approach requires. And designers may be able to minimize system monitoring by developing simple, forgiving vehicles with robust design margins.

Range Safety Requirements

An event associated with the testing of captured German V-2 missiles by the US Army provided the genesis for today's range safety infrastructure and command destruct systems. On 29 May 1947, German rocket scientists, working with Army and General Electric personnel, launched a V-2 that had been specially modified with an upper stage for ramjet research from White Sands Proving Ground, New Mexico. Round #0 of the Hermes II series started experiencing control problems four seconds into the flight, causing the vehicle to fly south instead of following its planned northern trajectory. The vehicle contained no destruct package, but ground personnel could have terminated thrust with a transmitted command. They delayed sending this command, however, to allow the missile to expend its propellant. As a result, it crossed the international border and impacted 76 kilometers (47 miles) south of the launch site near the city of Juarez, Mexico. No one was hurt, but it created an international incident and forced the Army to cease launch activities until much better range safety systems and procedures could be developed.[41]

During the launch stand-down, the Army installed a system that integrated radar data into an automatic plotting board, an impact computer that provided continuous trajectory predictions, and a visually-cued sky screen. These systems were installed to help keep missiles within the bounds of the proving ground and away from populated areas.[42] Technical descendents of these systems are still used today—and for the same purpose. Costly range safety systems are maintained at all US ranges. All launch vehicles, including the human-carrying Shuttle, have destruct packages that allow safety personnel to destroy any vehicle that goes off course so that populated areas will not be threatened.

It is worth noting that large commercial, military, and civil aircraft, filled with huge quantities of flammable jet fuel, routinely ply the skies directly over densely populated areas of the US. These aircraft carry no destruct systems, and they have no remote real time system-monitoring capability or the team of trained personnel to support it. However, they do communicate with aircraft controllers whose primary job is to keep proper distance between the huge number of aircraft flying at any one time. These aircraft occasionally have accidents, sometimes with significant loss of life to both passengers and people on the ground. Investigations ensue, but there is rarely any interruption of transport service. There is no national hue and cry, and passengers continue to travel by air. They are aware that there are risks involved in flying on commercial aircraft. They weigh those risks against the benefits that air travel provides, then make their decision whether or not to fly.

It is certainly true that launch systems have not yet demonstrated the kind of reliability typical of large transport aircraft. But it is also true that today's in-flight monitoring and range safety procedures are at least partially based on early missile reliability figures that were much worse than those exhibited by current launch vehicles.

An inelegant but cost-effective means of astronaut transport: an Apollo capsule returns from a mission and heads for a water splashdown.

An elegant but expensive means of astronaut transport: the orbiter *Challenger* makes the initial Shuttle landing at Kennedy Space Center.

The Space Shuttle main engine, ultra-optimized for maximum performance and minimum weight.

The patchwork quilt-like covering of tiles on the belly of the orbiter _Columbia_.

The expendable external tank for the STS-4 mission.

The gaseous oxygen vent hood undergoes tests at the KSC Launch Equipment Test Facility.

Installation of the Delta booster's solid-propellant strap-ons.

Hermes II, Round #1, very similar in configuration to the Round #0 vehicle that flew off-course and landed in a Juarez, Mexico, cemetery.

Summary

This chapter has discussed many of the causes of high launch costs. The early missile and space programs have handed down a proud, but expensive, design and operations legacy. Current design and manufacturing practices, along with a continuing drive for greater reliability, also contribute to high costs. Understanding why space launch is so expensive is an important step toward developing practical solutions. Another important step is to explode some myths about launch vehicle design and operations.

Notes

1. Jacob Neufeld, *The Development of Ballistic Missiles in the United States Air Force, 1945–1960* (Washington, D.C.: Government Printing Office, 1990), 108–09, 133–35.

2. Ibid., 47.

3. Gerard Elverum to John London, letter, 2 January 1993.

4. R. C. Truax, "The Commercialization of Space: Will It Ever Happen?" (Paper presented at Seminar on Private Sector Initiatives for Space Entrepreneurial Firms, Redondo Beach, Calif., July 1992), 2.

5. R. C. Truax, "Sea Dragon in the Manned Mars Mission," *The Journal of Practical Applications in Space,* Fall 1990, 14.

6. Robert C. Truax, "Shuttles—What Price Elegance?" *Astronautics and Aeronautics,* June 1970, 22.

7. James T. McKenna, "Endeavour Crew Begins Tests After TDRS Deployment," *Aviation Week & Space Technology,* 18 January 1993, 26.

8. Truax, "The Commercialization of Space," 2.

9. Ibid.

10. Truax Engineering brochure, "Project Private Enterprise: A Commercial Space Transport Program," Truax Engineering Inc., Saratoga, Calif., 1984, 2.

11. Marcellus G. Harsh, "Shuttle-C, Evolution to a Heavy Lift Launch Vehicle" (Paper presented at the AIAA/ASME/SAE/ASEE 25th Joint Propulsion Conference, Monterey, Calif., 10–12 July 1989), 1–2.

12. Steven J. Isakowitz, *International Reference Guide to Space Launch Systems* (Washington, D.C.: The American Institute of Aeronautics and Astronautics, 1991), 250.

13. Ibid., 188–89, 205, 208, 267–68.

14. Liz Tucci, "Plan to Build Lighter Shuttle Tanks Advances," *Space News,* 31 May–6 June 1993, 16.

15. William Harwood, "Launch Cost of a Shuttle: Take Your Pick," *Space News,* 30 November–6 December 1992, 29.

16. Jess M. Sponable, "Reliable Low Cost Space Transportation: Impossible or Intolerable?," *The Journal of Practical Applications in Space,* Summer 1990, 59.

17. "NASA: Shuttle Ground Operations Efficiencies/Technology Study Final Report," vol. 6, NAS 10-11344, in Sponable, "Reliable Low Cost Space Transportation," 59.

18. Isakowitz, 190–92, 206–9, 267–72.

19. Edward L. Keith, "Low Cost Launcher Viewgraphs," Microcosm, Inc., Torrance, California, 1992, Slide 2.3.

20. Ibid.

21. Edward L. Keith, "Low Cost Space Transportation: The Search for the Lowest Cost" (Paper presented at the AAS/AIAA Spaceflight Mechanics Meeting, Johnson Space Center, Houston, Texas, 13 February 1991), 6.

22. Frank Colucci, "Taurus Technology," *Space,* December 1992–February 1993, 22.

23. Edward L. Keith, "Low Cost Space Transportation: Hurdles of Implementation" (Paper presented at the AIAA/SAE/ASME/ASEE 27th Joint Propulsion Conference, Sacramento, California, 24–26 June 1991), 8.

24. Aerojet TechSystems, "Rocket Engine Combustion Devices Design and Demonstration NLB8DP," Sacramento, Calif., 23 September 1988, 4–9, in Keith, "Low Cost Space Transportation," 8.

25. Keith, "Low Cost Space Transportation," 8.

26. James R. French, "Paperwork is a Launch-Vehicle Roadblock," *Aerospace America,* April 1988, 18.

27. Keith, "Low Cost Launcher Viewgraphs," Slide 4.3.

28. Gregg Easterbrook, "Big Dumb Rockets," *Newsweek,* 17 August 1987, 57.

29. Colucci, 20.

30. Edward A. Grabis, "Progress on the National Launch System Demonstrates National Commitment" (Charts from presentation made at the World Space Congress, Washington, D.C., 31 August 1992).

31. Isakowitz, 204; J. F. Meyers, "Delta for the 1990s" (Paper presented at the World Space Congress, Washington, D.C., 31 August 1992), 7.

32. "Spacesaver," *Aviation Week & Space Technology,* 3 September 1990, S 6.

33. Keith, "Low Cost Launcher Viewgraphs," Slide 3.9.

34. Isakowitz, 206–8, 251, 253–54, 269–71.

35. Leonard David, "NASA Seeks Access to Strategic Defense Technology," *Space News,* 17–23 May 1993, 29.

36. Beth Dickey, "A Golden Opportunity," *Air & Space,* February/March 1993, 18.

37. Capt David C. Honhart, "Another Way of Thinking," *The Space Times,* November–December 1987, 13.

38. Jeffrey M. Lenorovitz, "Target Date Set for Restart of Atlas/Centaur Missions," *Aviation Week & Space Technology,* 26 October 1992, 72.

39. Jeffrey Lenorovitz, "Atlas/Centaur Targeted for March Launch," *Aviation Week & Space Technology,* 18 January 1993, 27–28.

40. Vice President's Space Policy Advisory Board, *The Future of the U.S. Space Launch Capability* (Washington, D.C.: National Space Council, November 1992), 31.

41. John R. London III, "Brennschluss Over the Desert—V-2 Operations at White Sands, 1946–1952" (Paper presented at the 38th International Astronautical Federation Congress, Brighton, UK, 10 October 1987), 9.

42. Ibid.

Chapter 5

The Necessity for Complexity Myth

There is a general belief in the US that launching rockets into space has been, is, and always will be a complex undertaking that requires extremely sophisticated equipment, large budgets, and personnel possessing the highest intellects in the land. However, we must focus on the fundamental demands of rocketry in order to develop an accurate understanding of the true requirements for space launch.

To place launch vehicles in proper perspective, we need to compare the designs of their powerplants to the designs of various aircraft propulsion systems. Despite the perception of complexity associated with launch vehicles in the US, Soviet launch vehicle designs and operating practices, along with the experience of German V-2 rocket engineers during World War II, indicate that simple design and manufacturing approaches are practical. A number of private experimental rocketry organizations have successfully built and flown solid, liquid, and hybrid propellant sounding rockets on shoestring budgets. There have also been several notable successes by the US aerospace industry in developing simple rocket engines and launch systems. These examples provide important precedents and lessons learned for building inexpensive space boosters. This chapter will debunk the notion that complexity is a necessary characteristic of space launch systems. It will support the idea that simple, very inexpensive launch vehicles are, in fact, possible.

Launch Vehicle Complexity: Myths and Realities

In the 1950s and 1960s, there was a widespread public fascination with space in general and with manned spaceflight in particular. The conquest of space was psychologically tied to the most exotic, cutting-edge technology in existence. Even today, this linking of space and complicated technology is reflected in popular colloquial expressions such as, "You don't have to be a rocket scientist to understand this problem." The term "space age" is a euphemism for anything associated with high technology.[1] This attitude has created an assumption and an expectancy, by both the man on the street and the aerospace engineer, that space systems will be highly complex.

Today's launch vehicles and spacecraft are surrounded by a powerful aura of elaborateness, of almost priceless value, and of fragility. Although these perceived characteristics are not without justification, they are amplified by our sense that space systems and their rocket-propelled launch vehicles must be of the utmost complexity. Anyone who has ever worked at a launch base such as Cape Canaveral or Vandenberg knows that you never touch space hardware unless you have a very strong justification (such as a work order in your hand). You don't need to be told; you just know not to do it. This is because space hardware is treated and handled with the utmost care, and workers are imbued with the sense, or even fear, that the slightest touch could result in millions of dollars in damage. Spacecraft are usually manufactured—as well as processed at the launch site—in a clean room environment, and this serves to reemphasize the high-tech nature of space systems.

Launch vehicles traditionally require a massive team of personnel to process and launch—at very high cost. Yet the complex and expensive Apollo program accomplished six lift-offs with a launch crew of only two people, and they did it from the surface of another world. The preflight checkout was accomplished from inside the cockpit of the launch vehicle, although the two-man launch team had plenty of remote monitoring and analysis support.

A launch vehicle's fundamental requirement is to lift its payload above the atmosphere, and to impart to the payload a velocity vector of sufficiently accurate direction and speed. An expendable launch vehicle must accomplish this requirement by working right once for a total of approximately eight minutes. Despite these seemingly less-than-stressing performance requirements, space launchers—including expendable boosters—are expensive, complex, machines that need very careful handling and benign operating environments.

One of the reasons for the complexity of launch vehicles, particularly with regard to the Space Shuttle and many of the new launch concepts NASA has proposed over the years, may be an institutional attitude within the space agency about technology development. Launch vehicle design consultant James R. French said:

> NASA is not interested in developing systems which do not require improvements in the state of the art. This is a matter of both natural bias and organizational charter. While NASA cannot really be criticized for this attitude, it certainly stands in the way of developing low cost operational vehicles.[2]

Navy Captain David C. Honhart, former president of the American Astronautical Society, said:

> We have a propensity in this country to strive for complex sophisticated solutions, when perhaps less complex systems would get the job done. Admiral Gorshkov of the Soviet Navy maintained that "Better is the enemy of good enough . . ." I think there is a lesson there for all of us.[3]

Rocket Engines and Aircraft Engines

To better establish whether extreme complexity and its attendant high cost are mandatory characteristics of space launch vehicles, it is helpful to review the development history of rockets and aircraft, and to compare rocket engines to various aircraft propulsion systems. Modern US aircraft engines are manufactured by the same aerospace industry that builds rocket engines; and these systems share enough commonality in design practices, materials usage, and performance requirements to allow at least a limited apples-to-apples comparison.

Rockets are not a product of twentieth century technological advances; they have been around for a long time. Solid propellant rockets have existed for many hundreds of years, the Chinese apparently having known of the technology since the eleventh century. They were probably the first to practically apply Issac Newton's third law of motion (long before the British scientist ever formulated it). This centuries-old heritage of black powder-based rocketry is reflected today in China's domination of the world's commercial fireworks market. The British used solid propellant rockets developed by William Congreve during the War of 1812; and both Union and Confederate forces used rockets similar to the British weapons during the American Civil War.[4]

On 16 March 1926, Professor Robert Goddard conducted the first successful flight of a liquid-propellant rocket near Auburn, Massachusetts, less than 23 years after the first powered flight of an aircraft. Goddard's rocket engine used liquid oxygen and gasoline, and propelled the rocket to a height of 12.5 meters (41 feet). The flight duration was a mere 2.5 seconds. Nevertheless, this important first step in modern rocketry was, in many ways, comparable to the Wright brothers' historic 1903 flight. Dr Goddard continued his work at a site near Roswell, New Mexico. Between 1930 and 1941, he made important contributions to the development of practical liquid-propellant rockets. Despite having to operate on a limited budget and receiving little interest from the US government, Goddard laid the groundwork for the liquid-propellant ballistic missiles and launch vehicles of the future.[5]

Although the first powered aircraft flew in 1903, its powerplant was based on reciprocating engine technology derived from the automobile engine, which had been developed in the late nineteenth century. Gas turbine aircraft engine designs, on which all modern jet engines are based, were not practically demonstrated until the World War II era. By that time, the Germans had V-2 ballistic missiles with 222,400-Newton-(50,000-pound-) thrust liquid rocket engines in mass production—under wartime conditions.[6]

The liquid rocket engine and the solid rocket motor are mechanically, in their simplest forms, much less complex than the simplest reciprocating engine or jet engine. Launch vehicle engineer Edward Keith has described the simple liquid-propellant rocket engine as "a one-cylinder engine with no piston."[7] The rocket engine experiences a thermal environment, propellent and exhaust gas-flow rates, and internal pressures that are generally more stressing than those of aircraft engines. Yet it remains a fundamentally simple device. The grammar school teacher who blows up a balloon and then releases it to illustrate the principle of jet propulsion is actually demonstrating something that is much closer in design to a rocket engine than to a jet engine.

A liquid rocket engine becomes complicated when engineers seek to maximize performance with enhancements. Examples of typical enhancements are very high combustion chamber pressures, ultra-lightweight materials that can still handle high thermal ranges, complex cooling systems, exotic and hard-to-handle propellant combinations, computers to optimize propellant mixture ratios, and very high-speed turbomachinery.

The Example of Russian Launch Vehicles

A comparison of US launch systems to those operated by Russia reveals important information about US and Russian design, manufacturing, and operational practices. Russian launch vehicles, which cost only one-half to one-fifth as much as US boosters, have demonstrated superior reliability records (see table 6). For example, the Vostok family of launchers, derived from the old Sapwood SS-6 ICBM, is comparable in performance to the Atlas Centaur, but it has a unit cost of only $17.3 million.[8] Between 1970 and 1990, Vostok boosters accomplished 1,108 launches with only three failures, resulting in a reliability of 99.73 percent.[9] Although some may try to dismiss the Vostok's low cost as simply a result of unreliable currency conversion calculations and Russian attempts to buy into the international launch market, the reliability figures speak for themselves. The Russians achieved these figures despite routinely launching in temperatures ranging from –48 degrees centigrade (–55 Fahrenheit) to 41 degrees centigrade (105 Fahrenheit), under blizzard conditions, and in high winds.[10]

Table 6

Vostok and Atlas Comparison

	VEHICLE COST ($M)*	LAUNCHES (1970–1990)	FAILURES (1970–1990)	RELIABILITY (1970–1990)
Vostok	17.3	1,108	3	99.73%
Atlas	80.0	100	10	90.0%

*Costs are in 1993 Dollars

During the same period (1970–1990), Atlas boosters were launched 100 times with 10 failures, for a reliability record of 90 percent;[11] and it is safe to assume that the Atlas launchers were manufactured with significantly superior parts and processes, and with more quality control measures (which partially explains the Atlas' higher cost).[12] Weather is always a major concern for any US launch vehicle, so launch support personnel must conduct a battery of meteorological measurements using balloons, sounding rockets, and other data sources prior to every launch. When an Atlas Centaur was destroyed in 1987 due to a lightning strike on the vehicle, the result was even tighter launch weather restrictions for all US boosters.[13]

Despite much cruder manufacturing practices—and operating sometimes in weather conditions that would close commercial airports—the Russian Vostoks are markedly less expensive and much more reliable than their US counterparts.[14] Nor are these characteristics unique to the Vostok-Atlas comparison;

they are generally true when comparing any Russian booster to a US launcher of commensurate performance.

Simple and Rugged Russian Booster Designs

To a large extent, engineers in the former Soviet Union were able to develop inexpensive and reliable boosters because economic conditions in their country forced them to. Compared to US launch vehicles that were designed for maximum performance and minimum weight, Soviet booster designs were suboptimized. However, "suboptimized" is a very relative term—the Soviet launchers got the job done, even though they were larger, heavier, and cruder than US launch vehicles with similar performance. Furthermore, they were cheaper and more reliable than corresponding American boosters.

Lacking the kind of scientific, engineering, and economic infrastructure that existed in the US, the Soviets used a few good, simple designs and modularized them. They could, therefore, be coupled together in various combinations to meet different mission requirements. This contrasts sharply with the traditional US approach, in which engineers typically start from scratch and custom design the system from top to bottom to meet specific and unique mission requirements. The Soviet design approach would not be very exciting to a US engineer who is eager to exercise his or her design skills against a challenging problem. But despite being somewhat boring technically, Soviet designs maximized the use of existing resources and minimized nonrecurring design and development costs.[15] James Oberg, an authority on the Russian space program and an engineer at NASA's Johnson Space Center, said, "We have spent our resources chasing the will-o'-the-wisp of maximum pressure and minimum weight. The [Russians] just build big, crude rockets and save their money."[16]

Aerospace historian Roger E. Bilstein, in his landmark history of the Apollo/Saturn launch vehicles, *Stages to Saturn,* superbly captured the dramatic differences between US and Soviet design philosophies.

> The tank skins and structural elements of American vehicles were kept at minimum thicknesses, shaving the weight of the structure as much as possible to enhance the payload capability. The first Western insight into the style of Soviet vehicle structure occurred in 1967, when the Vostok spacecraft and booster system were put on display in Paris. The Russians' series of A-type vehicles appear to have been exceedingly heavy. The Vostok launch vehicle arrived via Rouen, France, by sea, prior to shipment to Paris. To move the tank sections of the launch vehicle, workers hooked up cables to the opposite ends of the tank sections and picked them up empty, surprising many western onlookers who expected them to buckle in the middle. Their amazement was compounded when the Soviet technicians proceeded to walk the length of these tank sections, still suspended in mid-air, without damaging them in the least. The Russian vehicles were, if anything, extremely rugged.[17]

An Example of Simplicity—The Russian RD-107 Rocket Engine

An excellent example of a Soviet suboptimized design which is very cost-effective and highly modular, is the RD-107 rocket engine, the propulsion system for the Vostok booster strap-ons. The RD-107, like many Soviet rocket

The Rocketdyne MA series engines used by the Atlas launch vehicle.

engine designs, differs from Western engines by having multiple thrust chambers for each engine. Western rocket engines traditionally have one thrust chamber per engine. (The Rocketdyne MA series two-barrel booster engine used on the Atlas launch vehicle is one notable exception.[18]) The Gas Dynamics Laboratory-Experimental Design Bureau developed the RD-107 between 1954 and 1957.[19]

The RD-107 was derived from captured German V-2 rocket engine technology. It uses a liquid oxygen (LOX)-kerosene propellant combination, avoiding more exotic and energetic combinations like LOX-hydrogen.[20] The thrust chambers are not constructed from the bundles of tubes so common in regeneratively cooled US designs, but are made of low-grade stainless steel with a copper lining. This design simplifies the engine's manufacture, which is important since the Russians have averaged building at least four thrust chambers per workday for over 20 years.[21]

Although the four-chamber feature of the RD-107 caused the Vostok strapons to be wide at the base and heavier overall, the multiple-chamber design likely has provided an important benefit to engine production. By having to produce four smaller thrust chambers per engine instead of one large one, combined with the high production requirements for all Vostok subsystems, the Russians have been able to enjoy tremendous economies of scale by Western booster manufacturing standards. Since each RD-107 has only one turbopump assembly (albeit a higher-pressure system compared to Western designs of the 1950s), the Russians have had to produce only one-fourth as many of these relatively complex components as the simple thrust chambers. The gross size of the RD-107 turbomachinery indicates that it is probably much easier to manufacture than Western turbomachinery, which is designed for maximum power density.[22]

Each Vostok booster uses four identical RD-107-powered strap-ons and a sustainer core, which uses a slight modification of the RD-107 engine called the RD-108. The Russians have launched well in excess of a thousand Vostok-type boosters over the years, and this large number combined with the modular nature of the Vostok design has allowed high production rates of vehicle components.[23] In fact, the Russians have averaged a delivery every workday for over 20 years of at least one turbomachinery assembly, one strap-on or sustainer core section, and four engine thrust chambers.[24]

Systems like the RD-107 engine and the Vostok booster are good examples of designs that were used over and over in a very effective manner. This Russian penchant for reusing existing technology is reflected not only in their launch vehicles but also in their payload designs. The Vostok spacecraft, for example, was originally used as an early cosmonaut carrier but has been modified to perform a variety of unmanned missions, including biological research and photo-reconnaissance.

Russian Launch Operations—
Simple and Fast

Russian launch operations are very different from launch processing techniques commonly used for US launch vehicles. Russian boosters are typically built horizontally in enclosed buildings and then transported to the launch site by rail. At the launch site, the entire booster stack is erected to a vertical position, loaded with propellants, and launched. This approach is distinctly different from procedures used for US launchers; US procedures include significant and lengthy processing and testing that often result in vehicles being on the pad for months. The pad time for Russian launchers is typically measured in hours.

Russian launch practices were likely born out of necessity. The frequently harsh weather encouraged keeping outside activities as brief as possible, and the high launch rate did not allow launch pads to be tied up for extended periods. Also, the simple, rugged designs of the Russian boosters and payloads permitted engineers to gain acceptable confidence in mission success with only limited and brief testing and checkout. The Russian launch vehicles' short pad dwell times and high launch rates translate into greatly reduced per-mission launch costs when compared to US launchers.

The Russian Launch Program— Simple, Modular, and Robust

The Russians have achieved a low-cost, reliable launch capability because, first of all, they used simple, damage-tolerant designs that were less than optimum by Western standards (from a performance and weight minimization standpoint). The Soviet boosters and their subsystems were designed to be highly modular, allowing vehicle customization for various missions without always requiring completely new launch systems. Soviet launcher modularity also provided the opportunity for large manufacturing economies of scale for many components. Either because of pragmatic engineering judgment or because of economic necessity, the Soviets reused existing designs for decades, making minor modifications only when necessary.

Their launch operations emphasize off-line processing and minimum pad time; and their simple, rugged launch vehicles have required minimal launch pad testing. Also, Russian boosters have enjoyed high launch rates, thus enhancing manufacturing economies of scale and driving unit costs down. It is interesting to speculate on how well US industries would do if they applied these simple factors in a completely commercially-driven venture. After all, the reliable, low-cost Russian launch capability has been built by a country in which inefficiency and waste have been historically endemic.

The Lessons of the German V-2 Missile Program

The German V-2 ballistic missile offers another example of a rocket program that succeeded despite developmental, manufacturing, and operational conditions that were far less than ideal. The V-2 had few of the benefits that the development and production process for today's boosters routinely enjoy, but the program still achieved remarkable success despite these shortcomings. The V-2 design laid the foundation for modern liquid-propellant missiles and launch vehicles.

The Early German Rocket Program

On 17 December 1930, German army officers met to discuss the possible use of rockets as weapons of war. Since the Versailles Treaty did not expressly

A captured German V-2 ballistic missile.

71

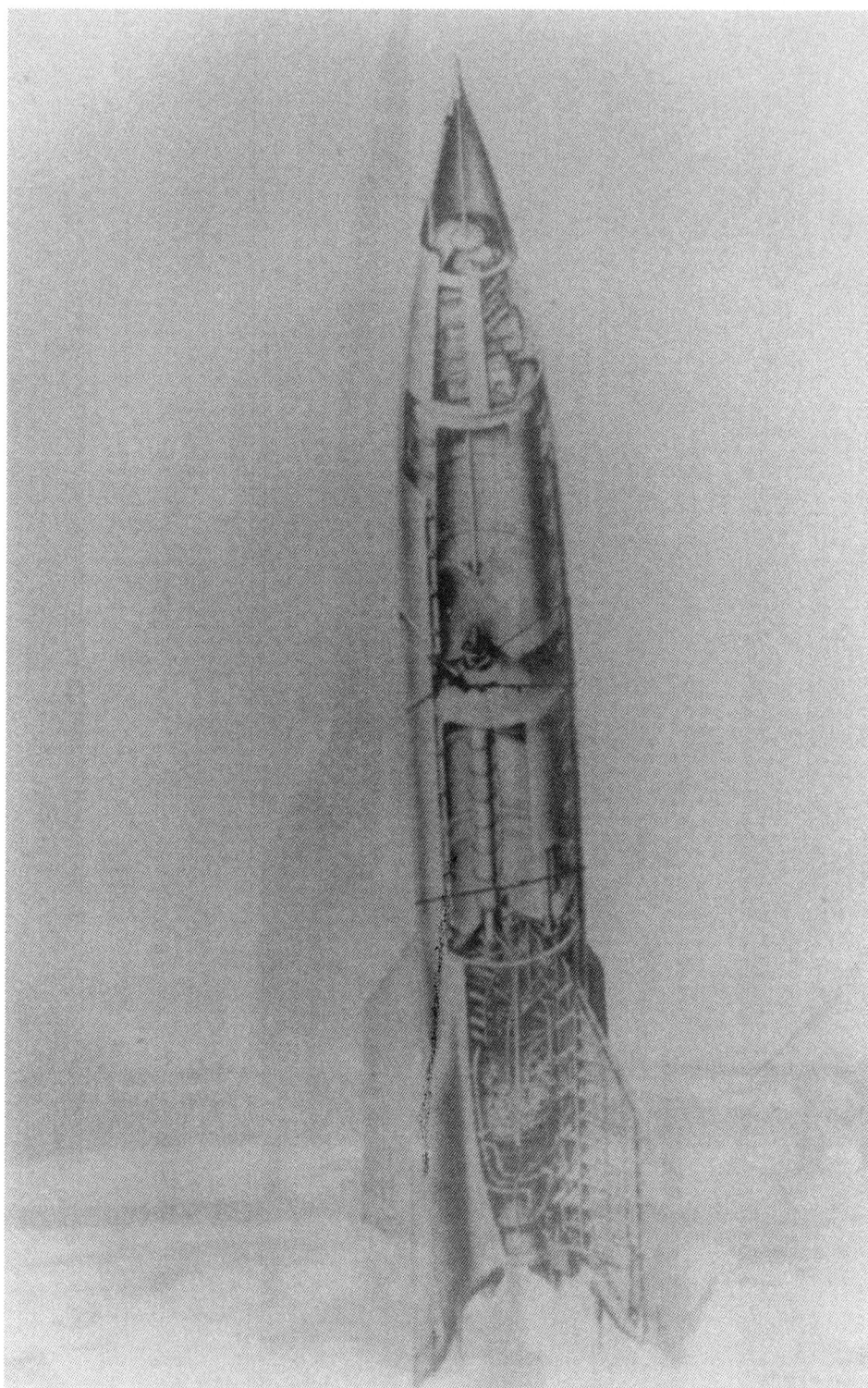

Cutaway drawing of the V-2's internal configuration.

72

The V-2 rocket engine.

forbid Germany's possessing rockets as weapons, Wehrmacht officers viewed them as a legitimate technology. The German army appointed Capt (later Maj Gen) Walter R. Dornberger to oversee the development of large military rockets and, in 1932, Dornberger hired Wernher von Braun to begin building experimental liquid-propellant rocket engines. Dornberger then assembled a capable team of engineers and technicians for the task at hand. Throughout the 1930s, the Wehrmacht's rocket program yielded progressively more powerful and capable prototype ballistic missiles.[25]

By 1937, most of the German technical team had moved to the new rocket research site at Peenemunde, on the Baltic Sea.[26] By this time, development of the A-4 missile was well under way. The Germans intended the A-4, with a planned warhead weight of 900 kilograms (2,000 pounds), to be an operational weapon. The missile's 222,400-Newton (25-ton) thrust engine used liquid oxygen and an alcohol-water mixture. The engine used the gas-generator cycle to power its turbomachinery. The A-4 was a tremendous engineering achievement. It pioneered a number of technologies, including inertial guidance techniques and the use of a hydrogen peroxide-fueled steam generator in conjunction with the LOX-alcohol turbopump.[27] Despite fluctuating funding

73

and a generally low priority within the German military, an A-4 was successfully launched for the first time on 3 October 1942.

Wartime Production of the V-2

Hitler ordered the A-4 to be placed in full production, and an underground factory was constructed in the Harz Mountains near Nordhausen in central Germany. The Germans formed a state-owned corporation called Mittelwerk to manufacture the A-4s (or V-2s, as they would become dubbed by the Nazi propaganda organization). The factory's manpower resources were largely provided by the collocated Dora concentration camp.[28]

The working environment in the underground Mittelwerk facility was appalling—the worst possible examples of SS-managed slave labor. Starving workers were subjected to severe physical abuse, and disease was rampant.[29] Despite these wretched conditions, a number of prisoners defiantly carried out an active program of sabotage against the production of the V-2s.[30] Jean Michel gives his eyewitness account of the concentration camp in Dora. He describes one instance where a prisoner had sabotaged 152 parts in a single day. Michel writes:

> I am even sure that the German scientists would have preferred to see their marvellous missiles made in more civilized factories and by a better treated work-force. They probably deplored the delays that our technical incompetence and our physical condition—not to speak of our sabotage—caused their programme.[31]

On 31 December 1943 the first few production V-2s rolled off the Mittelwerk assembly line. The factory built 50 missiles in January 1944, and produced a monthly high of 690 missiles a year later. Between January 1944 and March 1945, a total of 5,947 V-2s were fabricated in the subterranean factory. Of these, the Germans ultimately launched 3,600 against targets in England and on the European continent. Out of the 3,600 V-2s launched, 2,890 reached their targets, demonstrating a reliability of 80 percent.[32] The V-2 achieved this remarkably high percentage despite all of the liabilities working against its success.

The Germans mass-produced the V-2 under wartime conditions, with shortages in a variety of critical resources, materials, and components. The labor force that built the missiles was largely untrained, unmotivated, physically weak, and actively engaged in industrial sabotage. Working conditions could not have been much worse. The V-2 was a reasonably complicated vehicle, compared to other World War II weapon systems, and there was no manufacturing experience base for the missile's numerous design innovations. Also, the mobile V-2s were transported and launched in areas where the enemy had complete control of the air. Considering all of these factors, the V-2 had an amazingly successful and reliable track record.

Analyzing the V-2 in Today's Context

By today's US aerospace standards, the V-2 was a crude and unsophisticated missile. However, the missile's propulsion system was fundamentally

An Army Redstone ballistic missile lifts off from White Sands in the 1950s.

the same as the first stage propulsion systems of contemporary liquid-propellant US launch vehicles. The V-2 is widely recognized as the grandfather of all modern liquid-propellant missiles and space boosters. The US Army Redstone ballistic missile was a repackaged V-2 with a more advanced engine,

The Redstone was modified to serve as the booster for the initial two sub-orbital flights of the manned Mercury program.

and the Redstone served as the launch vehicle for America's first two manned space flights.[33]

The German V-2 program during World War II demonstrated that good liquid-propellant missile reliability is achievable, even using relatively complicated designs for vehicles that are manufactured and operated under terrible conditions. This experience offers the promise that outstanding liquid-propellant missile reliability is achievable using relatively simple designs for vehicles that are manufactured and operated under good conditions, without going to inordinately complicated and expensive lengths to make these conditions absolutely perfect.

The Private Experimental Rocketeers

The design, manufacture, and operation of liquid-propellant rockets are widely perceived to be highly complex undertakings that are possible only with large, well-funded technical organizations. However, some individuals have refused to assent to this view, and the most vivid demonstrations of the falsity of this conventional wisdom are the efforts of a few private rocket makers who build liquid-propellant rockets as an avocation. This discussion of these private rocketeers does not mean to imply that their efforts encompass the broad number of technical disciplines and system requirements that are fundamental to any launch vehicle capable of placing payloads into earth orbit. Guidance and control technologies, in particular, are not usually addressed by the rocket projects of these individuals. Nevertheless, their efforts do suggest that simple, low-cost liquid rocket engines and associated hardware are possible.

The California Societies

In 1943, George S. James founded a private experimental rocketry organization called the Southern California Rocket Society. The California-based organization was later renamed the Reaction Research Society (RRS). Its members were interested in designing, building, and flying high-performance, experimental rockets as an avocational pursuit. The RRS still exists as an active entity today, routinely testing and launching solid-, liquid-, and hybrid-propellant rockets. Two other notable experimental rocketry groups that have been in existence for many years and are still active are the Pacific Rocket Society (PRS) and the Rocket Research Institute (RRI). Like the RRS, both of these organizations are located in California.[34]

Each of these groups is unique when compared to pioneering US rocketry organizations such as Frank Malina's GALCIT team and the American Rocket Society (ARS), because elements of GALCIT and the ARS formed rocket engine manufacturing companies that received substantial government contracts.[35] These California experimental rocketry organizations have always been essentially private and nonprofit. We will focus on some of the significant accomplishments of these groups in building liquid-propellant rockets. In doing so, we will discover that liquid-propellant rockets can be, and are being, built in workshops and garages by individuals who are using very modest personal resources.

Examples of Successful Designs

In the late 1940s, RRS members David Elliot and Lee Rosenthal designed and built a liquid monopropellant rocket. The vehicle's propulsion system used concentrated hydrogen peroxide in conjunction with a solid catalyst. The rocket was optimized for simplicity, and it used nitrogen to pressure-feed the hydrogen peroxide through the catalyst. Elliot and Rosenthal used as many surplus parts and materials as possible to build their vehicle. The rocket was 1.78 meters (70 inches) long and 14.9 centimeters (6 inches) in diameter. On 14 May 1950, the rocket was launched near Rosamond, California. It reached a calculated altitude of 7.2 kilometers (4.5 miles) and travelled 12.5 kilometers (7.8 miles) downrange.[36]

The RRI's Spark Ia. Under the auspices of the Rocket Research Institute, some California aerospace engineers volunteered their time to build a simple pressure-fed liquid bipropellant rocket propulsion system. Constructed in the 1950s, the system was called the SPARK Ia. It used LOX and alcohol for propellants. Intended to serve as an educational resource for engineering students, the SPARK Ia was successfully static-tested on 1 December 1957 (with a thrust of 1,779 Newtons [400 pounds]).[37]

The PRS Acid/Alcohol Rocket. The Pacific Rocket Society developed a number of different hybrid propellant rockets in the 1940s and 1950s, using liquid oxygen as an oxidizer and a variety of solid materials for fuel. More recently, members of the society designed, built, and flew a bipropellant liquid rocket using hypergolic propellants. Dan Ruttle was the chief designer and fabricator of the rocket, and the propellant combination selected was nitric acid (oxidizer) and furfuryl alcohol (fuel). The propellants were fed through the engine's injector by pressurized gaseous nitrogen. Ruttle used a concentric propellant-tank configuration to minimize plumbing, consistent with the project's overall motto to "keep it simple."[38] The PRS successfully launched the rocket from Smoke Creek Desert, Nevada, on 19 July 1987, to an altitude of 3 kilometers (1.9 miles).[39]

Silver Bird II. The Reaction Research Society has been very active recently with a number of liquid-propellant rocket projects. Mark Grant built a pressure-fed, liquid-propellant rocket using LOX and kerosene. The vehicle, designated Silver Bird II, was 4.9 meters (16 feet) long. On 26 October 1991, Grant and his support crew successfully launched Silver Bird II from the RRS-owned Mojave test area near Mojave, California, to an altitude of 2.75 kilometers (1.7 miles).[40]

Dave Crisalli's Rockets. RRS member Dave Crisalli, while a midshipman at the Naval Academy in the mid-1970s, designed and built for his senior class project a sophisticated LOX/kerosene rocket that was 5.6 meters (18.25 feet) in length. The engine was regeneratively cooled, had a thrust of 4,000 Newtons (900 pounds), and was pressure-fed with gaseous nitrogen. Crisalli launched his rocket from White Sands Missile Range on 17 May 1976. Despite a premature deployment of the recovery system, which drastically limited the

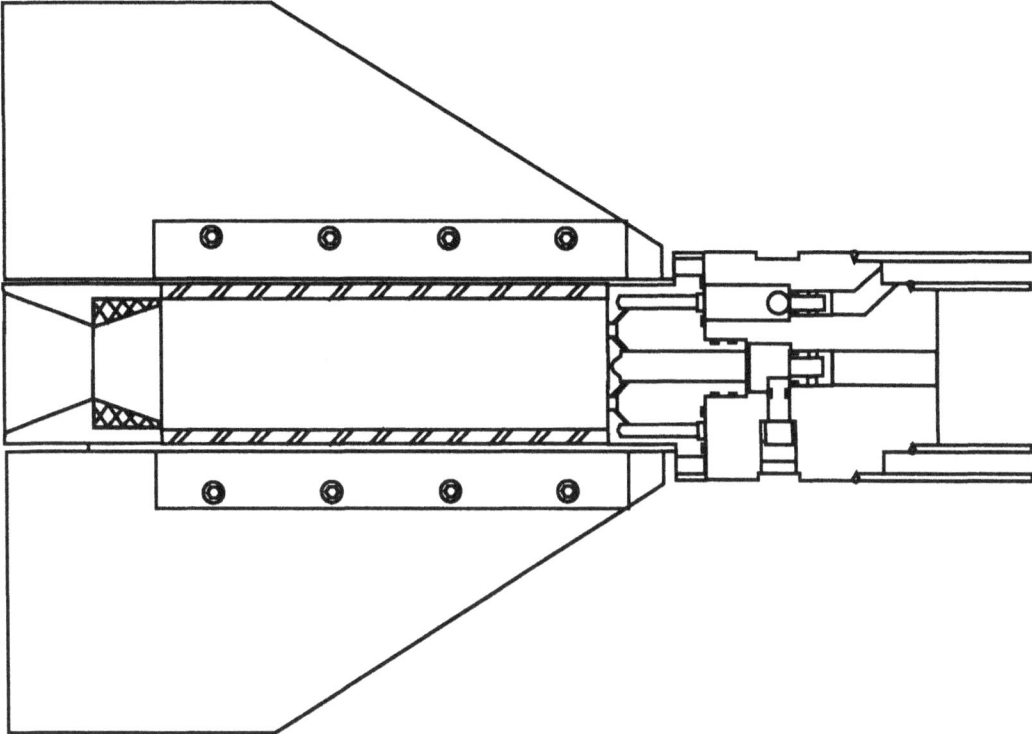

Figure 2. The engine and injector configuration of the PRS acid/alcohol rocket

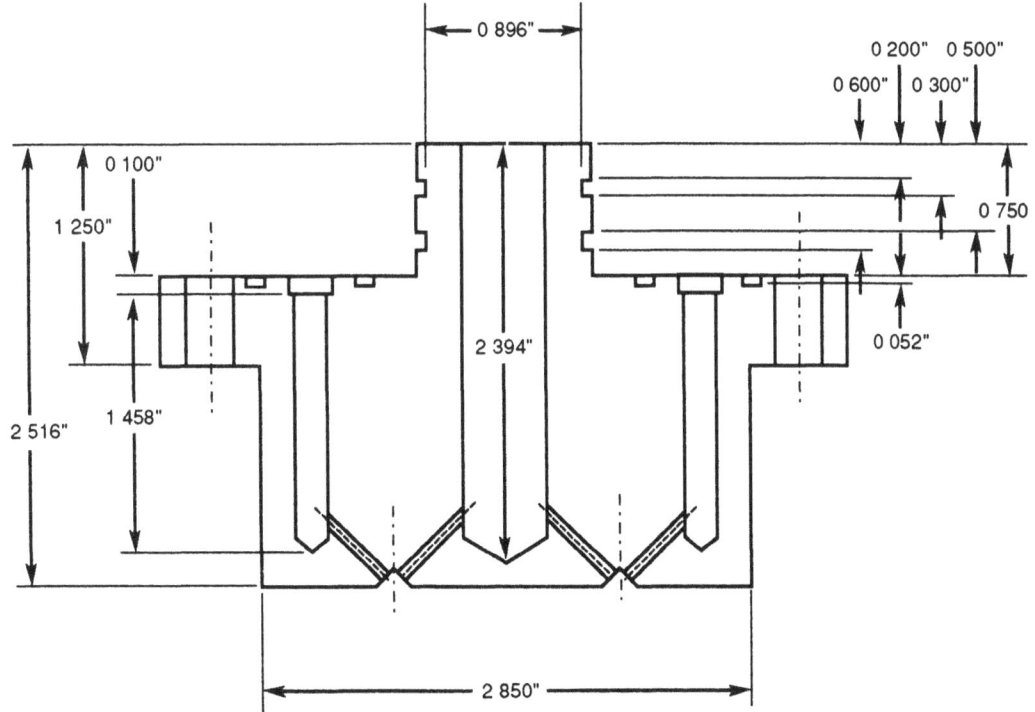

Figure 3. The rocket's injector dimensions and details

maximum altitude achieved by the vehicle, the rocket still flew to three kilometers (10,000 feet) and reached Mach 1.[41]

Dave Crisalli's LOX/RP-1 rocket at White Sands in 1976.

Recently, Crisalli has constructed another large LOX/kerosene rocket similar to his 1976 missile. This time, however, he has built and static-tested the rocket without the support of the Naval Academy or any other organization. The new rocket stands 6.3 meters (20.6 feet) tall and has a width of 31.75 centimeters (12.5 inches). The engine has a thrust of 4,500 Newtons (1,000 pounds), is regeneratively cooled, and uses LOX and RP-1 for propellants. Gaseous helium that is pressurized to 246 kilograms per square meter (3,500 pounds per square inch) pressure-feeds the propellants through the engine's injector. The entire propulsion system has been successfully static-tested for a full flight duration at the RRS's Mojave Test Area. The rocket should achieve a peak altitude of over 56 kilometers (30 nautical miles).[42] The total cost of Crisalli's project—including the cost of the rocket, the static test stand, the 18.3-meter (60-foot) launch tower, and the propellant ground-handling equipment—is about $6,000.[43] He planned to launch this latest rocket from White Sands Missile Range sometime in 1993.[44]

Tom Mueller's Rocket Projects. Tom Mueller, another RRS experimenter, has built and static-tested a 222-Newton-(50-pound-) thrust LOX/kerosene propulsion system for a small rocket, and successfully launched a complete rocket using this propulsion system design on 16 October 1993. His liquid rocket had a length of 1.9 meters (74 inches), and it achieved a maximum altitude of 2.45 kilometers (7,950 feet). Mueller is also working on

80

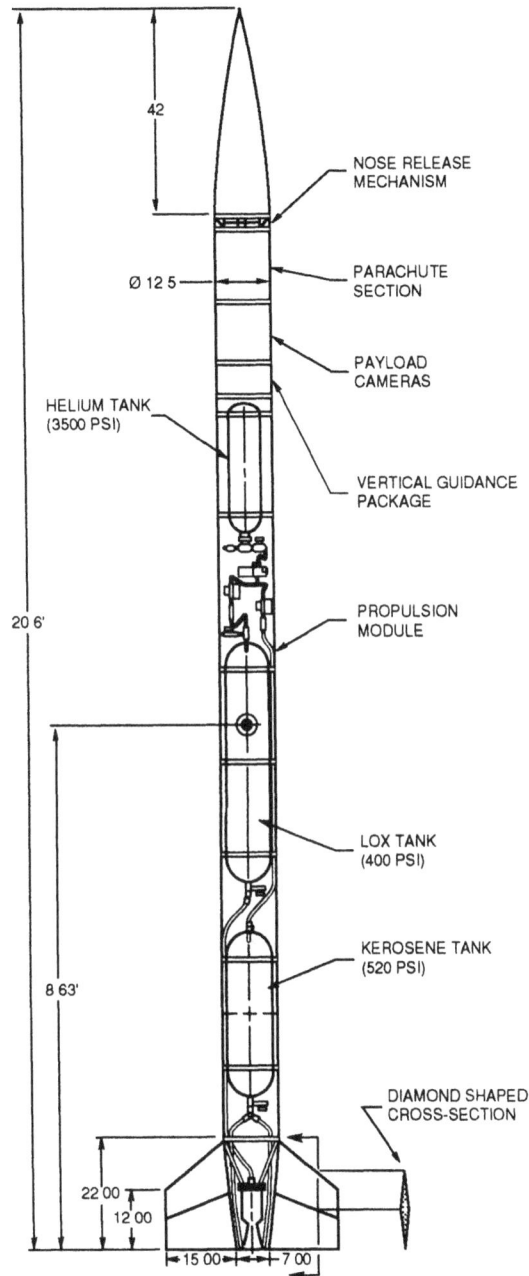

Figure 4. Crisalli's latest vehicle, which he planned to launch from White Sands Missile Range in 1993

a larger rocket that will use LOX and propane and have a thrust of 2,890 Newtons (650 pounds); it will be powered by a 44,480-Newton (10,000-pound) engine he plans to static-test in 1994.[45]

Ken Mason's Mobile Static Test Stand. RRI member Ken Mason is an experimental rocketry enthusiast who has been building and testing liquid-

81

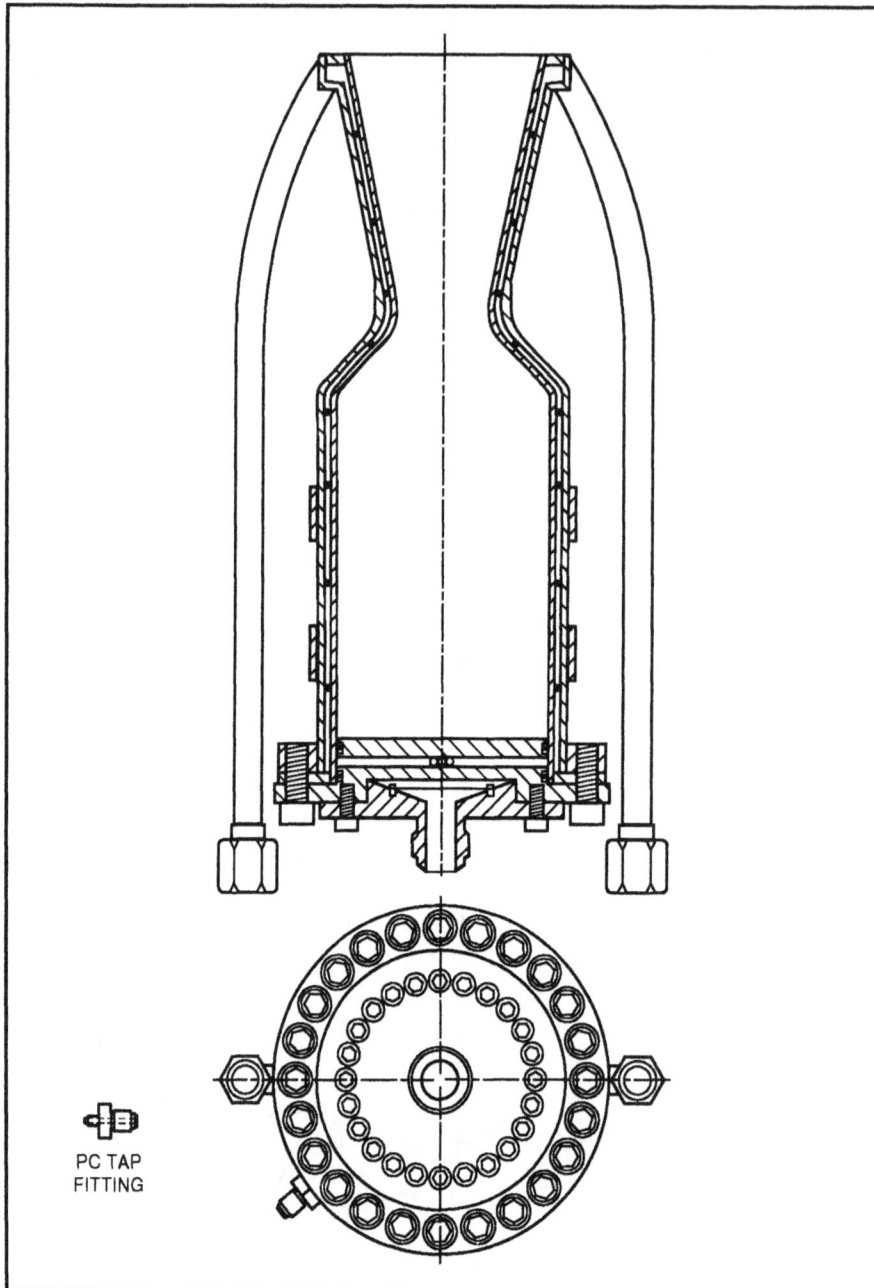

PC TAP
FITTING

Figure 5. Drawing details of the engine assembly for Dave Crisalli's current vehicle

propellant rocket propulsion systems for over 20 years. Mason constructed a mobile rocket propulsion system and static test stand from surplus components. The entire set of hardware is trailer-mounted and can be towed by any half-ton pickup truck. The mobile propulsion test system can accommodate a variety of liquid pressure-fed rocket engines up to 17,800 Newtons (4,000

50 LB THRUST EXPERIMENTAL LIQUID PROPELLANT ROCKET

VEHICLE

LENGTH:	74 INCH
DIAMETER:	3 INCH
WEIGHT (EMPTY):	6.0 LBM
WEIGHT (FULL):	7.5 LBM
FUEL:	KEROSENE (0.5 LBM)
OXIDIZER:	LIQUID OXYGEN (1.0 LBM)
PRESSURANT:	HELIUM @ 700 PSI
RECOVERY SYSTEM:	
– DROUGE:	18 INCH PARACHUTE DEPLOYED AT APOGEE
– PRIMARY:	58 INCH PARACHUTE DEPLOYED AT 2000 FT

ENGINE

THRUST:	50 LBF
CHAMBER PRESSURE:	400 PSIA
INJECTOR TYPE:	12 SPLIT TRIPLETS (F-O-O-F)
SPECIFIC IMPULSE:	220 LBF-SEC/LBM
BURN TIME:	6.0 SECONDS

PREDICTED PERFORMANCE

MAXIMUM ALTITUDE:	12,000 FT
MAXIMUM VELOCITY:	1100 FT/SEC (MACH 1.0)
FLIGHT TIME (TO APOGEE):	28 SECONDS
PLANNED LAUNCH DATE:	APRIL 1993

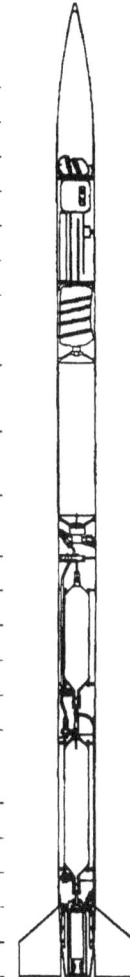

Figure 6. Tom Mueller's small liquid propellant rocket

pounds) in thrust, including 4,450-Newton-thrust Rocketdyne LR-101 Atlas vernier engines. Using his mobile system, Mason routinely performs static rocket tests at public gatherings. He also rents the trailer to various aerospace companies that are conducting small engine development and testing. For simple demonstrations, he uses a surplus Reaction Motors LR-11 engine powered by liquid oxygen and ethyl alcohol mixed with 25 percent water. (Chuck Yeager's Bell X-1 and early versions of the X-15 used the LR-11 in clusters for propulsive power.) The propellants are pressure-fed to the engine with gaseous helium. The LR-11 burns for 22 seconds, with a maximum thrust of about 9,350 Newtons (2,100 pounds).[46]

The Lesson of the Backyard Rockets

The accomplishments of these private experimental rocketry organizations argue against the notion that building liquid-propellant rockets has to be a complex

View of Mason's static test trailer with a Reaction Motors LR-11 mounted in firing position.

Static testing (by Mason) of a Rocketdyne Atlas Vernier engine.

and expensive undertaking that can be conducted only by the government-industrial complex of an economically-flourishing country with a strong technology base. These individuals have built their rockets in places like home garages, with a budget that came out of their own pockets, and with no support from government or industry. Their successful experimental liquid rocket projects have demonstrated that it is possible to develop and manufacture simple and inexpensive rocket propulsion systems.

Other Examples of Simple Rocket Engines

The Aerobee family of sounding rockets served as reliable research launchers for almost 38 years. The first Aerobee flew on 24 November 1947, and a total of 1,058 Aerobees had been launched when the last Aerobee lifted off on 17 January 1985.[47] Although there were a number of variants to the Aerobee rocket design, including the Aerobee 350 which employed a cluster of four Aerobee thrust chambers for its sustainer stage, the basic design of the propulsion system changed very little over a period of almost four decades. Developed by Aerojet, the Aerobee employed a short-burning, solid-propellant booster and a liquid-sustainer engine using hypergolic propellants. The liquid engine on most of the Aerobee variants used a mixture of aniline and furfuryl alcohol for fuel, and it inhibited red fuming nitric acid for an oxidizer. The propulsion system was extremely simple and inexpensively produced, using gaseous helium to pressure-feed the propellants.[48] Over the entire life of the program, the Aerobee achieved a success rate of 97 percent.[49]

When NASA engineers were defining the specifications for the propulsion systems that would be used by the Apollo command module and the lunar module descent and ascent stages, they demanded the maximum reliability possible. NASA knew there would be no recovery or rescue mode if any of these systems failed to operate in the proximity of the moon. To the contractors designing these propulsion systems, reliability translated to simplicity. The result was simple, pressure-fed designs using hypergolic propellants. Satellite liquid propulsion systems, in which maintenance-free, long-operating life is a paramount consideration, use similar, although smaller, designs. The simple design of the Lunar Module Descent Engine (LMDE) prompted the engine's manufacturer, TRW, to initiate a study that would apply a similar design philosophy to a larger rocket engine concept.

In 1966, TRW employed design-for-minimum-cost principles in designing a simple pressure-fed engine that would ultimately demonstrate a maximum thrust of 1,112,000 Newtons (250,000 pounds).[50] They contracted with a Gardena, California, commercial pipe and boiler fabricator to build the engine to "shipyard production tolerances."[51] The manufacturing cost of the entire propulsion assembly was $33,300, and the engine was built in about two months. Ablative liners were later added for an additional $62,175.[52] This engine was tested with a modified injector at

An Aerobee 150 sounding rocket without its solid-propellant booster motor.

The last launch of the Aerobee program.

One of TRW's lunar module descent engines undergoing preparations for the Apollo 10 mission.

222,400 Newtons (50,000 pounds) of thrust at the TRW San Juan Capistrano Test Site, and subsequently at its full thrust configuration of 1,112,000 Newtons at the Air Force Rocket Propulsion Laboratory.[53] Using the same design criteria, TRW successfully demonstrated other engines having 155,680-New-

TRW's 1,112,000-Newton pressure-fed engine being test-fired at Edwards AFB in the late 1960s.

ton (35,000-pound) and 222,400-Newton (50,000-pound) full thrust levels, and using many storable propellant combinations and LOX/RP-1. All of the engines demonstrated good combustion stability.[54] The total part count for the TRW 250,000-pound thrust engine was around two orders of magnitude lower than large pump-fed engines of that day.[55]

Summary

Despite the widespread belief that designing, building, and launching space boosters must be a highly complex and costly tour de force, a number of important precedents established over the last 50 years suggest otherwise. This chapter has touched on some of these precedents—the Soviet booster design and operations philosophy, the V-2 production and operations experience, examples of simple liquid-propellant rocket engines that were built as a hobby for almost nothing, and some aerospace industry programs which indicated that simple and inexpensive boosters are indeed possible.

Retired Air Force Lt Gen Richard C. Henry said:

Simplicity of operation without the frills has always been required to conquer a new frontier. In fact, simplicity can mean more reliability and increased affordability, a combination that would help ensure successful missions and be more responsive to the needs of taxpayers. We seem to have forgotten that is what always got us there in the past. It is time to apply the proven principles of austerity and simplicity to that short 100-mile trip to space.[56]

Rocket engines and their associated airframes and systems do not have to be complicated. Robert L. Stewart, retired Army brigadier general and two-time Space Shuttle astronaut, related the story of how he once observed technicians doing manufacturing finish work on the Space Shuttle main engines and was appalled that they were using dental tools to accomplish their tasks.[57] General Stewart said the US needed a heavy launch vehicle, and that this vehicle "must be cheap and built by workers in a foundry, not technicians in a clean room."[58]

Simple, inexpensive, and highly reliable launch systems like General Stewart envisioned are possible, but developing such systems will require a number of correct design choices. To help them make the right choices, launch vehicle system engineers will need to work through a long list of design trade studies that compare different options (the means) to achieve the program goals of low-cost space access (the ends).

Notes

1. Norman R. Augustine, "The Cost of Success," *Air & Space,* February/March 1993, 69.

2. James R. French, "AMROC Industrial Launch Vehicle: A Low-Cost Launch Vehicle" (Paper presented at the Aerospace Vehicle Conference, Washington, D.C., 8–10 June 1987), 2.

3. Captain David C. Honhart, "Another Way of Thinking," *The Space Times,* November–December 1987, 12.

4. *Colliers's Engyclopedia,* 1991 ed., v. 20, "Rocket," 120–129.

5. Roger E. Bilstein, *Stages to Saturn* (Washington, D.C.: National Aeronautics and Space Administration, 1980), 8.

6. Gregory P. Kennedy, *Vengeance Weapon 2* (Washington, D.C.: Smithsonian Institution Press, 1983), 27.

7. Edward L. Keith, presentation on ultra-low cost launch systems to the World Space Congress, Washington, D.C., 31 August 1992.

8. Steven J. Isakowitz, *International Reference Guide to Space Launch Systems* (Washington, D.C.: The American Institute of Aeronautics and Astronautics, 1991), 161.

9. Ibid., 160.

10. Microcosm Inc. presentation to NASA Headquarters, Washington, D.C., 1 September 1992, subject: Ultra Low Cost High Reliability Space Cargo Vehicle.

11. Isakowitz, 187.

12. Microcosm Inc. presentation, 6.

13. Isakowitz.

14. Microcosm Inc. presentation, 2.

15. Microcosm Inc. presentation to USAF Space and Missile Systems Center, El Segundo, Calif., 13 August 1992, subject: Concept for a Low Cost, High Reliability, 100% Available Space Delivery System, 13.

16. Gregg Easterbrook, "Big Dumb Rockets," *Newsweek,* 17 August 1987, 60.

17. Bilstein, 387–88.

18. H. M. Minami, "Atlas Engines—A History" (Paper presented at the AIAA/SAE/ASME 27th Joint Propulsion Conference, Sacramento, Calif., 24–26 June 1991), 1.

19. V. P. Glushko, *Development of Rocketry and Space Technology in the USSR* (Moscow: Novosti Press, 1973), 76.

20. Bilstein, 386.

21. Microcosm Inc. presentation to USAF, 12.

22. Ibid.

23. Isakowitz, 160, 163.

24. Microcosm Inc. presentation to USAF, 15.

25. Kennedy, 6–11.

26. Bilstein, 11–12.

27. Kennedy, 68–78.

28. Ibid., 16, 21, 23.

29. Ibid., 24.

30. Daniel Fischer, "Peenemunde Today," correspondence in *The Journal of the British Interplanetary Society,* July 1992, 310.

31. Jean Michel, *Dora* (New York: Holt, Rinehart and Winston, 1980), 97, 161.

32. Kennedy, 26–27.

33. Isakowitz, 288.

34. John R. London III, "The Liquid Propellant Rocket Project—A Key Space Education Resource" (Paper presented at the 39th International Astronautical Federation Congress, Bangalore, India, 8–15 October 1988), 2, 4.

35. Jacob Neufeld, *The Development of Ballistic Missiles in the United States Air Force, 1945–1960* (Washington, D.C.: Government Printing Office, 1990), 40, 47; Theodore von Karman and Frank Malina formed the Aerojet Engineering Corporation, later to become Aerojet General. Members of the ARS formed Reaction Motors Inc.

36. London, 2–3.

37. Ibid., 4.

38. George Morgan, *The Design, Construction, and Testing of a Bi-Propellant Liquid Fuel Rocket* (Santa Paula, Calif., GDM & Co., 1987), 9, 11, 13–14.

39. London, 4.

40. Kevin T. Brueckner, "Reaction to the Research," *Western Pyrotechnic Association Newsletter,* December 1991, 6–7.

41. David Crisalli, *The Design, Construction and Flight Testing of a Large Liquid Propellant Missile* (Annapolis, Md., Trident Scholar Project Report, no. 76, US Naval Academy, 1976), 34–35, 51–53.

42. David E. Crisalli, Amateur Liquid Propellant Sounding Rocket Project—Status as of October 1992, 3439 Hamlin Ave., Simi Valley, Calif., October 1992.

43. David Crisalli to John London, letter, 12 February 1993.

44. RRS Newsletter, "Project Status," Los Angeles, Calif., September–October 1992, 4.

45. Tom Mueller to John London, letter, 17 February 1993.

46. John Trumbo, "Thunderbolts and Lightning," *Auburn Journal,* 30 December 1988, A-1, A-8.

47. David W. Thomas, "Last Scheduled Aerobee Sounding Rocket Launch Set For January 17 From White Sands Missile Range," NASA News Release No. 85-1, Goddard Space Flight Center, Greenbelt, Md., January 1985.

48. *Aerobee ABS Handbook,* Space-General Corporation, 1969, B-1, B-9.

49. George Kraft, Aerobee Flight Histories Compilation, NASA Goddard Space Flight Center, Md., 1985.

50. Gerard W. Elverum, Jr., "Scale Up to Keep Mission Costs Down" (Paper presented at the 24th International Astronautical Federation Congress, Baku, USSR, October 1973), 23.

51. Ibid., 27; Easterbrook, 50.

52. Elverum, 27.

53. Gerard Elverum to John London, letter, 28 May 1993.

54. TRW Incorporated, *Low Cost Shuttle Surrogate Booster (LCSSB) Final Report* (Redondo Beach, Calif.: TRW Incorporated, 15 May 1981), 41.

55. Ibid., 44.

56. Richard C. Henry, "Launches Into Low-Earth Orbit Should Be Economical, Routine," *Aviation Week & Space Technology,* 27 November 1989, 96.

57. Interview with Brig Gen Robert L. Stewart, Maxwell Air Force Base, Ala., April 1990. General Stewart described how dental tools were used to deburr slots in the SSME combustion chamber.

58. "Vandenberg Shuttle Complex Will Go Into Mothball Status," *Aviation Week & Space Technology,* 2 May 1988, 27.

Chapter 6

Some Key Design Choices

Achieving drastic reductions in space launch costs starts with the right vehicle design. Developing this optimum design will require the engineering team to accomplish a number of trade studies that consider various design options. This chapter will address some of the key design choices necessary to arrive at a launch system that can provide the desired reductions in both acquisition and operations costs. As we examine each design choice (or trade) area, the discussion will provide general trends, considerations, and suggestions, but no hard and fast design decisions. It is not the intention of this chapter (or this study) to provide a single point design that would be the ultimate answer to low-cost space launch. Rather, there are several top level design paths that may lead to significant cost reductions—and various components within each of these approaches could potentially be mixed and matched to develop a large number of options.

Developing a system design for an inexpensive space booster that will provide a space exploitation breakthrough will require a level of effort that is well beyond the scope of this study. Nevertheless, each of the trade areas covered in this chapter will give some important ideas and advice to program managers and engineers on how they should craft requirements and specifications for a new, low-cost, launch vehicle.

Manned versus Unmanned

This initial design trade represents one of the first design decisions necessary in specifying the details for an inexpensive launcher. Chapter 3 described how the manned aspects of the Space Shuttle caused major increases in the launch system's complexity, weight, and reliability requirements. These increases, of course, led inexorably to higher development and operations costs. This study does not seek to debate the merits of human space flight. A continued human presence in space likely will be very important to future space exploitation and exploration. The issue we will address is whether launching people into space should be connected in any way with the inexpensive launching of payloads.

The Future of the Space Shuttle

The payload manifest for the Space Shuttle in 1993 illustrates the striking effect that the deletion of all commercial and military cargo has had on the program. Eight missions are planned or already accomplished: four are dedicated to on-orbit experimenting and testing that will use primarily nondeployable payloads onboard the Shuttle; one is a combination experiment and satellite retrieval mission; one is the Hubble space telescope repair mission; and two are large satellite deployment missions.[1] Both of the deployable satellites are NASA systems.

Once a US space station is in place and operational, all missions of the type flown on the Shuttle in 1993 (with the possible exception of the repair mission) could be largely accomplished without the Shuttle—and for much less money—by conducting them aboard the space station itself. The Shuttle does provide some unique benefits for certain experiments that would not be available with the space station; for example, a limited ability to customize mission orbital characteristics. But when NASA has an operational space station, we may not be able to afford maintaining the Shuttle as an orbital experiment host just to provide such benefits. Of course, if the NASA space station program is cancelled entirely, the Shuttle will be the only option available to accomplish these types of missions.

If the station were already deployed, almost all of the Shuttle's 1993 experiments and test activities could have been accomplished more efficiently and at a more leisurely pace on the space station than on the Shuttle during its brief stays in orbit. Neither of the deployable satellites requires a human presence to be launched and could be placed in orbit by existing or future unmanned boosters. The European Space Agency's Eureca spacecraft consists mostly of microgravity experiments that presumably could be accomplished aboard a space station and returned piecemeal if necessary.[2] Since a US space station is not yet up, there is justification for using the Shuttle to conduct these activities. It will, however, be difficult to rationalize using the Shuttle for such experiments and satellite deployments in the future.

Operations like the Hubble telescope repair mission may indeed require a large maintenance facility like the Shuttle's cargo bay. However, it is possible that even these activities could eventually be accomplished by astronauts traveling from the space station—although this would require the development of a piloted orbital transfer vehicle with a very robust propulsion system.

In any case, justification for continued use of the Shuttle beyond the deployment of space station components will diminish to being little more than a very expensive and inefficient taxi for astronaut crews, since space station logistics support could be accomplished for less money through the use of existing unmanned boosters. And if the redesign of Space Station Freedom (ordered by the Clinton administration) results in a reduced dependence on the Shuttle as a station hardware launch vehicle, the Shuttle's future utility will be further degraded.[3] These prospects provide a strong rationale for developing alternate and much less expensive means, in the near term, for getting crews into space. One possibility is the HL-20 Personnel Launch System proposed by NASA's Langley Research Center. Another is a capsule-like crew-ferrying vehicle.[4]

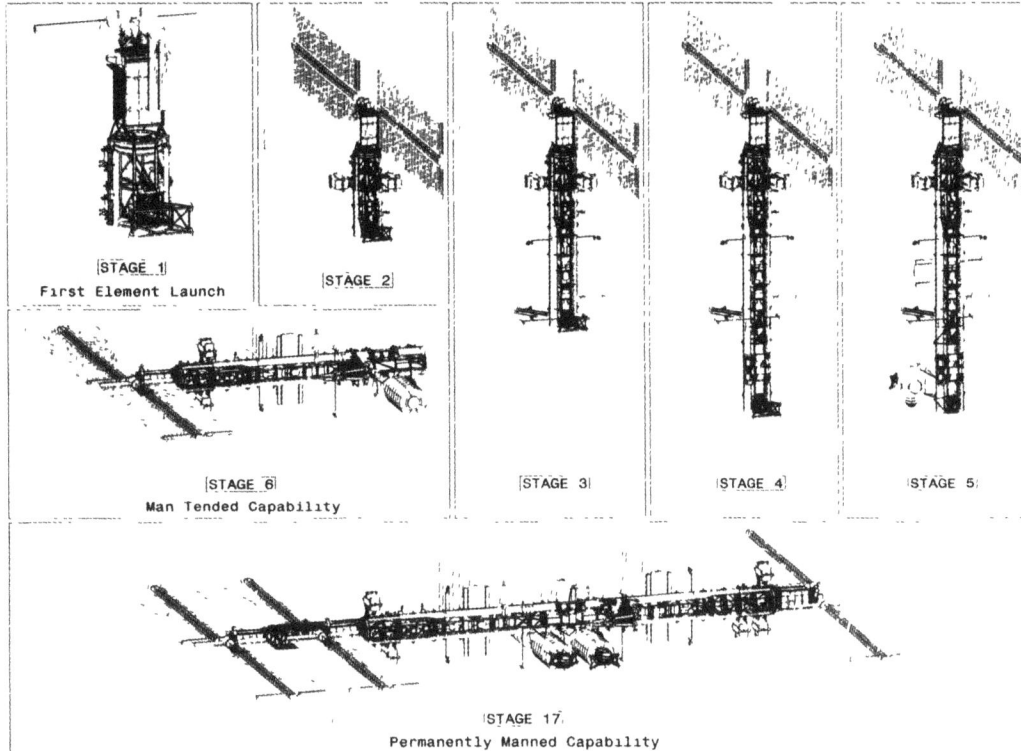

SPACE STATION FREEDOM
DESIGN ANALYSIS CYCLE CONFIGURATION

JULY 1992

STAGE 1
First Element Launch

STAGE 2

STAGE 6
Man Tended Capability

STAGE 3

STAGE 4

STAGE 5

STAGE 17
Permanently Manned Capability

The Space Station Freedom design.

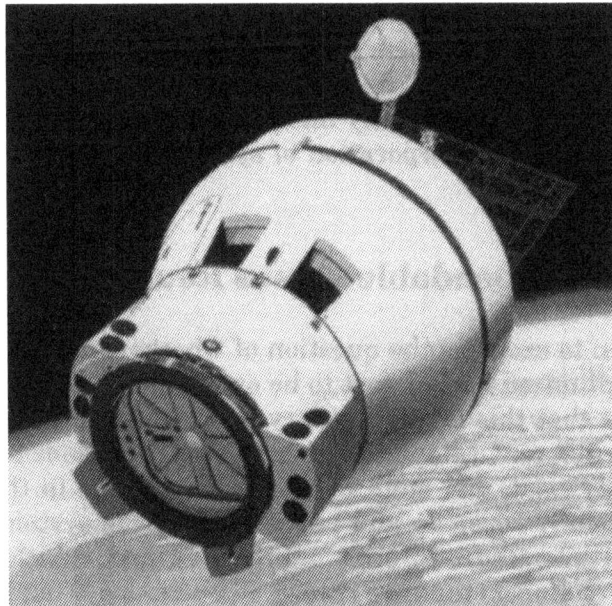

A British Aerospace concept of a crew-ferrying capsule.

95

The Advisability of Mixing People and Payloads

With the Space Shuttle's demise as a launch system an inevitability, we must examine future launch vehicle requirements for cargo and personnel. Both the National Launch System concept and the Spacelifter proposal recommended retaining the option of "man-rating" the launchers for use as manned spacecraft boosters.[5] This presumes that users of these boosters would always have the option to employ the launch systems for either unmanned or manned missions. This is not the case with the Shuttle, where the cargo and crew-carrying elements are integral to the same vehicle (i.e., both the payload bay and crew compartment are part of the Orbiter). Consequently, every Shuttle mission, regardless of payload, is flown with a crew. The approach put forward for the NLS and Spacelifter is a step in the right direction, allowing a level of "customization" relative to unmanned and manned missions.

When a launch system is designed to be man-ratable (as proposed by NLS and Spacelifter), however, the vehicle incurs certain liabilities. Regardless of how reliable the vehicle design is, man-rating will impose extra requirements that ultimately result in a more complex and expensive system. Costly additional launch base facilities and infrastructure will be needed if the launch system must support both unmanned and manned operations. To maximize the probability that a new launch vehicle will have the lowest possible development and operations cost, designers must resist the temptation to include the man-rated option. Otherwise, the vehicle designers will become captive to the demands of the manned spaceflight community. Therefore, the booster that is targeted to achieve drastic reductions in launch costs should be unmanned. Any complementary human launch system should be optimized for flight safety, not low cost. This does not mean that the complementary manned launcher has to be expensive, although case histories indicate it will be. Designing the manned launcher to be simple and reliable will enable the vehicle to also be safe and relatively inexpensive. Some added costs will come about, however, with the incorporation of systems such as emergency escape modules.

Expendable versus Reusable

When we begin to examine the question of whether it is better for a launch system that is optimized for low cost to be expendable or reusable, it becomes quickly apparent that this is not a binary black-and-white issue. First of all, there are many different categories of "reusable" systems. Various reusable concepts currently exist, and more will probably emerge in the future. These concepts include fully reusable and partially reusable systems, single-stage-to-orbit and multiple stages to orbit approaches, and vehicles (and in some cases their booster stages) that are recovered on runways, on landing pads, in catch nets, or in the ocean. Expendable launch systems normally deposit expended booster hardware in the ocean or on sparsely populated land areas.

This chapter will not address every known launch concept, but will provide some general discussions that are directly applicable to this topic.

The Space Shuttle's Reusable Solid Rocket Boosters

The Space Shuttle is a partially reusable (and therefore partially expendable) launch vehicle. The Orbiter lands on a runway, the Solid Rocket Boosters (SRB) parachute into the ocean and are reused (after extensive rework and re-casting of the solid propellant), while the External Tank is expended each mission. As discussed in chapter 3, designing the Shuttle Orbiter for airplane-like recovery created a negative effect on the launch system's payload fraction and added a host of additional subsystems that had to be designed, manufactured, and maintained. Although the Shuttle's SRBs once held the promise of helping to lower the system's launch cost through reusability, it is quite possible that making the SRBs reusable has actually compounded the Shuttle's problems of high operating costs.

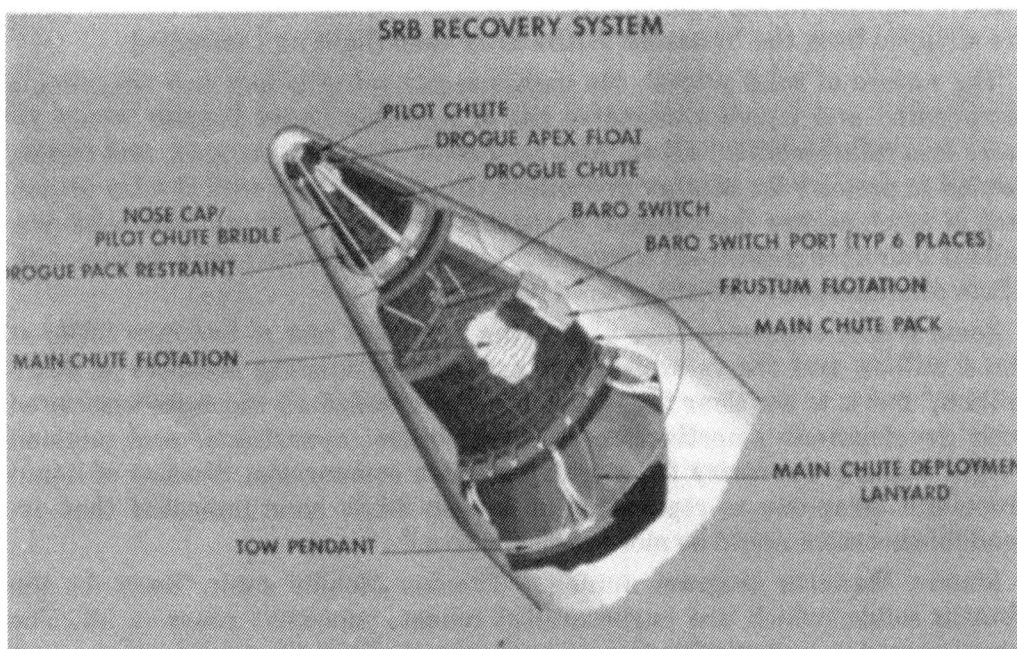

The SRB recovery system.

In making the SRBs recoverable from the ocean, NASA had to develop a dedicated ocean-going recovery capability and refurbishment operation. Two ships were specially constructed for this purpose. Ported at Cape Canaveral Air Force Station (AFS), they must be maintained and crewed year-round, regardless of what the Shuttle launch rate is. NASA built a large dock and refurbishment facility on the Banana River side of Cape Canaveral AFS to receive, rinse, clean, and disassemble the empty solid boosters after each mission and to prepare the motor casings for truck transport to the Kennedy Space Center (KSC). At KSC, the empty casings are loaded onto special rail cars and transported to Utah for reloading and the subsequent return to KSC.[6] The parachutes used to slow the SRBs' descent into the ocean are also recovered and reused. A dedicated facility at KSC refurbishes the parachutes for reuse on another mission. The booster thrust vector control system must also be refurbished in special facilities. NASA had to develop and procure all of the necessary equipment, facilities, and infrastructure, and now must maintain, operate, and staff it all the time. If the SRBs were expendable, none of this would be required.

By making the SRBs reusable, engineers had to make the motor cases thicker so they could endure water impact and continued reuse. The extra weight of these thicker cases, combined with the added weight of each SRB's parachute recovery system, reduced the Shuttle's effective payload capacity. By making the SRBs reusable instead of expendable, we have ensured much smaller production quantities, which has greatly reduced the opportunity to achieve manufacturing economy. And a number of non-reusable booster parts are stripped from the "reusable" SRBs after each flight and scrapped.

The nature of solid propellants makes motor refurbishing and reloading a complicated and logistics-intensive job. A reusable liquid booster would require less refurbishment effort, with only some cleaning, purging, and testing needed to prepare for another propellant fill. Further, the cost of solid propellant is much higher than that of cryogenic liquid propellants. The solid propellant therefore constitutes a sizable fraction of the overall solid booster cost, which diminishes the benefit of solid booster reuse.[7]

Some NASA estimates have placed the projected cost of two new SRBs at $66.4 million and the refurbishment cost of two existing boosters at $34.8 million,[8] but it is not clear that these figures included all the costs associated with development amortization, infrastructure, operations, and payload weight impacts necessary for a truly accurate comparison. Studies of liquid propellant strap-ons as replacements for the SRBs have indicated that expendable boosters would be more cost-effective.[9]

Martin Marietta program manager Thomas Mobley said: "Even for the Shuttle solids, which are [structurally] robust, you can't reuse it all. The record says you underestimate cost and overestimate the success of recovery [and reusability]."[10] Had the flight rate of the Shuttle ever reached its original projections, the tremendous investment for SRB reusability might have been recovered. However, the SRBs' huge logistics tail and the performance penalties they cause should provide an important lesson learned: solid propellant boosters are poor candidates for reusability.

Single-Stage-to-Orbit

The lure of a fully reusable launch vehicle that could attain orbit and return without having to shed any hardware during the flight is a dream that has been beckoning designers since science fiction authors began writing about such a vehicle many decades ago. One of the attractive aspects of the approach is that it emulates the operational concept of transport aircraft (i.e., take off—deliver cargo—return, having expended only propellant), and aircraft have certainly proven to be cost-effective and profitable.

NASP and SSRT. Two major US programs are pursuing single-stage-to-orbit technologies and concepts: The Air Force/NASA National Aerospace Plane (NASP) program and the Ballistic Missile Defense Organization's Single Stage Rocket Technology (SSRT) program. Both are developing technologies that could ultimately support the fielding of suborbital and orbital single-stage vehicles. The NASP program involves technologies necessary for a hypersonic aircraft that would take off horizontally from a runway, achieve orbit, and return to land horizontally on a runway. The SSRT team has built a subscale, suborbital flight demonstrator that will demonstrate many of the vertical takeoff, atmospheric flight, and vertical landing characteristics of a full-scale single-stage-to-orbit (SSTO) vehicle.[11]

Problems Common to All SSTO Vehicle Designs. In Chapter 2 we described some of the technical challenges associated with a NASP-type vehicle's having to fight through the "thermal thicket" of the atmosphere to achieve orbit. The SSRT/SSTO concept avoids most of that difficulty by using a much more vertical ascent. However, there are some technical difficulties that are common to all types of single-stage-to-orbit launch vehicles.

According to veteran rocket designer and builder Robert C. Truax:

> Using similar technologies (i.e., the same propellants and structural fraction), a two-stage-to-orbit vehicle will always have a better payload-to-weight ratio than a single stage designed for the same mission, in most cases, a very much better [payload-to-weight ratio]. Only when the structural factor approaches zero [very little vehicle structure weight] does the payload/weight ratio of a single-stage rocket approach that of a two-stage. A slight miscalculation and the single-stage rocket winds up with no payload. To get any at all, technology needs to be stretched to the limit. Squeezing out the last drop of specific impulse, and shaving off the last pound, costs money and/or reduces reliability.[12]

Edward A. Gabris of NASA Headquarters had similar thoughts about single-stage-to-orbit designs: "A minor miscalculation on the amount of thrust produced by a certain amount of fuel, the component weights, structural loads, or a host of similar items will easily reduce the payload capability to zero or below." Gabris further stated that a single-stage design engineer must seek maximum performance for every system, driving up the program's cost and technical risk. Also, since a maximum performance/minimum weight single-stage vehicle cannot be as reliable as a simple staged vehicle with its lower performance demands and greater design margins, it will be more prone to failure.[13]

Despite these obvious technical challenges to any single-stage rocket program, the concept still holds the promise of ultimately becoming a cost-effective system that uses routine, "airline-like," operations to place payloads into orbit at very low cost. However, getting to this point will require a large front-end investment for what must be considered a high-risk development program. Recent advances in materials technology notwithstanding, any single-stage booster design's low structural fraction demands will make it difficult, in the foreseeable future, for the vehicle to compete with simple staged rockets for the launching of heavy payloads (10,000 to 75,000 kilograms, or 22,000 to 165,000 pounds).

Suborbital Applications. Since the Ballistic Missile Defense Organization will likely have a number of suborbital payloads requiring flights in the coming years, the SSRT program could have a near-term payoff as an inexpensive suborbital sounding rocket.[14] Designing a reusable single-stage sounding rocket will not be nearly as technically stressing as designing a vehicle capable of orbital flight. The SSRT program is particularly appealing because the program managers seem determined to keep development and test operations costs minimized. They are using existing designs and surplus assets, a fast-track "skunkworks"-type development program, simple ground checkout and test equipment and procedures, and a very small test operations crew.[15] These kinds of initiatives may enable the fielding of a reusable suborbital single stage system that is affordable. The program is also laying the groundwork for future cost-effective single-stage orbital vehicles.

Expendable and Reusable Unmanned Staged Vehicles

We have seen that there are payload weight and system complexity penalties associated with winged recovery boosters, that manned vehicle designs result in complex systems with high reliability demands, and that single-stage booster programs bode of technical challenges and complexity. We are, therefore, left to consider the relative merits of unmanned expendable staged vehicles and unmanned reusable staged vehicles that employ simple recovery techniques in our pursuit of the lowest-cost launch system.

Unmanned expendable launch vehicles currently dominate worldwide launch activities, as they have throughout the entire history of space flight. In the US, these boosters have remained expensive over the years because of a variety of design and operational practices (for specifics, see chapter 3). In short, designing expendable launchers for maximum performance and minimum weight has made their manufacture and operation very expensive—and this high-cost hardware is thrown away with every launch. To solve this problem, we must either make expendable hardware so inexpensive that we don't care if we drop it to the bottom of the ocean each time we fly, or make the staged booster hardware recoverable so that it can be reused.

The Inexpensive Expendable Booster. By applying simple design practices, employing existing subsystems "off the shelf" to the maximum extent, and using inexpensive and available materials that do not require new technology, the US can develop an inexpensive expendable launch vehicle. This kind of design philosophy will result in a simple launch vehicle that will have a number of benefits. For example, a simple launch vehicle must necessarily have a simple design, resulting in nonrecurring development costs that are much lower than traditional aerospace systems. A simple design translates into fewer parts and interfaces, which translates into lower first unit and recurring manufacturing costs as well as lower operating costs. Inexpensive boosters will create a greater market demand for launchers, which will allow increased production runs and greater manufacturing economies of scale.

Achieving manufacturing economies of scale is one area in which expendable systems always have an advantage over reusable systems. Each launch of an expendable vehicle requires that booster be built. A reusable launcher requires far fewer boosters to be fabricated.

Flight Test Considerations. One argument for the development of reusable launch systems, particularly those with airplane-like operational characteristics, is that the vehicle can be taken through increasingly stressing flight regimes during the flight test program. This is not possible for an expendable booster, which necessarily experiences its entire flight profile during its first (and only) mission. Additionally, the expected low cost-per-flight of the reusable system would allow test engineers to develop a large amount of empirical flight data.[16] Clearly, there is more flight test flexibility with a reusable vehicle. But a very inexpensive expendable booster design could allow a launch system (but not an individual vehicle) to also develop a wealth of flight data.

Simple Reusable Vehicles. For a reusable unmanned staged vehicle to achieve maximum cost savings, the booster should have a very simple design. This "philosophy of simplicity" should be extended to the booster's recovery system, with the likely result that the vehicle stages will be configured to land in the ocean (using parachutes or some other velocity retardation device).[17]

Choosing an Expendable or a Reusable Design. The decision to make a staged vehicle expendable—or to make it reusable—will require a careful and dispassionate analysis. A host of factors will bear on this decision: the expected mission model and launch rate, the cost savings associated with manufacturing a few reusable boosters versus a large quantity of expendable boosters, the payload capacity reduction caused by the weight of the recovery system, the complexity and development cost of the recovery capability, and the cost of the facilities, infrastructure, and operations needed to support reusability.

Although proponents of reusability have often cited the fact that aircraft and ships are not thrown away after one use, the example of the cruise missile weapon system should also be evaluated when considering the advisability of expendable or reusable designs. The cruise missile is a relatively sophisticated aerospace system that could have been designed to be recoverable and reusable. The vehicle could have been configured to eject its warhead at the appropriate point in its mission, and then fly to a recovery site so it could be refurbished for another mission. Obviously, such a reusable feature would have had major design implications in the areas of propulsion, fuel capacity, guidance and navigation, airframe structure, recovery systems, and refurbishment infrastructure and logistics. The cruise missile system designers presumably considered these trades and determined that making the system expendable was the most cost-effective approach.

Since the high nonrecurring cost of launch vehicle development is a chief stumbling block to initiating a new booster capability, the best approach to bringing an inexpensive unmanned staged vehicle on-line is probably to make it initially expendable. An expendable booster will have lower front-end development costs than a reusable vehicle. As the flight rate increases due to an expanded demand for cheap access to space, the launch system can be reviewed for the selective application of recoverability. Reusable components could be phased into the vehicle design over a period of time, allowing the reusability support infrastructure to be brought along in something of a "pay-as-you-go" fashion.[18]

Solids versus Liquids versus Hybrids

There has been, and probably will continue to be, an ongoing debate among aerospace designers concerning the relative merits of solid propellant propulsion systems and liquid propellant propulsion systems (and combinations of the two). Recently, a third option—hybrid propellants—has entered the discussion. Hybrids combine elements of both solids and liquids. Recent static test successes (by AMROC) of large hybrid motors have renewed interest in this technology, which was first developed for large-motor applications in the 1960s.

Scope of the Trade Discussion

For the purpose of comparison, we will consider solid propellants using ammonium perchlorate for an oxidizer, powdered aluminum for fuel, and a rubber binder. We will consider liquid propellants that will use liquid oxygen (LOX) for an oxidizer and RP-1 (a form of kerosene) for fuel. We will evaluate hybrid propellants consisting of LOX as the oxidizer and solid polybutadiene as a fuel. There are a number of other propellant combinations that could be compared, especially in the liquids category. Most notably, hypergolics and LOX/hydrogen are liquid propellants that enjoy widespread application.

The use of both solid propellants and liquid propellants for space boosters is a well-developed engineering process, albeit a generally expensive one. Hybrid propulsion technology is much less mature, but it does hold certain advantages over solids and, to a lesser extent, liquids. The value of these advantages, of course, must be weighed against the technical risk that hybrids represent, since there is a lack of large-scale developmental and operational experience with hybrids. There are also some development and operational disadvantages to hybrids, especially relative to liquids. However, hybrid propulsion technology was promising enough to cause the National Research Council's Committee on Earth-to-Orbit Transportation Options to recommend a serious technology program: ". . . an investment should be made in demonstrating the technology necessary to validate the engineering practicality of the hybrid rocket motor for large, high-thrust, strap-on applications."[19]

Specific Impulse Comparison

Specific impulse is a measure of rocket engine, or motor, efficiency—the higher the value, the better. It tells how much thrust a rocket's propulsion system is delivering per unit mass of propellant expended over a specific interval of time. Specific impulse is traditionally expressed in "seconds," although it is not a measure of time. It is derived from (using the English measurement system) pounds of force (thrust) per pound of propellant mass per second. The "pound" units are usually cancelled for convenience.[20]

The Shuttle's solid rocket boosters provide a specific impulse of 268 seconds (in a vacuum).[21] The design goal for the AMROC H-1800 hybrid motor is 277.8 seconds in a vacuum, and the sea-level-optimized test motor delivered 276 seconds during a test on 17 February 1993.[22] Specific impulse values of the same propellant combinations will vary significantly as a result of varying propulsion system designs and other factors, and this is especially true of liquid systems. However, system efficiencies using LOX/RP-1 are typically in the 300-second range.[23] These figures indicate that liquid engines using LOX/RP-1 (or most any other liquid propellant combination) provide higher performance than solids or hybrids. Hybrid performance numbers are generally between those of solids and liquids.

Positive Attributes of Solid Propellants

Solid propellants offer a number of important benefits (see table 7). An attractive characteristic that solids have enjoyed over the years is that they

Table 7

Solid-Propellant Propulsion Systems

ADVANTAGES	
	High density impulse
	Storability
	Lower development risk
	Lower development cost
	Simpler designs
	Higher reliability
DISADVANTAGES	
	Development difficulties
	Lack of testability
	Inspection difficulties
	Safety concerns
	Environmental concerns
	Lack of throttability and thrust termination
	Rougher payload ride with higher acceleration
	Ground handling difficulties
	Weather concerns
	Higher propellant costs
	Manufacturing costs
	No engine-out applicability

provide a higher density impulse than liquid or hybrid propellants, which allows them to be packaged in smaller airframes. Combining this attribute with their inherent storability and instantaneous readiness for launch has made solids ideal for many military missile applications. Their high density impulse has also made them excellent candidates for upper and orbit insertion stages because they are conducive to volume-limited environments.

Lower Development Risk and Cost. One justification that engineers gave for the selection of solid propellant boosters for the Space Shuttle is that (they felt at the time) solids represented a lower development risk than liquid strap-on boosters.[24] Compared to most pump-fed liquid propulsion systems developed to date, solid boosters have, in fact, demonstrated lower development risk and cost, shorter development times, and lower recurring acquisition and operating costs (although not by a wide margin).[25] These are some of the reasons that rocket designers have selected solids for most sounding rocket, small launch vehicle, and booster strap-on applications.

Simpler Designs. Solid motor designs are generally simpler and have fewer parts than pump-fed liquid or hybrid designs. This translates into significantly reduced checkout requirements during prelaunch processing. Liquid systems that use high-speed turbomachinery for delivering propellants at the requisite pressure to the engine are the most complex type of propulsion systems. Hybrid complexity falls somewhere between solids and pump-fed liquids.

Higher Reliability. The inherent simplicity of solid motors has led to impressive reliability statistics. Through 1990, calculated on a per-launch basis, solids achieved a reliability record of 98.9 percent. Calculated on a per-motor basis for the same launches, solids had a 99.8 percent success rate. Solid propulsion systems accomplished this record despite the much publicized Shuttle 51-L and Titan 34D solid booster failures in 1986. Liquid systems had a slightly inferior record to solids over the same period of time.[26] Although hybrids have no flight record to calculate reliability statistics for, they have certain characteristics that have the potential of providing excellent reliability. In addition to their having a relatively simple design (especially if the LOX is pressure-fed to the polybutadiene grain), hybrid operations are generally insensitive to voids, cracks, debonds, and other imperfections in the solid grain (in sharp contrast to solid motors). This is because as the hybrid's solid fuel burns, it regresses normal (at a right angle) to the direction of the LOX flow. Solid propellants typically will burn (and regress) normal to *any* exposed grain surface—even those surfaces that are created by flaws.[27]

Negative Attributes of Solid Propellants

Despite their advantages and mostly positive track record, solid propellants also have some significant liabilities (see table 7). The development and operation of solid propellant launch systems is not cheap—and there is significant technical risk. The Strategic Defense Initiative Organization (now the Ballistic Missile Defense Organization) went through a troubling string of solid propellant suborbital rocket failures, and the Air Force's Solid Rocket Motor Upgrade (SRMU) program has had several setbacks. The SRMU, intended for use with the Titan IV launch vehicle, experienced a violent explosion during the first test firing in April 1991. Since then, there have been test delays, although the Air Force still hopes to have the new motor ready on schedule.[28] Because of a reduction in the number of required boosters and a fixed-price contract, SRMU builder Hercules Aerospace faced major financial losses. Congress directed the Air Force to help rectify Hercules' problems, and the result may be an additional $300–350 million paid by the US government to Hercules.[29] The Aerospace Corporation estimates that 46.1 percent of the total cost to procure a Titan IV vehicle with no upper stage will be expended on the two SRMUs alone.[30]

NASA's Advanced Solid Rocket Motor (ASRM) program was intended to develop new Solid Rocket Boosters for the Space Shuttle. The ASRM development effort had a number of political ups and downs in Congress, and it was finally cancelled in 1993. Between January 1988 and April 1993, the program budget grew from $1.67 billion with a first flight projected for 1994, to $3.7 billion with a first launch set for 2000.[31]

Lack of Testability. In addition to the comparatively lower performance that solids exhibit, solids are not amenable to testing prior to launch. (Liquid engines can be tested and calibrated relatively easily prior to their actual flight use; preflight hot-fire testing of hybrid motors is possible, but some percentage of the solid fuel would be expended.) The lack of solid motor flight unit testability and the high cost of full static testing for large solid rockets tends to limit confidence in the system's reliability, particularly if the motor is a new design.

Inspection Difficulties. It is difficult to verify the manufacturing process veracity of solid motors. Verification, however, is critical to establishing confidence in the motor's reliability because of the potentially catastrophic results of flying a solid motor with manufacturing flaws present. Consequently, manufacturing engineers must go to great lengths to determine the condition of the propellant grain after it has been poured—primarily using nondestructive inspection techniques. Test personnel have traditionally used radiography for the inspection of large rocket motors, but the propellant's density and the size of motor segments require very large radiographic facilities with powerful equipment. As aerospace companies develop new solid rocket motors, the need for improved inspection capabilities increases. These inspection systems are costly to develop and to operate. The Advanced Research and Applications Corporation (Aracor) is building a large real-time radiography system for NASA's Advanced Solid Rocket Motor program that sends detectors down the center of the motor. The Air Force's Wright Laboratory is working with Aracor to develop an X-ray computed tomography system for improved inspection of solid propellant motors.[32]

Liquid engines are more easily inspected than solids during manufacturing, and at all points in the processing flow.[33] Hybrids are less easy to inspect than liquids, but are much more tolerant of manufacturing casting flaws than solids. They therefore have less stringent inspection requirements than solid motors.

Significant Safety Hazard. Solids present a safety hazard because they are fully loaded with propellant when they come from the factory. They have the potential to ignite prematurely at anytime from when the propellant is poured into the motor casing until the booster has been launched. Liquid systems pose no hazard until they are fueled just prior to lift-off—and propellants are kept separated until they are loaded aboard the vehicle.[34] Hybrids are probably the safest of all, since they pose little hazard even after the LOX is loaded just prior to launch. There is never a potential for complete mixing of the solid fuel and LOX.[35] In fact, the Air Force has classified the AMROC hybrid boosters as having a TNT-equivalent explosive hazard of zero even when the vehicle is fully loaded with LOX.[36] The inherent safety of the solid fuel allows manufacturing and transportation of the hybrid motors that is free of many safety-restriction encumbrances.[37]

Environmental Impact Comparison

Another disadvantage of solids is that the exhaust effluent generated by the solid motors represents an environmental hazard. Concern about the exhaust products of solid propellants is focused primarily on three areas: ozone depletion, acid rain, and global warming.[38]

Ozone Depletion Associated with All Launch Vehicles. Ozone depletion in the stratosphere has been associated with solid propellants mainly because of the hydrogen chloride released into the atmosphere by the solid rocket exhaust plume. However, Russian research indicates that nitrous oxide production caused by the high temperatures and fuel-rich exhaust afterburning of all launch vehicles may be the primary ozone depletion culprit associated with space launchers. For example, the Russian data indicates that 75 percent of the ozone destruction caused by the Space Shuttle is a result of nitrous oxide, while only 25 percent is a result of hydrogen chloride.[39] NASA has employed, in conjunction with a number of Shuttle launches, the total ozone mapping spectrometer on the NIMBUS-7 spacecraft to measure for ozone depletion over the Kennedy Space Center area, and the spacecraft has never detected any depletion.[40]

The American Institute of Aeronautics and Astronautics reported that a launch rate of nine Shuttles and six Titan IVs annually could reduce ozone levels in the northern midlatitudes by up to 0.1 percent. Even this small amount is not trivial, and these calculations do not take into account the ozone depletion that would be caused by other US launch vehicles, sounding rockets, missiles, ground static tests, or non-US rockets. Nevertheless, the potential for ozone depletion by launch vehicles (at current or projected launch rates) does not appear to necessitate radical changes in solid propellant constituents.[41]

Acid Rain Associated with Solid Booster Exhaust. Acid rain results when hydrogen chloride gas from solid rocket booster exhaust is exposed to moisture and converted to a mist of hydrochloric acid. This occurs on a large scale during Shuttle launches when the solid rocket booster exhaust mixes with the large steam cloud created by the Shuttle's main engines and the Shuttle's hot exhaust gasses impinging on the huge amounts of sound-and vibration-attenuating water released at lift-off. The primary concern with solid rocket-produced acid rain is in the areas adjacent to the Shuttle's launch pad, although some native shrub damage has been detected as far as five kilometers (three miles) from the pad. Shallow water lagoons around the launch pad become acidic for a number of hours after each launch, resulting in the loss of as many as 1,000 fish.[42] The creation of acid rain can also cause operational limitations on booster tests and operations. For example, test crews delayed a scheduled 1 September 1992 test of a Titan IV Solid Rocket Motor Upgrade motor at Edwards Air Force Base, California, because wind speeds were not sufficient to carry the exhaust away from surrounding communities.[43]

Deposition from acid rain on the Launch Complex 39A service structure.

On a global scale, the acid rain produced by solid rockets appears to be insignificant. Although nine Shuttle flights and six Titan IV missions are estimated to generate three kilotons of acid-producing chemicals annually, this amount is less than 0.006 percent of that produced by US industries.[44]

Global Warming Associated with All Launch Vehicles. The amount of carbon dioxide generated by chemical rockets of all types, including solids, is less than 0.00004 percent of anthropogenic contributors. This amount makes a very minor addition to the increase in global carbon dioxide quantities that some scientists have associated with a possible global warming, or "greenhouse" effect.[45]

The exhaust products resulting from the combustion of LOX/RP-1 and those generated by hybrid motors are essentially the same: carbon dioxide, hydrocarbons, and water. Although liquid- and hybrid-propellant exhaust products do not contain the hydrogen chloride that causes acid rain, they deposit quantities of carbon dioxide into the atmosphere and cause some ozone depletion through plume heating and afterburning effects. As with solid propellants, though, the current and potential future effects on the global environment of operating liquid and hybrid propulsion systems appear to be insignificant.[46]

Research on Cleaner Solid Propellants. The Air Force's Phillips Laboratory is sponsoring research to develop "cleaner" solid propellants, and results have been promising. One demonstration indicated that sodium nitrate added to solid propellant produces sodium chloride (common table salt) instead of hydrogen chloride in the exhaust. The hydrogen chloride fraction in the exhaust products was reduced from 20 percent to less than one percent.[47]

Dutch scientists are working on a new solid propellant based on hydrazinium nitroformate with a glycidyl azide polymer binder. It promises not only to be environmentally cleaner than present solid propellants but also to have better performance.[48] However, making fundamental changes in the chemistry of a mature, solid-propellant experience base (like Phillips Laboratory and the Dutch are testing) has the potential of creating significant technical risk, causing manufacturing difficulties, and driving up acquisition costs.[49]

Comparison of Throttling Capability

It is difficult to provide throttling, early thrust termination, and restart mechanisms for solid-propellant boosters. Solid motors can be fabricated, through the casting of specific grain configurations, to provide an impulse profile with varying levels of thrust. However, this profile is unchangeable once the motor is ignited. In the case of the Space Shuttle, the lack of a thrust termination capability for the solid rocket boosters (SRB) means there is no viable abort mode for the Orbiter until the SRBs finish burning.

Liquid and hybrid systems can be easily throttled. Liquid propulsion systems can be designed for a wide range of throttle settings, although this does add complexity to the engine design. Engineers can provide a thrust termination and restart capability for liquid engines relatively easily.[50] Hybrids also can be easily throttled by varying the LOX flow rate. Also, terminating LOX flow will effect an engine shutdown, and resuming the supply of LOX to the solid fuel (with a proper ignition sequence) can provide a restart capability. Designing hybrid systems to have the ability to throttle, terminate, and restart thrust would likely be simpler than designing liquid systems with the same abilities, because only one fluid flow has to be regulated (compared to two for liquid engines).[51]

The ability of liquid and hybrid systems to throttle, shutdown, and restart allows more accurate orbital insertion and the exploitation of the earth's gravitational effects for high-altitude orbit insertions.[52] Because of the positional accuracies liquid upper stages can provide, many ICBM designs use liquid-propellant "post-boost" propulsion systems to achieve the desired accuracy for reentry vehicle release.[53]

Other Comparisons of Various Propellant Attributes

Liquid systems typically provide lower vibration, lower G-loading, and generally more benign launch conditions for payloads than solids. Acceleration conditions, especially at burnout, can be so severe on some solid-propellant launchers that certain classes of payloads cannot fly on them.[54] Payload designers that intend to use solid-propellant launch systems must take launch conditions into account, which can lead to higher payload acquisition costs. Hybrid launchers should be able to provide launch environments similar to those of liquids, since they are able to tailor their impulse profile by throttling.[55]

Launch Processing Handling Characteristics. Liquid systems remain devoid of all propellant until they are standing on the launch pad just prior to launch. Operators at the launch base can therefore handle liquid-propellant launch vehicles with much greater ease because they are so much lighter in weight than solids or hybrids, which come loaded with solid propellant from the factory. The lighter weight of liquid systems also makes them easier to manipulate at the factory and during transportation to the launch base.[56] The weight of large, solid-propellant boosters (along with manufacturing considerations) has typically required segmented case designs to accommodate transportation and handling requirements. Large liquid systems can have a larger overall bulk than solids or hybrids; however, that could create handling problems.

Weather Problems. Liquid-propellant launch systems, and probably hybrid launch systems as well, are less susceptible to weather problems than solid-propellant systems. Liquid systems can operate in a much wider range of temperature conditions than solids. The well-known problem of low ambient temperature that contributed to the *Challenger*'s SRB failure is a good example of solid motor operating temperature limitations. Additionally, solid-propellant boosters with segmented case designs seem to be particularly vulnerable to corrosion caused by exposure to the salt spray environment of coastal US launch sites. To prevent deterioration of its solid rocket motors (SRM), personnel destacked (in February 1993) a Titan IV booster that had been on the pad at Cape Canaveral's Complex 41. This particular vehicle had replaced a previous Titan IV whose SRM case joints had corroded while sitting on the pad during extended launch delays. Its SRMs had been stacked for more than 19 months.[57] Solid-propellant boosters are also subject to aging problems; they have a finite "shelf life."

SRB aft segments on the mobile launch platform in the Vehicle Assembly Building, Kennedy Space Center.

Propellant Costs. The LOX/RP-1 propellant combination costs much less than solid propellant—the price advantage can be as high as 44 to 1.[58] Hybrid propellant costs are between those of solids and liquids, and are likely closer to liquid-propellant costs. Although propellant price is not a major element of overall launch costs, it could become significant if the cost of launch vehicles decreases and the launch rates increase.

Manufacturing Characteristics. Low-cost boosters must be very inexpensive to manufacture, and simple liquid systems appear to have an advantage over solids in this area. Liquid-propellant rockets are conducive to being designed to be the cheapest vehicles possible. Without the proper design discipline, however, they can also end up being the most expensive. There is a considerable manufacturing requirement associated with the loading of solid propellants and, to a lesser extent, hybrid fuels.

Engine-Out Applicability. Neither solids nor hybrids are amenable to engine-out propulsion system designs, since the cast propellent or fuel of a failed motor cannot be used by other motors. Liquid systems, of course, can easily accommodate engine-out designs.[59]

Liquids Hold the Best Potential to Reduce Cost

To achieve truly drastic reductions in the costs required to put cargo into orbit, it will be necessary to make radical changes in the way we design, build, and operate launch vehicles. Considering all the factors we have discussed, liquids are the best choice to use in developing inexpensive launch vehicles. Liquid systems have advantages over solids and hybrids in the areas of performance, propellant cost, inspection, testing, and handling. Most important point of all, however, is that liquid propellant boosters hold the best *potential* of becoming the least costly launch vehicles to build and operate. Realizing this potential for low cost, however, is highly dependent on the right type of liquid launch system design. The manufacturing requirements, the cost of the hybrid booster's solid fuel component (the ease of loading and low cost of a liquid fuel like RP-1 compared to cast polybutadiene), and the hybrid's lack of a flight history create doubt about its ability to significantly bring down launch costs. Also, introducing reusability features into a liquid-propellant launch vehicle would be much more practical and less expensive than for hybrid designs. Still, the positive characteristics of hybrid systems make continued development seem prudent (to determine with greater confidence their applicability to low-cost launchers).

Pump-Fed versus Pressure-Fed

Rocketdyne engineers Dieter Huzel and David Huang, in their book *Design of Liquid Propellant Rocket Engines,* began the chapter on turbopump propellant-feed systems with the following statement: "In high-thrust, long-duration liquid propellant rocket engine applications, turbopump feed systems . . . generally result in lower systems weight and higher performance when compared to pressurized gas feed systems."[60] When it comes to designing maximum performance/minimum weight liquid boosters, there is little doubt that turbopump-fed propulsion systems are the way to go. The issue we will address is whether pump-fed or pressure-fed systems are the best choice for low-cost launch vehicles.

Engine Power Cycles

For many years, liquid-propellant rocket engines employing turbomachinery have been predominant in large US launch systems. To drive the turbomachinery and feed propellant to the engine combustion chamber, pump-fed engines have traditionally used one of three general "power cycles": the gas generator cycle (and other "open" cycles), the expander cycle, and the preburner or staged combustion cycle.[61] Each cycle has advantages and disadvantages relative to the other two. The Pratt & Whitney RL10 uses the expander cycle, the Atlas and Titan engines use the gas generator cycle, and the Rocketdyne Space Shuttle main engine uses the staged combustion cycle.[62] All three cycles employ turbomachinery, and are radically different from a fourth engine cycle that uses no turbomachinery whatsoever—the pressure-fed cycle. For the sake of brevity, we will lump together all three of the pump-fed cycles and simply compare pump-fed systems to pressure-fed systems.

The Rationale for Using Turbomachinery

The primary justification for using turbomachinery has been that turbopumps significantly increase the delivery pressure of the propellant as it is being routed to the rocket engine. The pressure of the propellant delivered to the engine combustion chamber injector is one factor that establishes combustion chamber pressure—and combustion chamber pressure is an important element in determining a rocket engine's specific impulse (the higher the pressure, the higher the specific impulse). Engineers seeking high-performance engines want high chamber pressures with their attendant high-performance turbomachinery. Using turbopumps to boost propellant pressures makes it possible to keep pressures in the large propellant tanks relatively low, allowing the tanks to have thin structural skins and to be lightweight. The task of a launch vehicle is in direct opposition to the force of gravity, so vehicle designers have traditionally sought to keep the weight of the vehicle as low as possible. The use of turbomachinery has been key to this effort.

Pressure-Fed Booster Designs

A launch vehicle that uses tank pressurization, as opposed to turbomachinery, to deliver propellant at the appropriate pressure to the engine combustion chamber injector is called a pressure-fed booster. The propellant must be pressurized by a high-pressure gas source, or some other mechanism, to a level that exceeds the required pressure at the combustion chamber injector. Compared to pump-fed boosters, a pressure-fed design requires structurally stronger (usually thicker-walled) propellant tanks, as well as engines that operate at lower chamber pressures (and have a lower specific impulse). Consequently, a pressure-fed booster with the same payload capacity to low earth orbit as a comparable pump-fed vehicle would be heavier and would need larger thrust engines to compensate for the heavier vehicle weights and lower engine efficiency. One source cites "propellant fraction" (the converse of structural fraction) values for typical pressure-fed designs of 0.89; structurally lighter pump-fed vehicles have propellant fraction values around 0.94.[63]

Pump-Fed versus Pressure-Fed Studies

In a mid-1980s study conducted for the Air Force Astronautics Laboratory (now part of the Phillips Laboratory) on low-cost expendable launch vehicles, pressure-fed boosters were eliminated from further trade study consideration. The study's analysis indicated that the booster's heavier tanks and engines, and the anticipated complexity of its pressurization system, would make it more expensive than a pump-fed booster with the same payload capacity.[64]

A study conducted for the Advanced Launch System (ALS) program as part of the ALS Phase I concept development had similar findings. The study stated that, in addition to the heavier structure and less-efficient engines, pressure-fed boosters raised questions about pressurization and combustion stability, and were not amenable to an engine-out capability. The study went on to say, "the lowest total systems cost is strongly influenced by the dry weight. Invariably, the lowest weight produced the lowest system cost by requiring less structure and propellant and smaller engines and facilities." For all of these reasons, but especially because the projected structural costs of the heavier pressure-fed design were more than twice the structural costs of competing pump-fed designs, pressure-fed engines were eliminated from consideration for the study's ALS reference design.[65]

The "Vehicle Weight Is a Cost Driver" Myth

In both of these studies, the primary basis for determining that pressure-fed systems would be more expensive than pump-fed systems was that overall system weight is a decisive cost factor. Many aerospace system cost-estimating models are predicated on system weight being a primary cost determinate, which helps to explain the strong bias in the aerospace community toward designing minimum weight systems.

The Number of Parts Is the Real Cost Driver. Longtime launch vehicle designer and analyst Paul Dergarabedian of The Aerospace Corporation has a different perspective:

> In 1968 (Apollo period) James Webb, NASA Administrator, requested a study to investigate the design of launch vehicles based upon achieving minimum cost. The reusable shuttle was the approach [selected and] which is in use today [although certainly not at low cost]. Another approach was to examine the reduction in cost through the use of a simplified design of an expendable system. This concept uses as its thesis that the primary cost is on the number of parts (and interfaces) and not the size (or weight) of the parts. Thus, complexity (developmental and operational

113

risk) results in a near-exponential increase in staffing and tends to overwhelm linear increases in material and propellant of similar designs.[66]

Dergarabedian developed a heuristically derived relationship to compare launch vehicles developed according to traditional maximum performance/minimum weight criteria with those optimized for minimum cost. His results indicated that a low-cost launch vehicle could be developed with the same payload capacity (and with a heavier overall booster weight) as the Saturn V, but having nonrecurring and recurring costs that are five-and-a-half times less. These cost reductions are enabled by the simplified low-cost vehicle's radical reductions in the cost of research and development, testing, and the required management of interfaces (since the interface count would be greatly reduced). The cost of direct labor (engineering, fabrication, assembling, testing, procuring, and documenting) and burden (overhead labor, capital equipment, facilities, and paid absences) would be reduced tenfold. In the case of the Saturn V, the cost of materials and propellants was only three percent of the total system cost, so the higher weight of the low-cost vehicle (relative to the Saturn V) would not come close to overwhelming its cost advantages in other areas.[67]

Low Weight Does Not Equal Low Cost. Retired TRW executive and rocket engine designer Gerard Elverum stated that for launch systems "cost as a design selection criteria . . . ought to be, in fact, the [dominant selection criteria] rather than high performance and low weight. In my opinion, low weight does not equal low cost. If you haul coal up and down the Mississippi River in a bunch of [speed boats] you've got low weight and high performance, but it's a very expensive way to move coal from one place to another."[68] Robert Truax said of traditional aerospace cost estimating techniques: "Most costing formulas are tied, directly or indirectly, to the *weight* of the product. For highly engineered devices, such as most launch vehicles, cost is *less* sensitive to weight than almost any other physical parameter."[69]

There are a number of cases in which smaller and lighter vehicles cost more than larger systems, a fact which tends to invalidate the idea that weight has a dominant influence on vehicle cost. For example, the Thor ballistic missile was approximately 10 times larger than the Agena upper stage but actually cost less. Since both were liquid-propellant, single-engine rockets, factors other than weight were making major contributions to vehicle cost.[70] Similarly, the Delta launch vehicle, which is much larger than the solid-propellant Inertial Upper Stage, costs about half as much.[71]

The cost of raw materials for fabricating a liquid-propellant booster is a very small percentage of its overall cost. The initial thickness (and cost) of propellant tank raw material for a pump-fed design has a good chance of being greater than that of a comparable pressure-fed design. Often, pump-fed tankage is designed with waffle ribs for stiffness, so the raw tank stock must be milled down to the required lighter gage at a large additional expense.[72] Space historian Roger Bilstein described the process used to manufacture the propellant tanks for the third stage of the Saturn V launch vehicles:

A Delta II launch vehicle.

With a design goal for very thin but rigid walls, Douglas [Aircraft Corporation] finally settled on an integrally stiffened shell structure, using special equipment to literally "carve out" ribs from the inside walls of the tank. . . . The waffle recesses were about 7.5 centimeters square, bounded by ribs that increased the buckling strength of the tank walls.[73]

115

An inertial upper stage and the Magellan spacecraft being deployed from the Shuttle cargo bay.

If a pressure-fed vehicle is designed to be water-recoverable, its thicker and heavier propellant tank structure affords a less-than-obvious benefit: Locking up the residual tank pressure prior to water impact would make the vehicle structure very strong. It would also preclude water intrusion to the vehicle interior, which would simplify the recovery and refurbishment process.[74]

Treating vehicle weight as a primary cost driver does not appear to be necessarily applicable to launch systems. Other, less obvious, influences tend to dominate launch vehicle costs. The central justification for avoiding pressure-fed systems has always been the attendant increase in vehicle weight; but since weight is not a primary factor in determining vehicle cost, this justification is likely not valid. Therefore, the use of pressure instead of turbopumps to deliver propellant to the engine deserves a closer look. Retired Aerospace Corporation launch vehicle designer Arthur Schnitt said:

> We were designing every stage as if it went into space. For the top stage, which is small and extremely valuable, minimum-weight designs made sense. For the lower stages it was nonsense. Why spend millions on high-efficiency engines when you could substitute a less efficient engine and simply make it bigger?[75]

Horizontal installation of an SSME.

The 70,000-piece-part SSME, during processing at KSC.

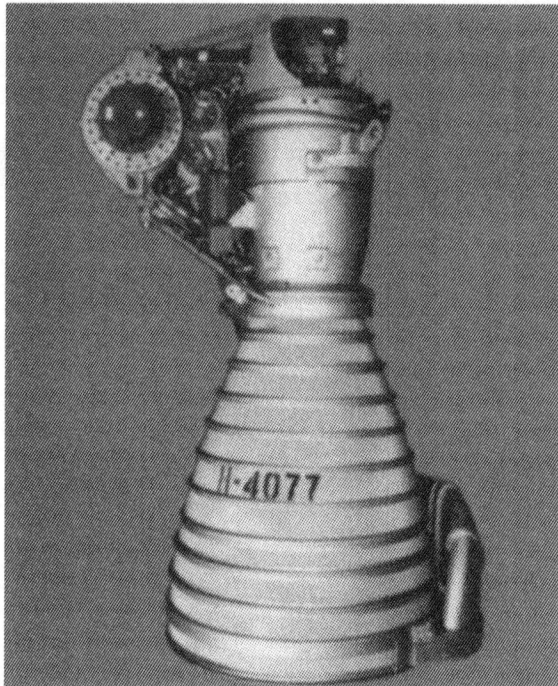

The Rocketdyne H-1.

118

SSME and STME Complexities and Part Counts

Of all the rocket engine turbomachinery ever produced, the highest performance, most complicated, most expensive, and most demanding of exacting manufacturing tolerances is that used by the Space Shuttle main engines (SSME). The SSME has had an excellent reliability record due to the dedicated efforts of many individuals at NASA's Kennedy, Marshall, and Stennis centers, as well as at Rockwell and Rocketdyne. However, it has exacted a heavy toll in operational turnaround costs and time. A contributing factor to the SSME's complexity and cost, of course, is the fact that the engines are reusable. A much more significant influence, however, is the high performance and low-weight demands put on the SSME designers. R. D. McKown of Rocketdyne said of the SSME:

> Clearly, design decisions in the early days of SSME were weight driven. . . . Things like scalloping flanges between bolt holes and machining lightening pockets in low stress areas became part of the engineering drawing. Producibility studies were limited to: "Can the component be produced at any cost" rather than "how to produce at low cost."[76]

The Space Shuttle main engine consists of 5,807 major component parts.[77] Its turbomachinery has both high-and low-pressure turbopumps for the liquid oxygen and liquid hydrogen sides of the engine. These four turbopumps have a total major component part count of 2,700, representing 47.3 percent of the total number of SSME component parts.[78]

SSME/STME Comparison. Developers of the Space Transportation Main Engine (STME), which was intended for use with the National Launch System vehicle, made noteworthy progress toward reducing engine complexity and improving ease of manufacturing. Despite being pump-fed and using a LOX/hydrogen propellant combination, the STME design had a major component part count of 3,047 and a drastically reduced number of required welds (as compared to the SSME) using near-net shape processing (e.g., casting components to such tolerances that they require little to no assembly or machining).[79] The reduction in STME complexity and performance requirements has often been dramatically illustrated by comparing the new engine concept to the highly complex, performance-driven SSME. Comparing the STME design with a variety of engines and engine designs employing different propellant combinations, various power cycles including pressure-fed techniques, and a spectrum of performance requirements would provide a more complete perspective. For example, the Rocketdyne H-1 LOX/RP-1 engine that (in a cluster of eight) powered the Saturn IB launch vehicle first stage is a good example of a simple pump-fed engine. It had a total of two electrical interfaces with the booster: one to start the engine and one to shut it down.[80]

SSME/Pressure-Fed Engine Comparison. McDonnell Douglas and TRW engineers estimate the total piece part count for the SSME to be around 70,000 individual items and the number of welds to total 3,000. In contrast, a pressure-fed engine with similar performance would have 100 piece parts and 20 welds.[81]

The Cost and Complexity of Turbomachinery

Estimates of the cost impact of turbomachinery (including gas generators or preburners and other associated hardware and plumbing required to operate the turbopumps) on the total cost of liquid engines range from 35 percent to 53 percent.[82] Even these percentages can be misleadingly low. Edward Keith of Microcosm said:

> The fatal assumption on parametric trade studies is that a pressure-fed engine must be just like a pump-fed engine, without the pump. We found that this is not always true. We found that pressure-fed engines could be so much less complex and demanding that they could be manufactured in a commercial manner . . . the turbo pumps drive the engine cost with their high tolerance and fine material demands. Likewise, high cost engines are cost drivers for rocket vehicles.[83]

Since turbomachinery has large numbers of high-speed moving parts that require precise manufacturing tolerances, it clearly represents a major component of engine cost. The development cost of a pump-fed engine is certainly higher than that for a pressure-fed engine, even if both engines are designed for the same chamber pressure. This is because the thrust chamber assembly of a pump-fed engine is usually developed on a pressure-fed test stand, separate from the turbomachinery. The turbine, pumps, and gas generator are typically developed on hydraulic facilities; and the thrust chamber and turbomachinery must then be integrated into a single engine package. The development cost for this integration is about equal to the cost of developing the thrust chamber or the turbomachinery. Therefore, the development cost for a pump-fed engine is about three times that of a pressure-fed engine. If the pump-fed system is designed for greater chamber pressures (as most are), the heat transfer problems go up proportionally. This results in the requirement for regeneratively-cooled, complex thrust chambers, which drive development costs even higher. Additionally, pump-fed engines consist of several subassemblies (thrust chamber, turbopump, and gas generator), which result in a net engine reliability that is much lower than the reliabilities of the individual subassemblies.[84]

Because of the higher quantity of parts, interfaces, and subassemblies that pump-fed systems possess relative to pressure-fed vehicles, the requirements for instrumentation, checkout, testing, documentation, and other operational activities will be correspondingly higher as well. This equates to greater post-fabrication costs, both at the factory and at the launch base.[85]

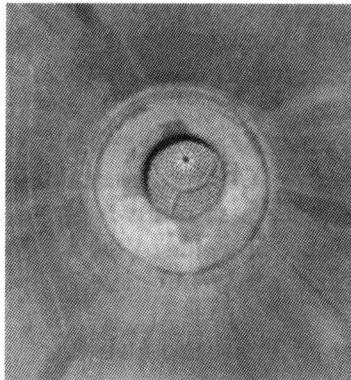

The business end of an SSME.

Examples of Turbomachinery-Induced Problems

Some examples of actual incidents will highlight the complexity, operational overhead, and high cost that pump-fed hardware can create for launch systems. These particular examples involve the Space Shuttle and the Atlas/Centaur.

Shuttle SSME Turbomachinery Problems. In the first case, technicians could not find the documentation required to determine which variety of tip seal retainers had been installed on the Shuttle's SSME high-pressure oxidizer turbomachinery blades, and one version needed more frequent inspections than the other. This problem resulted in an on-the-pad removal and replacement of each engine's high pressure oxidizer turbopumps and a two-week-plus delay in the launch of STS-55, a German spacelab mission.[86]

Due to maintenance and durability concerns about the high-pressure fuel and oxidizer turbopumps originally developed by Rocketdyne for the Space Shuttle's main engines, NASA contracted in 1986 with Pratt & Whitney to develop alternate turbopumps that could be installed on existing SSMEs as line replaceable units.[87] The pumps were originally scheduled to fly by the end of 1991 at a development cost of $200 million, but problems with cost growth caused a work stoppage on the fuel turbopump in January 1992. This left only the oxidizer pump effort continuing. Development difficulties with this work have resulted in costs increasing to $1.1 billion and the first flight of the hardware slipping to mid-1995.[88]

The Space Shuttle *Columbia* experienced a shutdown of its three SSMEs three seconds prior to lift-off on 22 March 1993, after the Number 3 SSME's oxidizer preburner failed to ignite. (Preburners drive the main engine tur-

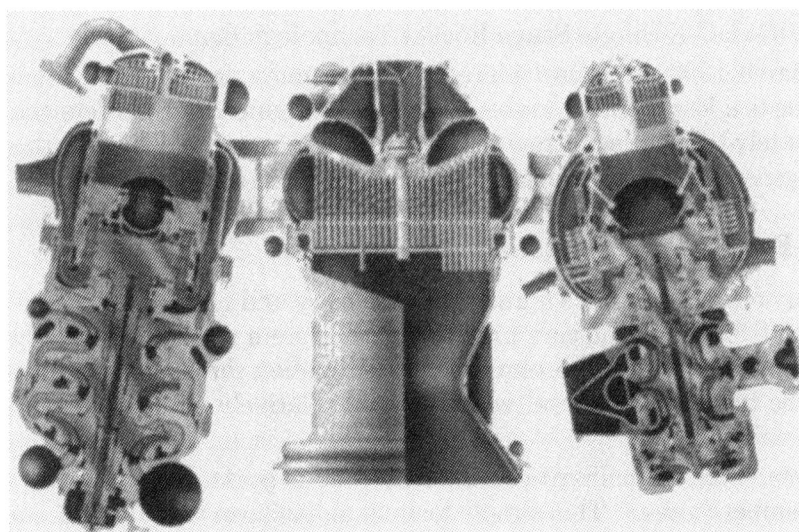

FUEL TURBOPUMP   OXIDIZER TURBOPUMP

Pratt & Whitney high-pressure fuel turbopump and oxidizer turbopump replacements for the SSME.

121

bopumps.) This was the third on-pad abort after main engine start that the Shuttle program had experienced.[89]

Technicians removed and replaced a relatively high-time, high-pressure fuel turbopump from the Shuttle *Endeavour*'s main engine Number 1 on 4 May 1993. The turbopump was changed out because a turbopump with similar run time experienced a failure of its turbine inlet during tests at the Stennis Space Center in Mississippi.[90]

A problem with an SSME high-pressure oxidizer turbopump forced a two-week delay in the planned 3 June 1993 launch of *Endeavour* to inaugurate the spacelab module and retrieve the Eureca spacecraft. Concern over the potential failure of a turbine bearing preload spring installed in the Number 2 engine prompted a change-out of the engine's turbopump in early June.[91]

Atlas Centaur Failures. The cause of two Atlas Centaur launch vehicle losses in April 1991 and August 1992 has been traced by analysis and test to a check valve that, in both failures, stuck and allowed outside air to be sucked into the cryogenically-cooled engines. Moisture in the air probably froze on the turbomachinery impeller blades of the Centaur RL10 engines, preventing the pumps from turning and the engines from starting.[92]

It is important to note that these two failures were the first for the RL10 program, which has achieved a remarkable reliability record since the initial flight of the RL10 in 1962. This record is particularly impressive when one considers that the engine uses relatively exotic liquid hydrogen for fuel, is pump-fed, employs two side-by-side engines on the Centaur stage, and flies missions that routinely require engine shutdowns and restarts.[93] The engine has been used on the Atlas, Saturn, and Titan launch vehicles; and also serves as the propulsion system for the Ballistic Missile Defense Organization's (BMDO) DC-X Single Stage Rocket Technology demonstrator.

On 25 March 1993 an Atlas 1 placed a Navy communications satellite in a useless orbit due to a loss of thrust in the Atlas booster engine. Analysis determined that an inadequately-torqued set screw led to a decrease in oxygen flow to the booster engine gas generator, which supplies power to the engine turbomachinery.[94]

Pressure-Fed Booster Pressurization Systems

Some previous studies have found the complexity and high development costs of the pressure-fed launch vehicle's pressurization system to be a potentially significant problem.[95] Providing the required pressurization for a large launch vehicle would not be trivial, but several workable and relatively simple alternatives appear to be available.

Stored gas (such as helium) could be used as a pressurant, possibly even at cryogenic temperatures.[96] This simple technique has been widely used. For strap-on stages, even stored nitrogen has been shown to be cost-effective as a pressurant.[97]

The use of Tridyne is another possibility. Developed by Rocketdyne, the Tridyne concept uses a nonexplosive mixture of an inert gas (like helium) and small quantities of hydrogen and oxygen. Passing the mixture through a catalyst bed produces

Pratt & Whitney's standard RL10 (left) and the RL10A-5 used by BMDO's SSRT demonstrator.

heated helium (and a small amount of steam), which is an effective pressurizing gas.[98]

A third alternative is to use decomposed hydrazine as a pressurizing agent, although this approach could represent some significant risk. Both helium and hydrazine are expensive, but they seem to provide good pressurization solutions for large pressure-fed launch systems.[99]

In at least one respect, pump-fed pressurization systems are more complex than pressure-fed systems. In order to regulate high-pressure gas down to the head suppression pressures needed by pump-fed engines, two-stage regulators must often be used; pressure-fed systems require only single-stage regulators.[100]

Pressure-Fed Engine Combustion Stability

Some studies comparing pump-fed and pressure-fed systems have raised a concern about the potential for combustion instability of pressure-fed engines that are scaled up for large booster applications.[101] The simple, inexpensive pressure-fed engine that TRW developed in the late 1960s, and tested to 1,112,000 Newtons (250,000 pounds) of thrust, showed no signs of stability problems at any of the tested thrust levels.[102] The coaxial pintle injector design that was pioneered by TRW for use on the lunar module descent engine has been used on a number of other subsequent TRW engines, including the 1,112,000-Newton engine. No engine using this injector technology has ever had a catastrophic failure—whether during ground test or in flight—and no trace of combustion stability difficulty has ever been noted.[103]

Historical Pump-Fed/Pressure-Fed Comparisons

Some historical comparisons between pump-fed and pressure-fed rocket engines are instructive and worth reviewing. The pressure-fed rocket engine used on the Bomarc surface-to-air missile had twice the thrust of the pump-fed RL10 but cost only one-sixth as much to produce. The pressure-fed Apollo Service Propulsion System had a thrust level comparable to the RL10, with development costs less than one-fourth those of the RL10. One of the factors in the RL10's higher cost is its use of the powerful, but persnickety, liquid hydrogen fuel. Another factor, of course, is that the RL10 employed turbomachinery.

In cases where both pump-fed and pressure-fed engines have been developed for the same application, the pressure-fed engine came out ahead in the categories of cost and schedule. For example, the Navy's Lark surface-to-air missile used both pressure-fed and pump-fed engines, and the X-1A research aircraft used a pump-fed version of the four-chamber engine system that operated in a pressure-fed mode on the X-1. In both cases, the programs using the pressure-fed systems were completed much quicker than those using the pump-fed systems.[104]

A Survey of Pressure-Fed Engines

Some studies have cited the fact that pressure-fed engines have seen only limited use for space launch applications, and those that have been used are relatively small in size. They have argued that, because of this, pressure-fed engines are not practical candidates as propulsion systems for large launch vehicles.[105] In a design climate where performance and weight-savings are critical considerations, it is not surprising that pressure-fed engines have not been considered for space launch use very often. Nevertheless, a number of moderate-sized, pressure-fed systems have been developed over the years for a variety of applications, including space launch. This study will survey some of the better known liquid-propellant, pressure-fed systems, whether currently in use or used in the past, confining the survey to engines with a thrust in excess of 4,450 Newtons (1,000 pounds) (see table 8). All thrust levels will be for high altitude or vacuum conditions unless otherwise noted.

Table 8

US Pressure-Fed Engine Survey

	ENGINE	THRUST LEVEL
AEROJET ENGINES		
	Aerobee Sustainer	11,600–72,300 N (2,600–16,260 lb)
	Vanguard AJ10-37	33,400 N (7,500 lb)
	Able AJ10-101	34,700+ N (7,800+ lb)
	AbleStar AJ10-104	34,700+ N (7,800+ lb)
	Delta AJ10-118	43,800 N (9,850 lb)
	Transtage AJ10-138	71,200 N (16,000 lb)
	Apollo SPS AJ10-137	95,600 N (21,500 lb)
	Shuttle OMS-E AJ10-190	26,700 N (6,000 lb)
OTHER ENGINES		
	TRW LMDE VTR-10	43,800 N (9,850 lb)
	TRW Delta TR-201	44,000 N (9,900 lb)
	Rocketdyne LMAE RS-18	15,600 N (3,500 lb)
	Marquardt Saturn MA 118-XAB	9,800 N (2,200 lb)
EXPERIMENTAL AND TEST ENGINES		
	TRW Low Cost Engine Family	up to 1,112,000 N (250,000 lb)
	Rocketdyne XLR117-NA-1	53,400 N (12,000 lb)
	GE Plug Nozzle Engine	277,600 N (62,400 lb)
	Aerojet Sled Engine AJ10-51	677,200 N (150,000 lb)
	Aerojet Shuttle Sub-Scale Strap-On	890,000 N (200,000 lb)

Aerojet Engines. Aerojet has produced a large number of pressure-fed engines over the years. Some of the first were various versions of the Aerobee sustainer engine that had thrust levels ranging from 11,600 to 72,300 Newtons (2,600 to 16,260 pounds). A very large number of these engines were built over a three-decade-plus period. The Navy's Vanguard second stage used the 33,400-Newton (7,500-pound)-thrust Aerojet AJ10-37. The Able and AbleStar stages used the AJ10-101 and AJ10-104, respectively, each of which delivered a thrust of over 34,700 Newtons (7,800 pounds). Aerojet delivered 40 of these systems to the Air Force between 1957 and 1963.

The Able and AbleStar engines formed the basis for the AJ10-118 and follow-on variants. Two of these variants power the Delta II second stage and the Japanese N-II second stage. The AJ10-118 has a thrust of 43,800 Newtons (9,850 pounds). The Titan Transtage propulsion system, designated AJ10-138, employed twin engines very similar to the Delta second stage engine that delivered 71,200 Newtons (16,000 pounds) of thrust for the third stage of the Titan III and 34D launch vehicles.

The Aerojet 95,600-Newton (21,500-pound)-thrust AJ10-137 Apollo Service Propulsion System served as the primary propulsion system for the Apollo command and service module. The Space Shuttle Orbiter uses two AJ10-190 OMS-E orbital maneuvering subsystem engines, each of which produces 26,700 Newtons (6,000 pounds) of thrust. A pump-fed version of this engine has been considered by NASA, but it is not currently in use.[106]

125

Pressure-fed thrust chamber assembly for Aerojet's Delta second stage engine.

TRW, Rocketdyne, and Marquardt Engines. TRW built the VTR-10 lunar module descent engine (LMDE), which provided 43,800 Newtons (9,850 pounds) of thrust for the Apollo program's lunar lander. TRW also manufactured an earlier version of the Delta launch vehicle second stage engine,

Aerojet pressure-fed engine that was used in pairs on the Transtage upper stage vehicle.

designated TR-201, which was a fixed thrust version of the LMDE that produced a thrust of 44,000 Newtons (9,900 pounds). Rocketdyne produced the
15,600-Newton (3,500-pound)-thrust RS-18 lunar module ascent engine. The
RS-18 was based on a Bell Aircraft design, with a Rocketdyne-designed injec-

OMS/RCS AFT PROPULSION SUBSYSTEM

The Space Shuttle's OMS propulsion system and aft reaction control system.

tor. Marquardt built a propellant ullage control engine (designated the MA 118-XAB) that had a thrust of 9,800 Newtons (2,200 pounds) and was used on the Saturn S-IVB (Saturn V third stage) vehicle.[107]

Experimental and Test Engines. As mentioned previously, TRW developed a family of simple, low-cost, pressure-fed engines in the late-1960s that demonstrated thrust levels up to 1,112,000 Newtons (250,000 pounds) during sea-level ground tests. Rocketdyne built an experimental pressure-fed engine known as the XLR117-NA-1 in the late 1950s for the Nomad upper stage. Using liquid fluorine and hydrazine, it developed a thrust of 53,400 Newtons (12,000 pounds). General Electric built an experimental engine using a plug nozzle configuration that had a thrust of 277,600 Newtons (62,400 pounds). Aerojet's AJ10-51 engine, built for rocket sled applications, had sea-level thrust capabilities up to 667,200 Newtons (150,000 pounds).[108]

The Diamant Pressure-Fed Booster. In the early 1960s, the French government developed a low-cost satellite launcher called Diamant that used a pressure-fed liquid propulsion system for the first stage and two solid-propellant upper stages.[109] In its initial launch attempt, the Diamant placed France's first satellite into orbit on 26 November 1965. Launched out of Hammaguir, Algeria, this mission made France the third nation (after the Soviet

128

TRW's pressure-fed engine for the Delta launch vehicle second stage.

Union and the US) to establish an orbital capability. The French launched a total of 12 Diamant boosters (of three different variants) on orbital missions from Hammaguir and from Kourou, French Guiana, between 1965 and 1975. Ten of the missions were successful, and the two failures were attributed to the solid-propellant upper stages. The pressure-fed first stage of the largest Diamant variant, Diamant BP4, had a thrust of 392,000 Newtons (88,000 pounds). This booster could place 200 kilograms (440 pounds) into low earth orbit.[110]

Aerojet Pressure-Fed Engine Technology. In 1989, NASA's Marshall Space Flight Center contracted the Aerojet Propulsion Division to develop low-cost pressure-fed engine technologies for potential space launch applications. This effort was an outgrowth of studies accomplished in the late 1980s to examine the feasibility of using liquid-propellant strap-on boosters for the Shuttle (instead of continuing to depend on the solid rocket boosters). NASA originally intended the technology effort to develop a full-size test engine using LOX/RP-1 propellants and having a thrust of 3,336,000 Newtons (750,000 pounds), but budget limitations allowed Aerojet to build and test only a subscale engine. Nevertheless, Aerojet demonstrated the subscale engine at thrust levels of slightly over 890,000 Newtons (200,000 pounds) with no spontaneous combustion instabilities. Engineers designed the subscale injector to be easily scalable to larger engine applications. The program final report states:

> This NASA-MSFC sponsored program has successfully developed the technology for a low cost [pressure-fed] LOX/RP engine. Using the design and production approaches developed in this program, very simple and low cost LOX/RP thrust chamber assemblies (TCAs) can be developed at minimum risk.[111]

Other Simplification Possibilities

A compromise between high-performance/lightweight pump-fed vehicle designs and cost-optimized pressure-fed vehicles with heavier structure is a possibility, by using pressure-fed engine designs with simple, low-pressure turbopump assemblies. This approach retains the simple, inexpensive engines typical of pressure-fed vehicles, but it uses low-cost pumps to avoid the heavier pressurized tank structure needed by pressure-fed boosters. McDonnell Douglas is pursuing such an approach with TRW and Allied Signal, using Allied Signal's simple foil-bearing pump technology.[112] Rocketdyne has also developed a simple turbopump called the Simple Low Cost Innovative Concept (SLIC) turbopump. Rocketdyne said the pump was designed and built for one-fifth the cost and schedule of today's typical turbomachinery.[113] Another alternative that could simplify the design and lower the cost of pump-fed engines is to adopt the Soviet/Russian design strategy of incorporating multiple thrust chambers with a single set of turbomachinery.

A relatively recent technology development that may make pressure-fed systems an extremely attractive option is the use of graphite/epoxy in the fabrication of large propellant tanks. The experience gained in developing graphite/epoxy motor cases for the Shuttle's solid rocket boosters and other motor case and pressure vessel development programs would be applicable to the manufacture of large graphite/epoxy propellant tanks for pressure-fed launchers. Graphite/epoxy tanks could be an enabling design feature that would allow pressure-fed systems to decrease their structural fraction considerably. Of course, the higher cost of using graphite/epoxy would have to be traded off against heavier (but cheaper) materials like steel. Dr John Davis of NASA's Langley Research Center, speaking at a workshop on low-cost space transportation systems sponsored by the Office of Technology Assessment, said, "It appears that graphite/epoxy would be the [best] choice of materials for the pressure fed booster."[114]

Pressure-Fed Systems Offer the Possibility of Lower Costs

Turbopump-fed rocket engines have dominated the large launch system arena in the US throughout the history of the space age. However, simple pressure-fed systems offer possibilities for achieving drastic reductions in the cost of getting to orbit through simplified manufacturing processes and easier operations. There are some drawbacks to using pressure-fed propulsion systems, but the potential for major reductions in launch costs makes a compelling case for seriously investigating this design approach. A pressure-fed design will certainly allow the development of inexpensive small launch vehicles, and it may be the key to producing low-cost large boosters as well.

Summary

The right design choices will allow the US to develop inexpensive space launchers; the wrong choices will perpetuate high launch costs. This chapter has sought to delve into some of the key design choices that have the greatest influence on booster development and operating costs. When making such choices, the launch system designer must consider the expense of development and manufacturing, as well as the cost of operations. New launch proposals that require big development costs with a promise of out-year savings and pay-back may not survive in the current budgetary environment. Making the right choices will not always be easy, especially if they break with longstanding conventions and practices that have succeeded in the past, albeit at high cost. However, these choices are essential to successfully field simple, inexpensive, and highly reliable launch systems. Arriving at the correct design decisions that will enable major launch cost reductions may require new ways of thinking within both government and industry.

Notes

1. "1993 Shuttle Manifest," *Space News,* 22-28 February 1993, 11.
2. "ESA Rescues Eureca from Low Orbit, Tests Payload for 9-Month Flight," *Aviation Week & Space Technology,* 10 August 1992, 61.
3. Andrew Lawler, "Station Panel Leader Awaits New Guidelines," *Space News,* 1–7 March 1993, 3.
4. Theodore A. Talay, "The HL-20 Personnel Launch System" (Paper presented at the AIAA Space Programs and Technologies Conference, Huntsville, Ala., 24–27 March 1992), 1–2.
5. A. Prince, "National Launch System Comparative Economic Analysis" (Paper presented at the AIAA Space Programs and Technologies Conference, Huntsville, Alabama, 24–27 March

131

1992), 2; Vice President's Space Policy Advisory Board, *The Future of the U.S. Space Launch Capability* (Washington, D.C.: National Space Council, November, 1992), 31.

6. Thiokol Corporation Marketing brochure, "Building the Space Shuttle Redesigned Solid Rocket Motor," Thiokol Corporation, Brigham City, Utah, 1989, 20.

7. Robert C. Truax, "The Pressure-Fed Booster—Dark Horse of the Space-Race" (Paper presented at the 19th International Astronautical Federation Congress, October 1967), 3.

8. R. C. Truax, "Sea Dragon and the Manned Mars Mission," *The Journal of Practical Applications in Space,* Fall 1990, 12.

9. Richard DeMeis, "Liquid Lift for the Shuttle," *Aerospace America,* February 1989, 22.

10. Ibid., 25.

11. Leonard David, "Unorthodox New DC-X Rocket Ready for First Tests," *Space News,* 11–17 January 1993, 10.

12. Robert C. Truax, "One Stage to Orbit—Or Two" (Unpublished paper, Truax Engineering, Inc., 2614 Temple Heights Drive, Oceanside, Calif., 5 March 1992).

13. Edward A. Gabris, "SSTO vs. Airplanes," letter in *Space News,* 8–14 February 1993, 14.

14. David.

15. J. R. Wilson, "Designing the DC-3 of Space?" *Interavia Aerospace Review,* January 1992, 41–43.

16. Malcolm A. LeCompte, "SSTO Vehicle: Low-Cost Alternative," *Aviation Week & Space Technology,* 8 March 1993, 57.

17. R. C. Truax, "Cheap Transportation for Cheap Satellites" (Paper presented at the AIAA/DARPA Meeting on Lightweight Satellite Systems, Monterey, Calif., 10 May 1990), 5.

18. It should be noted that this was the original plan for Ariane, but it has not yet proven to be cost-effective to do so.

19. Paul Estey, "Hybrid Rockets," *Aerospace America,* December 1992, 62.

20. Dieter K. Huzel and David H. Huang, *Design of Liquid Propellant Rocket Engines* (Washington, D.C.: National Technical Information Service, 1967), 10–11; lecture by Lt Col Doug May, Kennedy Space Center, Fla., January 1982.

21. Thiokol Corporation marketing brochure, "Space Shuttle Redesigned Solid Rocket Motor (RSRM)," Thiokol Corporation, Brigham City, Utah, 1988, 6.

22. Michael A. Dornheim, "AMROC Hybrid Motor Tests Aimed at 1995 Flight," *Aviation Week & Space Technology,* 1 March 1993, 51.

23. Rick Fleeter, Frank Mcloughlin, and Ray Mills, "A Low-Cost Expendable Launch Vehicle for 500-Pound Class Satellites," marketing brochure, PacAstro, 520 Huntmar Drive, Herndon, Va., 26 May 1992, 4.

24. Office of Technology Assesment, Congress of the United States, *Big Dumb Boosters—A Low-Cost Space Transportation Option?* (Washington, D.C.: Government Printing Office, February 1989), 12.

25. W. Geary Andrews and E. G. Haberman, "Solids Virtues a Solid Bet," *Aerospace America,* June 1991, 24–26.

26. Andrews and Haberman, 26.

27. Jerry R. Cook et al., "Hybrid Rockets: Combining the Best of Liquids and Solids," *Aerospace America,* July 1992, 31–32.

28. Vincent Kiernan, "Trouble-Plagued SRMU Rocket Motor Faces Further Delay," *Space News,* 15–21 February 1993, 7.

29. Michael A. Dornheim, "USAF May Pay Hercules for SRMU Losses," *Aviation Week & Space Technology,* 1 March 1993, 24.

30. "Launch System Costs" (Briefing prepared by The Aerospace Corporation, El Segundo, Calif., 23 May 1991), 12.

31. Liz Tucci, "Lockheed, Aerojet Regroup on ASRM," *Space News,* 3–9 May 1993, 3.

32. Breck W. Henderson, "X-Ray Inspection Advances to Include Large SRM," *Aviation Week & Space Technology,* 14 September 1992, 79.

33. Pacific American Launch Systems, Inc., "Evaluation of an Innovative Propulsion Concept (EIPC)—Final Report," vol. 2, USASDC contract DASG60-88-C-0056 (Menlo Park, Calif., 24 May 1989), 2-5, 2-6.

34. Fleeter, McLoughlin, and Mills, 4–5.

35. Michael D. Griffin and Joseph H. Jerger, "Preliminary Design of the Industrial Launch Vehicle" (Paper presented at the AIAA/DARPA Meeting on Lightweight Satellite Systems, Monterey, Calif., 4–6 August 1987), 242.

36. Cook et al., 30.

37. James R. French, "AMROC Industrial Launch Vehicle: A Low Cost Launch Vehicle" (Paper presented at the Aerospace Vehicle Conference, Washington, D.C., 8–10 June 1987), 3.

38. "No Sign of Ozone Loss from Launches," *Science News,* 12 October 1991, 237.

39. Allan J. McDonald, "The Impact of Chemical Rocket Propulsion on the Earth's Environment" (Paper presented at the World Space Congress, Washington, D.C., 28 August–5 September 1992), 8.

40. Ibid.

41. "No Sign of Ozone Loss from Launches."

42. Steven Aftergood, "Poisoned Plumes," *New Scientist,* 7 September 1991, 35.

43. "Weather Delays Titan Test," *Military Space,* 21 September 1992, 3.

44. McDonald, 9.

45. Ibid., 11.

46. Ibid., 2, 8.

47. Dawn Scovell, "Solid Rockets," *Aerospace America,* December 1992, 48.

48. "Dutch Scientists Produce Environmentally Safer Rocket Propellant," *European Space Report,* February 1993, 4.

49. McDonald, 2.

50. Fleeter, McLoughlin, and Mills, 5.

51. Cook et al., 32.

52. Fleeter, McLoughlin, and Mills.

53. Pacific American Launch Systems, Inc., 2-3.

54. Paul Dergarabedian, The Aerospace Corporation, telephone conversation, author, 6 January 1993.

55. Cook et al.

56. Pacific American Launch Systems, Inc., 2-6.

57. "Crews to Destack Titan 4," *Aviation Week & Space Technology,* 15 February 1993, 17.

58. T. J. Frey, Jr., "Sea Launch and Recovery (SEALAR): Responsive and Affordable Access to Space" (Paper presented at the AIAA Space Programs and Technologies Conference, Huntsville, Ala., 24–27 March 1992), 2.

59. Gerard Elverum to John London, letter, 28 May 1993.

60. Huzel and Huang, 175.

61. J. E. Dyer et al., "Low Cost Expendable Propulsion Study," AFAL Report No. TR-87-020, General Dynamics Corporation, San Diego, Calif., August 1987, 99; Leland B. Piper, "Advanced LO2/LH2 Engines: Cycles and Selection Options," *Chemical Propulsion Information Agency Bulletin,* March 1993, 7–9.

62. The Aerospace Corporation, Space Transportation Analysis and Design (El Segundo, Calif.: Report No. TOR-92(2464)-1, 15 March 1992), 5-5.

63. Huzel and Huang, 35.

64. J. E. Dyer et al., 102, 107.

65. Andrew J. Stofan and Steven J. Isakowitz, "Design Challenges for the Advanced Launch System" (Paper presented at the AIAA/ASME/SAE/ASEE 25th Joint Propulsion Conference, Monterey, Calif., 10–12 July 1989), 14–15.

66. Paul Dergarabedian, "Cost-Model Considerations for Launch Vehicles" (Unpublished study, The Aerospace Corporation, El Segundo, Calif., 14 November 1991), 1.

67. Ibid., 2–4.

68. G. W. Elverum, Jr., "Boosters" (Transcript of a talk presented at the Aerospace Productivity Conference, The Aerospace Corporation, El Segundo, Calif., 1987), 4.

69. Robert C. Truax to John London, letter, 24 September 1992, 1.

70. Robert C. Truax, "Thousand Tons to Orbit," *Astronautics,* January 1963, 44.

71. William Harwood, "TDRS, Training Spacewalk on First '93 Shuttle Flight," *Space News,* 4–10 January 1993, 9.

72. Ibid., 2.

73. Roger E. Bilstein, *Stages to Saturn* (Washington, D.C.: National Aeronautics and Space Administration, 1980), 165.

74. Truax, "Sea Dragon and the Manned Mars Mission."

75. Gregg Easterbrook, "Big Dumb Rockets," *Newsweek,* 17 August 1987, 48.

76. R. D. McKown, "Low Cost Design Approaches for the Advanced Launch System (ALS) Propulsion System" (Presented at the AIAA/ASME/SAE/ASEE 25th Joint Propulsion Conference, Monterey, Calif., 10–12 July 1992), 2.

77. Edward A. Gabris, Ronald J. Harris, and Stephen A. Rast, "Progress on the National Launch System Demonstrates National Commitment" (Presented at the World Space Congress, Washington, D.C., 31 August 1992), 6.

78. A. Csomor, "Low Cost, Reliable ALS Turbopump Concept" (Paper presented at the AIAA/ASME/SAE/ASEE 25th Joint Propulsion Conference, Monterey, Calif., 10–12 July 1989), 4.

79. Gabris, Harris, and Rast.

80. Conversation with James R. French, Washington, D.C., 1 September 1992.

81. J. P. Henneberry et al., "Low-Cost Expendable Launch Vehicles" (Paper presented at the AIAA/SAE/ASME/ASEE 28th Joint Propulsion Conference and Exhibit, Nashville, Tennessee, 6–8 July 1992), 9.

82. John Wooten and Arthur Weiss, "Low-Cost Design Approaches for Earth-to-Orbit Propulsion" (Paper presented at SAE Aerospace Atlantic, Dayton, Ohio, 23–26 April 1990), 2; Aerojet Tech Systems briefing, "STME/STBE Configuration Study," 28 March 1989 in Edward L. Keith, "Low-Cost Space Transportation: The Search for the Lowest Cost" (1991 AAS/AIAA Spaceflight Mechanics Mtg.).

83. Edward L. Keith, "System Analysis and Description of an Ultra-Low Cost Ground to Low Earth Orbit Cargo Delivery System" (Paper presented at the World Space Congress, Washington, D.C., 31 August 1992), 3.

84. Truax, letter, 1–2.

85. Ibid.

86. "Shuttle Launch Delay," *Aviation Week & Space Technology,* 15 February 1993, 17.

87. J. P. Mitchell and J. L. Price, "Space Shuttle Main Engine (SSME) Alternate Turbopump Design and Development" (Paper presented at the World Space Congress, Washington, D.C., 28 August–5 September 1992), 1.

88. Andrew Lawler, "Litany of NASA Overruns Described to Congress," *Space News,* 22–28 March 1993, 4.

89. James T. McKenna, "Launch Abort Has NASA Scrambling," *Aviation Week & Space Technology,* 29 March 1993, 23–24.

90. "Turbopump Fails Test; Unit Removed From Endeavour," *Aviation Week & Space Technology,* 10 May 1993, 63.

91. James T. McKenna, "Eureca Hits Snags, Shuttle Launch Slips," *Aviation Week & Space Technology,* 31 May 1993, 27–28.

92. Jeffrey Lenorovitz, "Atlas/Centaur Targeted for March Launch," *Aviation Week & Space Technology,* 18 January 1993, 27–28.

93. Daniel A. Heald, "LH2 Technology Was Pioneered on Centaur 30 Years Ago" (Paper presented at the World Space Congress, Washington, D.C., 28 August–5 September 1992), 3.

94. "Loose Set Screw Cited in Atlas Launch Anomoly," *Aviation Week & Space Technology,* 14 June 1993, 34.

95. Stofan and Isakowitz, 14.

96. A. Schnitt and Col F. W. Kniss, "Proposed Minimum Cost Space Launch Vehicle System," The Aerospace Corporation report no. TOR-0158(3415-15)-1, El Segundo, Calif.: 1 July 1968, 3–12.

97. Elverum to London, letter.

98. Ibid.

99. Microcosm, Inc. presentation to NASA Headquarters, Washington, D.C., 1 September 1992, subject: Ultra Low Cost High Reliability Space Cargo Vehicle.

100. Truax, letter, 3.

101. Stofan and Isakowitz.

102. TRW, "Low Cost Shuttle Surrogate Booster (LCSSB)," TRW Redondo Beach, Calif. NASA contract report, 15 May 1981), 40.

103. Pacific American Launch Systems, Inc., 3–7.

104. Truax, letter, 2, 3.

105. Stofan and Isakowitz.

106. Aerojet Propulsion Division marketing booklet, "Engines Thrust Chambers Turbopumps Valves and Actuators Engine Controllers" (Sacramento, Calif.: Marketing booklet June 1990, 6–8, 10, 12.

107. Chemical Propulsion Information Agency, *Liquid Propellant Engine Manual* (Laurel Md.: Applied Physics Laboratory, Johns Hopkins University, February 1987), 49, 97, 180, 207.

108. Ibid., 64, 74, 82.

109. Pacific American Launch Systems, Inc., 2-2.

110. Steven J. Isakowitz, *International Reference Guide to Space Launch Systems* (Washington, D.C.: The American Institute of Aeronautics and Astronautics, 1991), 284.

111. Aerojet Propulsion Division, "Pressure Fed Thrust Chamber Technology Program—Final Report" contract NAS 8-37365, Aerojet Propulsion Division, Sacramento, Calif., July 1992 2–3, 10–11, 15, 58, 81.

112. Henneberry et al., 1.

113. News Breaks, *Aviation Week & Space Technology,* 10 May 1993, 17.

114. John G. Davis, Jr., "Materials and Structures for Low Technology Boosters" (Unpublished paper presented at the OTA Conference Center, Washington, D.C., 1 December 1987), 3.

Chapter 7

Cultural Changes

In 1988, Air Force Col John Wormington, program director for the Advanced Launch System (ALS), characterized the ALS as a launch system that "doesn't use new technology that much" but would bring about "design and cultural changes" in the way launch vehicles are made and operated. Colonel Wormington said that existing technologies not used for launch systems would be investigated for possible application to the ALS. Speaking of the ALS engine requirements, he said the program planned to develop a "truck engine—robust and low cost." Colonel Wormington stated that contractors would be expected to "spend weight to save money. This is a cultural shock for designers. We're not interested in [wringing out] the last second of specific impulse, the last 100 pounds of weight, or the maximum chamber pressure. When cost is a performance variable in design, the challenge is different."[1] This chapter will discuss in some detail the "cultural changes," or new approaches and mind-sets, that are necessary for the US to field a drastically cheaper means for getting payloads into orbit.

Recent Launch System Proposals

Designers intended the ALS to be the product of a "clean sheet" approach to designing, developing, and operating a space launch system.[2] The program was to represent a radical departure from the development methods used for such boosters as the Apollo Saturn V moon rocket and in which political exigencies made the program schedule the paramount consideration. According to Charles Murray, coauthor of *Apollo: The Race to the Moon,* managers posted the slogan "waste anything but time" in NASA facilities during the 1960s, reflecting a period of budgetary extravagance that is foreign to space programs today.[3]

Unfortunately, as the ALS design studies progressed and the program grew, it became clear that the ALS design that was beginning to emerge would be unaffordable in the fiscally-constrained environment of the 1990s. The program was cut back to become the Advanced Launch Development Program with primary emphasis on developing a new LOX/hydrogen engine, the Space Transportation Main Engine.[4] In a paper presented at the World Space Congress in August 1992, the authors stated: "In an Utopian world of infinite monies, the clean sheet Advanced Launch System would have been the launch vehicle of choice; however, with the international shrinking economic reserves for space systems ALS set the groundwork for future vehicles and provided the essential technologies for the NLS [National Launch System]"[5] In other words, ALS cost too much. Consequently, the Air Force and NASA revamped the program to focus ". . . on previous investments and existing hardware and infrastructure to limit development costs for a family of vehicles to complement the existing launch vehicle fleet."[6] Thus, the National Launch System (NLS) came into being.

NLS and Spacelifter

Despite the intention of NLS planners to use existing designs and assets, Congress canceled the NLS program in 1992 primarily because the program would cost too much and did not offer a sufficient return on investment. The "Spacelifter" concept that Pete Aldridge's National Space Council working group developed in the wake of the NLS cancellation is more focused than the NLS "family" of launch vehicles and promises to reduce the cost of launch by half. However, the proposal has been branded a repackaged NLS by some members of Congress. Representative Dana Rohrabacker, R-California, said: "We canceled NLS because it was a bad buy. . . . We failed to put a stake all the way through its heart [and completely kill NLS]. . . . A duck is a duck, and Spacelifter is NLS." Representative Jim Sensenbrenner, R-Wisconsin, stated: "Money is getting scarcer and scarcer. Getting a new launcher authorized is going to be even harder than the [NLS], which was canceled. . . ."[7]

SSRT and NASP

Recent efforts to develop a new launch system for the US that is more reliable and much less expensive to procure and operate than current systems have continued to evolve through several incarnations from the original ALS "clean sheet" concept. However, Congress appears to be seeking a new launcher proposal that incorporates significantly different design approaches and will be much less expensive than previous boosters. One method to achieve these ends is to use radically different techniques to achieve orbit, such as those embodied in the Single Stage Rocket Technology (SSRT) and National Aerospace Plane (NASP) programs. Both of these programs plan to achieve major reductions in launch costs through low operating expenses; but they would eventually depend on lengthy, high-dollar, high-risk, technology-intensive development efforts to get there. Either an SSRT-derived single-stage-to-orbit vehicle or a NASP vehicle, as currently envisioned, would indeed bring about dramatic cultural changes in the way we operate launch systems and may be the ultimate solution to providing low-cost, routine access to space. However, their front-end development costs will be difficult to accommodate in the current budgetary environment.

The most important aspect of the Ballistic Missile Defense Organization's (BMDO) SSRT program is not the DC-X vehicle or the vertical takeoff and landing concept it is designed to demonstrate. Far more significant is what the SSRT program has accomplished for the allocated budget and schedule. The Strategic Defense Initiative Organization awarded a $58.9 million two-year contract to McDonnell Douglas Space Systems Company in August 1991.[8] BMDO has used a one-person government program office to manage the effort. It is nothing short of phenomenal that the SSRT team has designed, fabricated, and flight tested a liquid oxygen/liquid hydrogen-powered aerospace vehicle incorporating a number of design innovations—all in under two years and for a lot less than $100 million.[9] The program's success has been enabled in part by using very streamlined management techniques, as well as employing existing technology throughout the design and existing hardware and software whenever possible.[10] This streamlining philosophy has flowed down into the SSRT's launch operations requirements, which specify a minuscule amount of personnel and ground equipment. These are the kinds of programmatic cultural changes that will be necessary to develop any launch system that achieves a breakthrough in launch cost reductions.

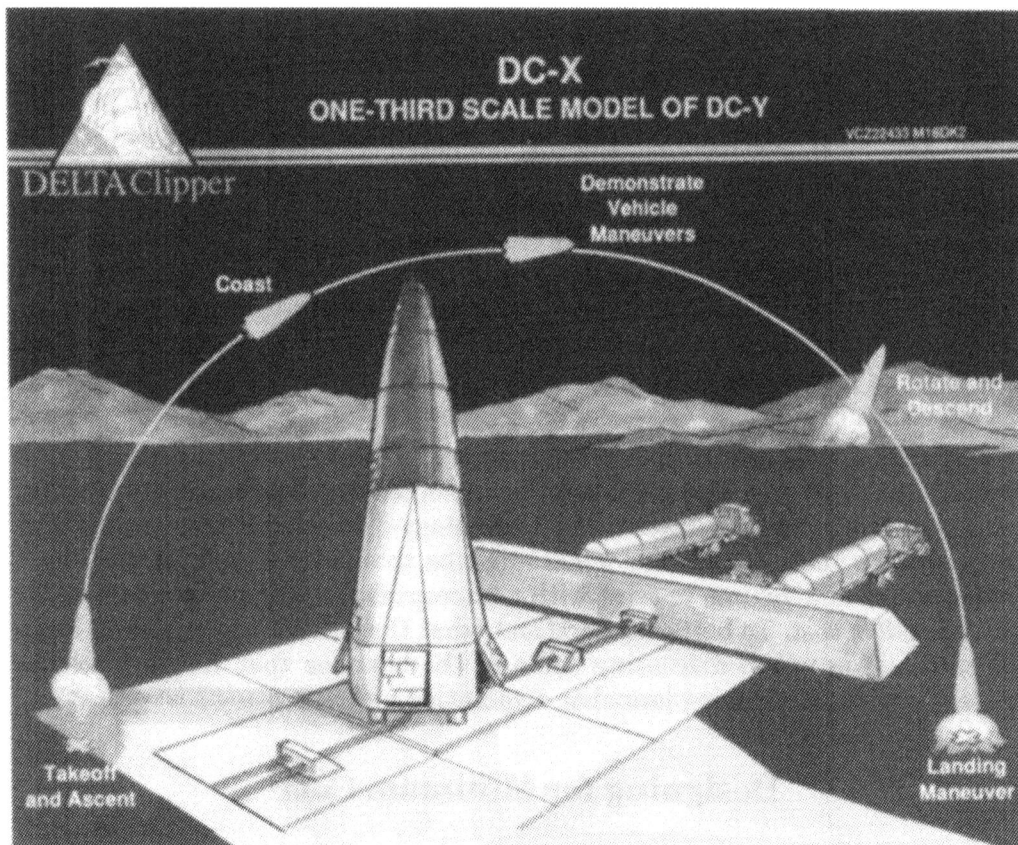

The McDonnell Douglas DC-X: a remarkable achievement in program management and aerospace system development.

Cultural Changes to Get a Space Truck

An alternative method to provide a new launcher that incorporates different design approaches and will cost significantly less is to recapture Colonel Wormington's vision of a rugged space truck, much like the Air Force and NASA intended the original ALS to be. Colonel Wormington spoke of cultural changes needed to develop an inexpensive booster that spanned the entire spectrum of the system's life cycle—from concept development through mature and stable operations. Development of such a system will necessarily *require* a clean sheet approach, despite the findings of the original ALS/ALDP/NLS team that such an approach would be cost prohibitive. To incorporate existing hardware and infrastructure would void the program's ability to establish true changes in design, manufacturing, and operational methods, and would ensure the perpetuation of the current development and operating practices that are at the root of high launch costs. The clean sheet effort must have an affordable development budget, and the current wisdom says this will be difficult if not impossible. The current wisdom, however, is based on previous launcher development experience, so cultural changes in how we develop launch vehicles will be essential to bringing about drastically lower design and manufacturing costs.

The practice of designing launch vehicles to have the maximum performance that technology can possibly provide, along with the lightest possible weight, has a heritage that reaches back to early ICBM development. Major General Joseph S. Bleymaier, deputy director of the Manned Orbiting Laboratory program in the late 1960s, said this about traditional design approaches for launch vehicles: "Customarily, we have designed for minimum weight and maximum performance. We use the finest lightweight alloys. We demand the highest order of skills in design, production, and retest, to get results that are the utmost in precision and sophistication."[11] General Bleymaier made his comments in 1969, and the design of our current launch vehicles still reflects this approach.

The cultural changes Colonel Wormington alluded to could be broadly summarized as using only the *necessary* technologies and operational practices, and not performance-optimized and technology-driven practices, to achieve the program's goals. And these goals must be to deliver a certain minimum payload mass and volume to orbit with an acceptable injection accuracy *at the lowest possible cost.* To better understand what these "cultural changes" actually entail, it is worth discussing some of the changes that would have the greatest impact in reducing launcher acquisition and operating costs.

Designing for Minimum Cost

To achieve big reductions in launcher development costs, we need to move away from the design-for-maximum performance/minimum weight philosophy and embrace the design-for-minimum-cost (DFMC) approach pioneered by

The Aerospace Corporation in the 1960s. The fundamental premise that the DFMC concept rests upon is that, by using a clean-sheet design approach, a space launch vehicle can be optimized for minimum cost, instead of being designed like current launch vehicles, which are optimized for maximum performance and minimum weight.[12]

Writing in a 1970 report prepared for the Air Force's Space and Missile Systems Organization in Los Angeles, Walter Tydon of The Aerospace Corporation described the DFMC, or minimum cost design (MCD) methodology:

> The MCD methodology is a process whereby costs/weights are optimized without compromising quality or reliability. Proper application of technology becomes a most important factor, as meaningful results can only be obtained when trade-offs of candidate designs, possessing low-cost characteristics, are iteratively analyzed. The MCD methodology must extend throughout the entire life cycle of the system, encompassing both the recurring and the nonrecurring costs. This necessitates an organizational approach utilizing all the skills—design, manufacturing, launch support, quality assurance, facilities, etc.—starting with the conceptual phase. The paramount impact is on the designer (heretofore minimum-weight-oriented), who must become knowledgeable of costs, down to the component level.[13]

Credit for the development of design-for-minimum-cost criteria for launch vehicles belongs to Arthur Schnitt, who began working on the concept in 1959 while working as an engineer for Space Technology Laboratories in Los Angeles.[14] Continuing his work with The Aerospace Corporation, Schnitt refined his concept in the mid-1960s and coauthored a report that detailed the DFMC criteria and proposed a candidate MCD booster.[15] This report formally established a methodology for a decision-making process that could be used when trading off cost and weight and that became the basis for a number of follow-on studies.

Speaking about DFMC, General Bleymaier said:

> There is little doubt . . . that the concept of . . . design for minimum cost . . . must be a main current of our thinking on future space boosters. . . . If a new booster is to survive the stringent cost-effectiveness evaluation that will precede its approval, it must indeed be designed from the outset for rock-bottom minimum cost.[16]

The DFMC design criteria run counter to almost everything an aerospace engineer has been traditionally taught is sacred, and it takes a big mental adjustment to operate in the MCD mode. Fortunately, through the use of computer-based cost engineering tools, engineers can more effectively accommodate this design approach today than they could in the 1960s. With these tools, the engineer and the cost estimator work together as a team to integrate system design and cost estimating, allowing detailed design/cost sensitivity analyses. Commercially available software packages such as *Javelin* are available for this purpose. *Javelin* is an intuitively structured database/spreadsheet program that will run on an IBM-compatible personal computer.[17]

The Effects of DFMC Application

The aircraft industry has always put a premium on minimizing vehicle weight. Aerospace historian Richard Smith said, "Weight is at the heart of every airplane's purpose and problems, its success, assignment of mediocrity, or condemnation to failure. . . ." Smith compared a number of aircraft based on their "load:tare" ratio in which load is the useful load, such as cargo, passengers, and/or expendable armament; and tare is the tare weight that represents the aircraft structure, engines, fuel, and crew.[18] The obvious goal for aircraft designers is to maximize the percentage of useful load relative to the gross takeoff weight of the aircraft. Normally this is accomplished by minimizing the weight of the aircraft structure, engines, and other components (the tare).

When Aerospace Corporation engineers began applying the DFMC criteria to the design of space boosters, they discovered a startling result: contrary to the minimum weight imperative of aircraft design, the weight of the launch vehicle and its propellant (the tare) was not so critical as long as the primary goal was to design the lowest-cost vehicle possible. This was due to a number of factors. First of all, rockets do not depend on aerodynamic lift for flight as aircraft do. Aircraft, because of their dependence on lift for flight, have much more sophisticated structures with complex, weight-sensitive geometries. DFMC-designed boosters would have very simple structures and engines whose costs would not increase correspondingly with weight increases. In the case of an aircraft, more weight means more of a lift requirement, which means more drag, which means more of an engine power requirement. Under these circumstances, the horsepower demands can escalate very rapidly, helping to explain the highly weight-sensitive nature of aircraft. Rocket designs can usually address additional energy requirements by adding propellant. Aircraft are essentially single-stage vehicles, and an increase in weight causes a one-to-one reduction in payload. Increases in weight to the lower stages of staged rockets do not cause this same one-to-one payload reduction.[19]

By applying the DFMC criteria to the launch vehicle design, we are seeking the simplest, least expensive booster possible that meets the system performance specifications. We are not overly concerned about the launcher's performance per kilogram of gross weight. This approach generally results in a bigger and more cost-effective booster design as opposed to a smaller, better performing, and more expensive booster with the same overall capability. General Bleymaier stated:

> If we use heavier hardware, of lower unit cost and inherently higher reliability, then greater simplicity of design becomes possible. Subsystems can then be substantially reduced. Tolerances can be increased optimally. A propulsion system can be selected which results in a lower propellant mass fraction but does not require structural complexity, high-speed machinery, a multitude of parts, supporting subsystems, and/or high launch service costs.[20]

This larger and more "beefy" design resulting from DFMC application has a number of benefits.

The MCD vehicle will have larger design margins, making for a more rugged launcher overall. From an airframe structure perspective, this means that there will be opportunities for greatly simplified manufacturing processes. For example, there will be much less pressure on the design and manufacturing engineers to "lightweight" the booster structure by machining off (or even removal by chemical processes) every possible kilogram of material. Thicker structural material of less-complex shapes will allow robust weld seams and fewer, less-complicated welds. In addition to reducing fabrication costs, this may open the door for a reduction in weld inspection requirements. Heavier, more structurally sound launcher airframes will also be less susceptible to costly launch delays due to weather constraints.

Simplicity/Robustness Instead of Redundancy

Aerospace engineers who design launch vehicles have, as a matter of course, depended on the use of redundant systems to achieve reliability goals and enhance confidence in mission success. Redundancy, however, carries a heavy price—both figuratively and literally. Adding redundancy increases the overall complexity of a launch system, increasing the cost to design, build, operate, and monitor it.

Redundancy means more subsystems, more components, and more interfaces—and this means a larger work force and increased documentation to support these items throughout all phases of the launch vehicle's life cycle. Redundant systems increase the overall weight of a booster and decrease its effective payload capacity, which translates into a degradation of the booster's payload fraction (the ratio of the gross lift-off weight of the launcher to the maximum payload it can carry to low earth orbit). Redundancy adds additional systems, which increase the number of possible failure modes. This would not be so bad if redundant systems were treated as true backups that were not required unless the primary systems failed to function. Unfortunately, redundant systems are treated as primary systems prior to launch, and numerous launches have endured costly scrubs because a redundant system failed late in the countdown, when the primary system was operating perfectly and was completely capable of supporting the launch.

Launch systems are not generally designed with their complete complement of redundant systems included from the very beginning. Many redundant systems are added incrementally as a result of "redundancy creep," increasing the development costs accordingly.

An alternative to redundancy to achieve increased reliability is to use simplicity of design, coupled with wider and more robust design margins. This is typically the kind of design solution the MCD criteria provide. This is *not* the typical design philosophy for boosters today, so a change in thinking would be necessary if this approach were to enjoy widespread application by launch vehicle engineers.

Simplicity of design would reduce the number of subsystems, components, and interfaces—and the size of the work force and the amount of documentation needed to support them. The benefits of this simplification would flow down through all aspects of the launch vehicle program. Simplification combined with large design margins would increase confidence in the system's performance, would allow increased use of "single-string" design practices and would allow a reduction in testing requirements. Simplification would reduce the number of potential failure modes, and increased design margins would decrease the probability of failure in those that remained. Selective redundancy could still be incorporated into the launcher's design, but only in limited areas and in a very judicial manner.

Vehicle Instrumentation and Range Operations Changes

Current launch systems are highly instrumented machines that provide a withering amount of prelaunch and flight data to an army of technical personnel through sophisticated telemetry receiving and computational equipment. Launch vehicles with simple designs and large design margins would allow a scaling back of vehicle instrumentation and the ground systems and support staff required to receive, store, and analyze the data coming from it. This reduced instrumentation would also provide savings during the vehicle's design and manufacture. These reductions would be enabled by design simplifications that reduce the total number of vehicle systems and subsystems the booster has and, therefore, the total number to be monitored. The larger vehicle design margins would also allow reduced instrumentation requirements by lowering the failure probability of booster systems and components, which would presumably cut back on the need to monitor them. The scaling back of vehicle instrumentation and the amount of data available for analysis would represent a major change in the way launch vehicles have been processed almost since their inception.

A network of downrange tracking and telemetry receiving stations, sometimes augmented by ship-based systems and the advanced range instrumentation aircraft (ARIA), is required to support US launches. All of these downrange systems are expensive to operate and maintain. An alternative approach would be to use the NASA Tracking and Data Relay Satellite System (TDRSS) to receive and relay telemetry data from boosters in flight and to use the Global Positioning System (GPS) in conjunction with receivers and processors on board the launch vehicles to provide accurate tracking data. These changes would eliminate the need for the terrestrial-based tracking and telemetry systems.[21] This space-based tracking and telemetry relay capability would also allow systems like the Pegasus to operate independently of existing range infrastructure, providing greatly increased flexibility in the selection and use of launch points and azimuths.

Another alternative to the current network of telemetry collection and relay systems is to employ a data recording and transmission device on the uppermost stage of the launch vehicle. The device would record all instrumentation data during the flight of the launch vehicle and then "dump" the data in its entirety to a ground station or data relay satellite. The relatively short delay in receiving the data as compared to the current real-time downlinks should not be a big problem to analysts. In case of an in-flight mishap, the recording device would operate in a mode similar to the "black box" on an aircraft and could be ejected for recovery in the same manner that film capsules were recovered from boost-

NASA's Tracking and Data Relay Satellite space vehicle.

ers during the Saturn program. The requirement for this contingency should become increasingly rare, since the increased reliability afforded by the DFMC process (combined with the system design maturity achieved by many flights) would bring about a marked reduction in launch vehicle failures.

There would clearly be some front-end development costs for either of these alternatives, but the investment should pay for itself quickly by allowing for the elimination of a significant amount of range infrastructure. Instituting changes like this will not be a trivial matter, of course, since they would represent a shift in traditional range operation methods that have been developed and that become deeply ingrained in people's thinking over a period of 45-plus years.

Current range safety practices call for destruct packages to be carried on all space boosters operating from US launch sites. To support this capability to destroy manned or unmanned launch vehicles if they deviate from their prescribed flight trajectory, each operational range must maintain significant instrumentation, computational, radar, optical, telecommunications, and personnel assets at all times. These practices were established during an era in the 1940s and 1950s when missile and space booster reliabilities were dramatically lower than they are today. Furthermore, boosters designed to MCD standards should provide large reliability improvements over even today's typical percentages. As launch vehicle reliability numbers begin to converge on those that have been posted by the commercial aviation industry, we should move away from this universally applied range destruct policy. This is especially true if we continue to conduct orbital launches only from coastal sites with trajecto-

145

ries that carry the vehicles over broad ocean areas. At some point, we must develop enough confidence in our launchers that these range safety practices become unnecessary, and we should start planning toward this today.

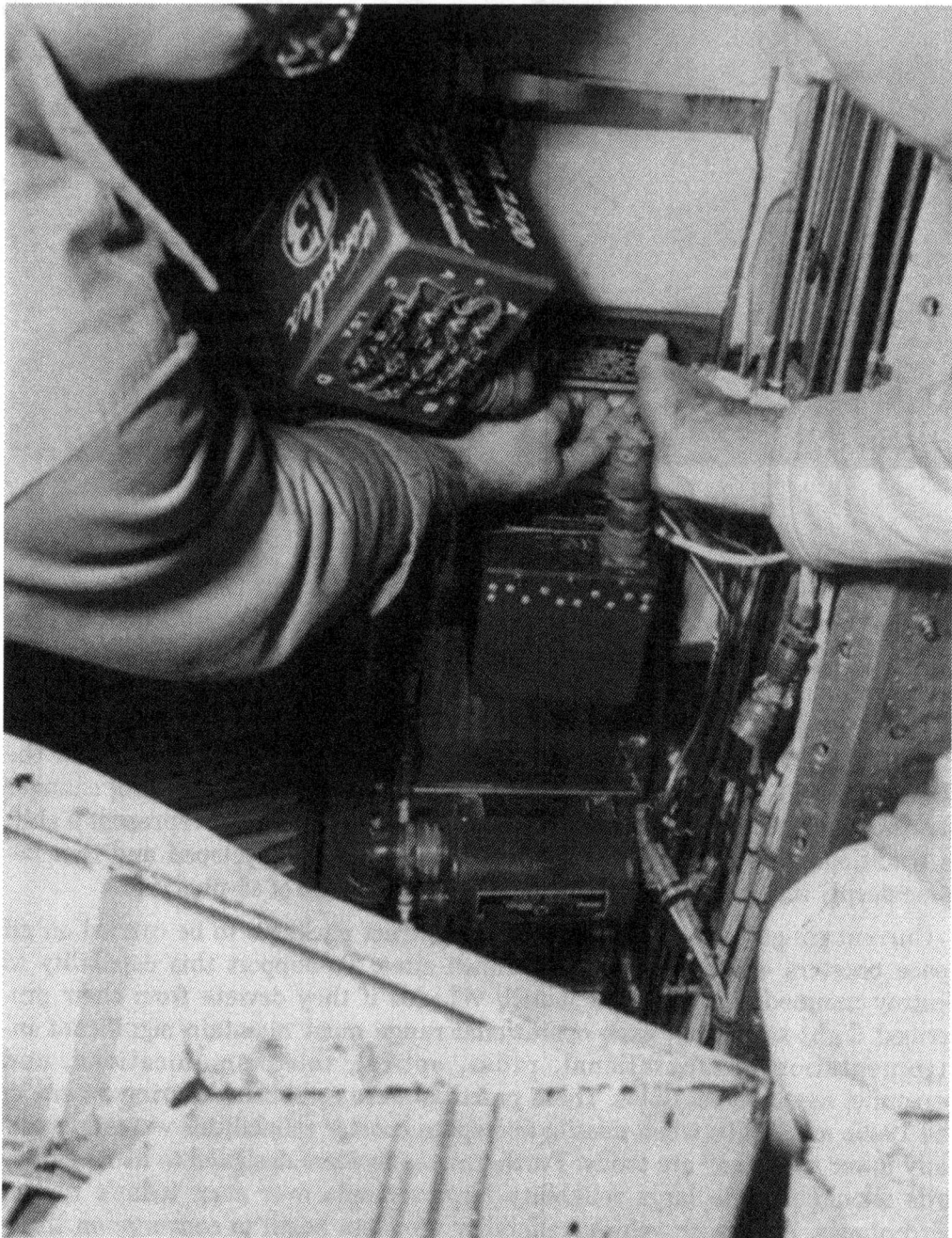

Early photograph of a launch vehicle destruct system.

Using Commercial Manufacturing Techniques

Because of the high cost of launch vehicles and their payloads, there is a resulting low demand (due to these systems' lack of affordability) that translates into very low production rates. Consequently, launch vehicles and spacecraft tend to be unique, handmade articles that are constantly modified because of the dominance of engineers in the manufacturing and test process.[22] There has been some progress recently in involving manufacturing personnel early and throughout the development of aerospace systems through the use of concurrent engineering practices. However, these efforts must be taken to the next level of application for launch vehicle development so that manufacturing interests can begin to have a dominant influence.

Boosters designed to the DFMC criteria will provide less-expensive access to space, which will fuel an increase in the payload market and, thus, demand for the launchers. The change in emphasis from engineering toward manufacturing during the development process will allow the booster design to be amenable to large production runs and greater economies of scale. Although the market demand may have to "catch up" before the benefits of these manufacturing-oriented design features come to full fruition, a lack of manufacturing foresight will eliminate the ability of a booster's production rate to expand to meet increases in market demand.

For the booster design to take full advantage of the DFMC criteria, the vehicle must be designed and manufactured to commercial standards, using commercial—and not government/aerospace industry—specifications, tolerances, and practices.[23]

A classic example of this approach is the tremendous cost and performance success TRW experienced when the company designed, built, and tested their 1,112,000-Newton (250,000 pound)-thrust liquid engine in the late 1960s. The total cost of this effort was far less than the expense of most paper studies in the aerospace business.

The common argument against the use of commercial standards for space boosters is that no self-respecting owner of the large satellites worth hundreds of millions of dollars would ever let their spacecraft ride on top of a booster built to those standards. This implies that launch vehicles built using commercial practices would not be as reliable as current boosters. But as we have discussed already, the simplicity and design margin robustness of MCD-developed boosters would more than offset any possible liability incurred by not building to aerospace standards. Despite this, it may require a number of successful flights by the MCD booster before owners of expensive payloads develop confidence in the launch system. In the meantime, the MCD boosters may be forced to fly less-expensive payloads. As we will discuss in the next chapter, however, the availability of cheap access to space provided by MCD launch vehicles may enable the development of a completely new breed of inexpensive, yet highly capable, satellite systems.

Shedding the Fear of Failure

A final area needing cultural change to achieve lower launch costs is one that cuts across virtually every part of government and the aerospace industry that is involved in space system development and operations. In the February/March 1993 issue of *Air & Space* magazine, Martin Marietta chairman and chief executive officer Norman R. Augustine said: "We should not be so preoccupied with avoiding failure that we lose interest in trying to succeed. Especially at times of challenge, we must guard against becoming more focused on what can go wrong than on what can go right—more concerned with investigation than invention."[24] NASA administrator Goldin referred to the fear of failure as "a pervasive societal malady."[25]

Fear of failure, and the consequent lack of tolerance for it, dominates the thinking of many engineers and aerospace managers to the point of having major effect on the design and operation of space systems. This attitude is due largely to the fact that the media, Congress, and the general public are not very forgiving of spectacular aerospace mistakes. This is not meant to imply that we should relax our efforts to make space systems extremely reliable, especially if they are manned. But this inordinately conservative approach to space system development and operations has caused the cost of such activities to rise so high as to budgetarily prohibit most new initiatives.

The fear of failure has not always been such an influential part of the US space program. Norm Augustine stated that by the end of 1959, two-thirds of all US attempts to orbit satellites had ended in failure. He also stated that, during the 1960s, 10 of the first 11 US missions launched to gather data for lunar landing sites were failures.[26] Yet, despite these setbacks, the US fashioned a space program that, by the end of the 1960s, was a technological marvel and the envy of the world. Today's space leaders in this country need to recapture the spirit and vision of bold adventurism and risk acceptance to open avenues for reductions in space system costs and new space program starts. This will require strong courage by space managers as well as politicians to weather the storms of inevitable failures and continue to press forward. To help ameliorate the emotional, political, and financial impact of failures, the launching of cargo and the launching of people should be forever separated as soon as possible. As the cost of space launch comes down, launches (at least those that are unmanned) will become more routine and more plentiful. This frequent and common unmanned launch activity will allow any occasional accident that does occur to be treated with no more significance than any other accident that does not involve a loss of life or injury to people, or damage to the environment.

Summary

Sikandar Zaman of the Pakistan Space and Upper Atmosphere Research Commission, in a paper delivered in 1989 at the Symposium on Space Commercialization in Nashville, Tennessee, captured the essence of the type of launch vehicle that would result from application of the DFMC criteria:

> Instead of designing for minimum rocket weight, the launch vehicle should be designed for minimum cost. The innovative design should not be based on exotic materials, such as titanium alloys, where mild steel would do. The rockets do not have to be small and lightweight; they do not have to be fast or on the leading edge of technology. They can be clumsy, heavy, and slow but safe, as long as they are cheap. High performance and "handmade" high cost are not necessary. Humble rockets might do the job as well at a much lower cost. The true criterion and benchmark for optimality [of a] satellite launch vehicle should be the unit production cost rather than gross lift-off weight: reduced efficiency in exchange for greater ease of design integration and lower operational cost.[27]

This statement highlights the radically different ways of thinking that will be required to achieve major space launch cost reductions.

Speaking about the development of a new, cost-effective launch system, Malcolm Wolfe of The Aerospace Corporation stated: "The time is ripe to take space transportation out of the performance-oriented, specialized-launch, labor-intensive operations of today and into the low-cost, highly-operable, routine operations of tomorrow."[28] To achieve this goal, it will be necessary to bring about major cultural changes within the aerospace community relative to space launch systems. Some of these changes may be difficult to establish because of certain methods and attitudes that have become institutionalized over the years, but with proper leadership they can become the way to break down the barriers that have prevented inexpensive space access.

Notes

1. Richard DeMeis, "Sweetening the Orbital Bottom Line," *Aerospace America*, August 1988, 27, 28.
2. Roger A. Chamberlain, "ALS: A Unique Design Approach" (Paper presented at the AIAA Space Programs and Technologies Conference '90, Huntsville, Ala., 25–27 September 1990), 1.
3. "Saturn V's Successor," *Popular Mechanics*, January 1990, 29.
4. Elaine J. Camhi, "Space-Launch Alphabet Soup," *Aerospace America*, March 1993, 5.
5. Edward A. Gabris, Ronald J. Harris, and Stephen A. Rast, "Progress on the National Launch System Demonstrates National Commitment" (Presented at the World Space Congress, Washington, D.C., 31 August 1992), 3.
6. Ibid.
7. "Launch Proposal Gets Cool Reception," *Military Space*, 22 February 1993, 4.
8. McDonnell Douglas news release, Huntington Beach, Calif., 16 August 1991.
9. Simon P. Worden, "DC-X: Trouble for the Status Quo," *Space News*, 7–13 June 1993, 19.
10. Otis Port, John Carey, and Seth Payne, "Is Buck Rogers' Ship Coming In?" *Business Week*, 21 June 1993, 120.
11. Maj Gen Joseph S. Bleymaier, "Future Space Booster Requirements," *Air University Review*, January–February 1969, 44.
12. R. M. Allman, "Minimum-Cost-Design Space Launch Vehicle," briefing to The Aerospace Corporation Board of Trustees ad hoc committee on space systems cost, El Segundo, Calif., 25 September 1987.
13. Walter Tydon, "Minimum Cost Design Launch Vehicle Design/Costing Study," Aerospace Report TOR-0059(6526-01)-2, vol. 1 (The Aerospace Corporation, El Segundo, Calif., 31 July 1970), 3.
14. Arthur Schnitt to Daniel S. Goldin, NASA Administrator, letter, 18 May 1992.

15. A. Schnitt and Col F. W. Kniss, "Proposed Minimum Cost Space Launch Vehicle System," Aerospace Report TOR-0158(3415-15)-1 (The Aerospace Corporation, El Segundo, Calif., 1 July 1968).

16. Bleymaier, 45.

17. John R. London III, Jack R. Weissman, and R. Curtis McNeil, "Brilliant Eyes—Developing Small Space Systems in a New Environment" (Presented at the World Space Congress, Washington, D.C., 4 September 1992), 4.

18. Richard K. Smith, "The Weight Envelope: An Airplane's Fourth Dimension . . . Aviation's Bottom Line," *Aerospace Historian,* Spring/March 1986, 31–32.

19. Gerard Elverum, telephone conversation with author, 5 July 1993.

20. Bleymaier.

21. ESMC 2005, *Functional Area Requirements and Technology Data,* Eastern Space and Missile Center/XR, Patrick Air Force Base, Fla., 24 July 1990, 3-36, 3-41.

22. Edward L. Keith, "Research and Findings in Lower Cost Space Transportation," briefing charts, Microcosm, Inc., Torrance, Calif., June 1992, 8.

23. Edward L. Keith, "Ultra Low Cost High Reliability Space Cargo Vehicle" (Presentation to NASA Headquarters by Microcosm, Inc., 1 September 1992), 24.

24. Norman R. Augustine, "The Cost of Success," *Air & Space,* February/March 1993, 68.

25. Beth Dickey, "A Golden Opportunity," *Air & Space,* February/March 1993, 18.

26. Augustine.

27. Sikandar Zaman, "Low-Cost Satellites and Satellite Launch Vehicles" (Paper presented at the Symposium on Space Commercialization: Roles of Developing Countries, Nashville, Tenn., 5–10 March 1989), 8.

28. Malcolm G. Wolfe, "Joint DoD/NASA Advanced Launch System: Pathway to Low-Cost, Highly-Operable Space Transportation," paper no. A91-38939, The American Institute of Aeronautics and Astronautics, 215.

Chapter 8

Booster/Spacecraft Cost Relationships

Spacecraft designers and operators have always known that the satellite was the launch vehicle's raison d'être. Even though the booster's ultimate purpose is to provide a service to the satellite customer, efforts to lower the cost of space systems and operations need to begin with the launch vehicle and not the spacecraft. Some aerospace managers believe that the high cost of space activities is primarily attributable to the expense of developing and operating satellites and other space-faring craft, and that high launch costs make only a minor contribution to the overall space budget. Nevertheless, there is strong design and operational linkage between the launch vehicle and the cargo it is carrying. This chapter will examine how this linkage affects the cost of both booster and satellite. Specifically, we will discuss the potential effects that the availability of a large, low-cost launch vehicle (at least an order of magnitude decrease in cost, compared to current large US boosters) could have on the design, operation, and overall cost of future orbital space vehicles.

In recent years, a number of aerospace companies have succeeded in developing highly capable, low-cost, small satellites. They used simple design and manufacturing techniques, and they took advantage of the increasingly compact electronics and computer systems that are now available. Despite the development of these low-cost spacecraft, however, the cost to launch them has not decreased in a corresponding fashion. In fact, the cost of small launch vehicles that are optimized for the small satellite mission, based on a dollars-per-kilogram comparison, has been approximately twice as much as the cost of large boosters. This is partly due to the economies of size that larger boosters enjoy. Nevertheless, the availability of low-cost small satellites has not been a driving force in reducing launch costs, and it is highly questionable whether the availability of large low-cost spacecraft would motivate important launch cost reductions. On the other hand, the availability of a large low-cost launch vehicle could enable and motivate the development of significantly lower-cost space vehicles.

The Russian space program has had a history of much higher launch rates than the US. Space officials in the United States, when confronted with such statistics, have traditionally rationalized the launch rate disparity by citing the fact that US spacecraft are much more sophisticated, capable, and long-lived than their Russian counterparts. As details of the many low-cost Russian boosters and their inexpensive spacecraft continue to emerge, and as the US continues to pay stratospheric prices for satellites and their launch services, the validity of these traditional rationalizations has become suspect. Low-cost boosters and their attendant lower-cost payloads would allow a new mind-set, akin to the Russian approach, that could enable a wave of increased US space activity.

Lowering Spacecraft Cost through Weight/Volume Growth

A 1988 Hughes Aircraft study on design considerations for future space vehicles intended for the Advanced Launch System described the impact of existing launch systems on satellite costs:

> Payload costs have been driven to a large extent by the limited lift capability and restricted payload volume available on current boosters. These constraints have forced payload designers into sophisticated designs which use expensive, light-weight materials, high packaging density and complex configurations involving numerous deployable appendages. The resulting designs are costly to build and involve significant amounts of analysis and testing to validate their design.[1]

Eric Hoffman of the Johns Hopkins Applied Physics Laboratory said that high launch costs are responsible for about one-half the total cost of new satellite systems. According to Hoffman, "Today's high launcher costs dictate longer satellite life, higher reliability, redundant subsystems, more and stricter test programs, lengthy schedules, and so on up the cost spiral."[2]

Edward Keith described the reason that spacecraft structure and subsystems must weigh so little: "Space-grade hardware is very light weight. With the price for space transportation to low earth orbit starting at about $5,000 per pound, space hardware has to be very light weight. Aerospace products are also very fragile. That is the price for making them as light weight as possible."[3]

Mike Griffin, NASA's chief engineer, said that the time span from the time a company submits a formal proposal for a typical complex new space system until the system achieves an initial operational capability is about 16.5 years.[4] This excruciatingly long development period is usually a result of satellite system complexity and the ponderous nature of the government acquisition system. The satellite complexity, in turn, is at least partially caused by high launch prices. The ultimate results of this lengthy system gestation period are lost operational availability, major costs to maintain the program for an extended period, and large personnel expenses that are required to keep the development work force in place for over a decade and a half. Clearly, the US needs a solution to the high cost and lengthy development of satellite systems; sharply reduced launch costs may be the key to finding an answer.

The Lessons of Russian Spacecraft Design

Reports out of Russia indicate that the Russian space industry giant NPO Energia plans to build a new class of communications satellite for launch on the Energia booster. The satellite, called Globis, is projected to weigh around 19,000 kilograms (41,890 pounds) and to operate in geostationary (or Clarke) orbit. A satellite of this size would be about 10 times heavier than typical existing communications satellites. Jeff Manber, vice president for marketing at Energia U.S.A., said the Energia launch vehicle's lift capability allows the Globis designers to abandon traditional spacecraft design practices, which have always put a premium on costly miniaturization. Manber stated that "[the Russian satellite designers] believe that if size were not an issue, the cost of the satellite could go down dramatically."[5] This lack of concern about the satellite's weight is a luxury afforded by the power and low cost of the Energia booster.

This design philosophy is not a new innovation for the Russians—it is reflected in many of their launch systems and space vehicles. The Phobos interplanetary spacecraft represented a Soviet-sponsored effort that involved a number of Western countries as well. The Soviet Union built the spacecraft bus (the portion of the space vehicle that includes the structure and nonmission unique subsystems) and some of the payload instrumentation. Additional payload instrumentation was provided by other countries. Jochen Kissel of (the former) West Germany, a member of the Phobos program's scientific council, said of the Soviet design approach, "We could use standard printed circuit boards rather than ultraminiaturized parts. . . . It made everything cheaper and simpler."[6] Although the Phobos program ultimately ended in failure due to human operator error and lost communications, this example still illustrates the value of generous weight and volume margins.[7]

Benefits of Spacecraft Weight Growth

In 1990 the Office of Technology Assessment (OTA) issued a background paper on design and launch alternatives for affordable spacecraft. The paper stated:

> If payloads were allowed to be much heavier, a manufacturer could forego expensive processes for removing nonessential structural materials, as well as expensive analyses and tests for assuring the adequacy of the remaining structure. Standardized subsystems, which could be produced economically in quantity, could be used instead of customized subsystems designed to weigh less.[8]

Michael Callaham was the principal analyst for the OTA study on affordable spacecraft. In a technical paper presented in 1990 he wrote:

> Many experts find it plausible that a payload could be designed to perform a function at lower cost if it were allowed to be heavier. Several ways of exploiting an increased weight allowance to reduce cost have been proposed . . . standard (or previously developed) subsystems could be used to avoid the costs of developing customized lighter ones . . . designers could allow greater strength margins [to avoid costly testing].[9]

Gerard Elverum of TRW stated:

> It would appear that very significant cost reductions should be possible by making the spacecraft and instrument payloads larger and heavier in order to make use of

low cost fabrication methods, eliminate expensive weight reduction exercises, and minimize expensive man-hours in both development and production.[10]

Sikandar Zaman gave some important steps designers should take to reduce the cost of spacecraft:

> Borrowing reliable commercial systems and technologies for use in space systems; keeping the design as simple as possible, based on off-the-shelf, mass-produced, and commercially available components and subsystems; and designing for minimum cost rather than minimum weight. . . . Staying close to the known designs and using well-known and less exotic materials can go a long way to reducing the ultimate cost of the spacecraft.[11]

As we will see later in this chapter, the implementation of the OTA's, Callaham's, Elverum's, and Zaman's cost-cutting ideas for spacecraft must be coincident with the availability of very inexpensive access to space, which does not currently exist. According to Elverum, "Obviously a family of launch vehicles having large payload capacity at much lower launch costs would provide high leverage on reducing total costs. Not only would the launch vehicle cost be reduced, but it would permit spacecraft weights to more closely approach their cost-optimized values."[12]

Studies on Spacecraft Weight/Volume Growth Benefits

The aerospace community has made several attempts to examine, at a top level, the potential cost reduction benefit of allowing spacecraft to be heavier by providing generous design margins, using existing subsystems, and employing less-exotic structural materials. In 1968 Arthur Schnitt of The Aerospace Corporation and Gene Noneman of TRW engaged in a short design-for-minimum-cost study for spacecraft. Using the existing VELA spacecraft as a baseline, Noneman changed the satellite's design to fit a spectrum of launch costs. The study indicated that, as launch costs go down, the optimum sophistication and cost of the spacecraft will decrease as well.[13] Schnitt discovered that a large percentage of a spacecraft's gross weight is structure, which, along with the power subsystem, is amenable to a cost-weight trade-off. He worked with TRW in developing six separate designs of an existing spacecraft, steadily increasing weight and decreasing cost with each design iteration. The results indicated that major cost reductions were possible by allowing increases in vehicle weight.[14]

Studies examining the potential benefits of weight increases on satellite costs have been conducted by the RAND Corporation (1969), Lockheed (1971), Boeing (1988), and Hughes Aircraft Company (1988). Each study concluded that some amount of spacecraft cost reduction would occur if the vehicle weight increased. The amount of cost savings projected by the different studies varied; for example, the Boeing report estimated the cost of spacecraft could be cut in half if weight was allowed to grow by 30 percent. However, these figures may have been impacted by some atypical design assumptions for Boeing's hypothetical spacecraft, such as designing the power system to consist of solar cells only (with no batteries).[15]

Despite all of these efforts, no one has accomplished a thorough and exhaustive study of this concept. Michael Callaham writes: "There have been few attempts to estimate how much cheaper spacecraft could be, if allowed to be heavier, or to estimate the optimal weight—the weight at which the total cost of producing and launching a spacecraft would be minimal."[16] The OTA background paper on affordable spacecraft stated that "the United States has never designed and built two payloads, one heavy and the other light, that perform the same functions equally well, in order to compare actual costs."[17]

Simply allowing a spacecraft design to increase in weight does not guarantee cost reductions. Normally, when a spacecraft design gets heavier, the opposite is true. This is because the weight gain is a result of added capability and/or performance. The OTA background paper cited the Milstar satellite as being the antithesis of the "grow bigger and cheaper" design philosophy. Milstar is a huge space vehicle, but its size is necessary to contain all of the satellite's advanced communications and other supporting subsystems.[18] To achieve cost reductions through heavier satellite designs, the weight increases must be a result of design simplification, increased design margins, and application of previously developed subsystems that are suboptimized for weight and volume.

Opportunities for Increased Reliability

One of the main reasons for the high cost of today's satellites is the burdensome demand for extreme reliability. Dr Mark Chartrand succinctly stated the rationale behind this kind of reliability requirement: "With a very few exceptions, no one makes housecalls to repair satellites, so they must be designed with reliability in mind."[19] (Of course, if a means were developed for placing astronauts in orbit that was much less costly than the Shuttle, "housecalls" could become more practical.) Traditional methods to achieve high levels of system, subsystem, and component reliability fall into three general categories: fault avoidance, fault tolerance, and functional redundancy.[20]

Fault avoidance makes spacecraft reliable by providing generous design margins for structure and for mechanical, thermal, and electrical subsystems. Unfortunately, providing these kinds of margins is in direct opposition to achieving the lowest possible weights, which has also been a traditional spacecraft design demand. Designers avoid failures by specifying very high quality parts that are 100 percent acceptance tested and by using careful record-keeping techniques for these parts (thus providing lot control and detailed compliance documentation). The very costly Class S parts are manufactured under carefully controlled, thoroughly inspected and tested processes.[21]

Engineers use the second method, fault tolerance, to achieve reliability by designing the spacecraft, utilizing redundant subsystems and components, to continue operating even after certain failures have occurred. The third method used to achieve high reliability, functional redundancy, is accomplished through the use of dissimilar systems and techniques to accomplish the spacecraft's mission when primary systems have failed.[22]

The redundancy requirements for spacecraft are much different from the redundancy needs of launch vehicles. This is not only because of the radically different functions of the two systems, but also and especially because the operating lifetime of an expendable booster is measured in minutes, whereas the on-orbit design life of a spacecraft is measured in years. The more pressing need for redundancy on spacecraft comes with a significant design penalty. Herbert Hecht said in *Space Mission Analysis and Design,* "The [redundant] components add to the cost, weight, volume, and frequently to the power and thermal control requirements of the spacecraft."[23] The impacts to the power and thermal control systems serve to magnify the effects of cost, weight, and volume growth.

By providing a significant increase in lift capacity through the use of large, low-cost boosters, new opportunities for additional redundancy would be created. Adding redundancy for certain critical operations might help to reduce the requirements for the large amounts of exhaustive testing currently required to assure mission success of satellite systems, although the requirement to test all combinations and permutations of the additional redundant modes could also actually increase net testing demands.[24] Also, the benefits of adding such redundancy must be carefully weighed against the liabilities of increased complexity that such redundant subsystems and components (and their attendant added weight, volume, and cost) would bring to the overall spacecraft design.

Opportunities for Increased Design Weight Margins

Spacecraft designers have traditionally incorporated a certain amount of weight "margin" into initial spacecraft weight estimates. Designers do this to avoid a situation late in the development phase in which the actual spacecraft weight has grown so far beyond the original estimates that it can no longer be carried by its designated launch vehicle. The impact of such an occurrence can be severe. When this happens, engineers must either redesign the spacecraft to weigh less (a very costly procedure, especially late in development) or reconfigure the spacecraft to fly on a larger and more expensive booster (usually even more costly than redesigning for weight reduction).[25] Gerard Elverum said, about the cost of redesigning spacecraft to reduce weight, "We have at TRW, since our business is building payloads [and] not launch vehicles, spent numbers like [$185,000] a pound trying to get the last few pounds out of a spacecraft."[26]

Design engineers initially include a contingency amount of weight margin that represents the amount the designers expect in weight growth because the early design estimates are immature.[27] Initial weight estimates are almost always lower than what the spacecraft's actual weight ends up being. TRW, with many years of spacecraft development experience, typically includes a contingency weight budget that adds 15 percent to the initial weight estimate. As the design matures and the spacecraft weight increases as expected, the contingency percentage is refined downward.[28]

Ground processing of TRW's DSCS II spacecraft.

TRW may also allow an additional 15 percent weight margin, over and above the allocated contingency margin, to cover unexpected weight growth.[29] These unexpected increases can be caused by a number of reasons, such as customer requests for added capability and/or increased performance, technology development difficulties, and changes to accommodate new flight safety requirements. New, very high technology payloads can consume weight margins with extraordinary rapidity, causing redesigns and schedule slippages that are measured in many months or even years. This can cause a redesign spiral, as changes force additional redesigns. Schedule delays of six to eight months, causing a cost growth of 10 to 25 percent, are not at all unusual.[30]

If satellite designers had a booster available to them that had twice the lift capacity (and volume) they initially required, and that cost 90 percent less than current boosters of the class their spacecraft would typically require, they could enjoy the luxury of very generous weight and volume margins. Under these circumstances, the designer would be able to "spend weight to save money and/or reduce risk," as opposed to the costly exercise of fighting to keep spacecraft weights within limits, which is commonplace today.[31]

Another TRW military spacecraft—the Defense Support Program vehicle during processing at the Cape.

Booster/Spacecraft Interface Standardization

Spacecraft designs have traditionally placed great demands on the launch vehicle for various services, both prior to the flight and during ascent to orbit, as well as forcing many electrical, mechanical, fluid, and structural accommodations from the booster. Mike Holguin and Mike Labbee of General Dynamics said, "Since the number of payloads is so large and their launch support requirements so diverse, interfaces between the launch vehicle and the payload(s) can become major cost drivers."[32] The 1986 Space Transportation Architecture Study, conducted by the Air Force and NASA, identified widely varying spacecraft-to-booster interface requirements as a significant contributor to high launch costs.[33]

Holguin and Labbee cited the Atlas Centaur as an example of the kind of impact that numerous spacecraft interface requirements have had on launch vehicles:

> Today's Atlas/Centaur has grown tremendously, sprouting a variety of interfaces for power, electrical, command and control, bolt circle patterns and adapters, and environmental and GSE [ground support equipment] controls. Provisions for each of the interfaces have driven the cost and complexity of payload interface support up an order of magnitude from the initial [launch vehicle] programs. Support operations, engineering analysis, and mission-peculiar redesign for the interfaces and associated launch vehicle systems must be accomplished before the payload can be successfully integrated with the vehicle. The schedule for integration of a payload begins at 36 months prior to an Atlas/Centaur launch. The one-of-a-kind launch vehicle designs for every different payload complicates the integration process, and varying customer demands on each of the payload interfaces can delay programs beyond even the lengthy "nominal" integration schedule.[34]

In the commercial transportation world, transportation vehicles (trucks, ships, and airplanes) normally do not make special provisions for the cargo they are carrying; the cargo is usually expected to conform to the accommodations provided by a given transportation vehicle. It would be highly impractical to expect an aircraft, for example, to make structural and electrical modifications prior to each flight for the sake of the different types of cargo assigned to the aircraft. Extrapolating this commercial transportation philosophy to space launch would require future payloads to be much more autonomous and self-contained. When program personnel were drawing up the original specifications for the Advanced Launch System (ALS), this is exactly what they had in mind.

The mechanical interface on the ALS was planned to provide for all payloads; it was a simple mounting plate with a standard bolt-hole pattern. The payloads were to provide payload adapters, separation systems, and all attachment hardware. The ALS would not have provided any power to the attached payload, either from the ground or from the booster's internal power systems. The only electrical interface planned was a connection for discrete timer signals that would be sent from the booster to the space vehicle. All other command and data interfaces to the payload were to be via radio-frequency transmission through the payload fairing. The ALS plan did provide

FLTSATCOM spacecraft being enclosed in an Atlas Centaur payload fairing.

air conditioning to the payload shroud, thus relieving individual payloads from having to carry their own environmental conditioning systems. Although this required the launch system to provide ground air-conditioning to the fairing and a quick-disconnect mechanism for launch, ALS planners deemed

160

this a good trade since most payloads would require some kind of conditioned air while sitting inside the fairing.[35]

The interface philosophy espoused by the ALS program, if adopted by a future low-cost booster system, would provide many benefits. Such an approach would give the new low-cost launch system a much higher degree of payload manifest flexibility than current boosters can provide. The booster could accommodate changes in the sequence and schedule of planned payload launches with much less impact to the overall launch schedule or booster availability. A standardized booster interface would allow much shorter and less costly payload integration, resulting in a potential for increased launch rates. Interface standardization would also allow launch vehicle engineers to avoid the costly booster redesigns, analyses, testing, and operational constraints that are associated with adapting for unique spacecraft interface requirements.[36]

Enacting this new payload/booster interface philosophy would place an added burden on the satellite community and result in added development expenses and larger space vehicles. However, all of the many different satellite designs are seeking the cheapest launch possible, and standardizing the booster would reduce launch costs. The additional spacecraft costs resulting from this standardization should be more than offset by the reduced launch vehicle procurement and integration costs.

Making the satellite responsible for services that had previously been provided by the launch system will force the satellite designer to carefully reevaluate whether all of these services are truly essential, and will allow opportunities for consideration of simpler alternatives. Additionally, by having a large and inexpensive booster with lots of weight and volume margin available for satellite engineers to design to, they can more easily and cheaply provide for the added space vehicle requirements caused by the interface standardization. Holguin and Labbee said:

> The launch vehicle can no longer serve as a luxury liner that accommodates every payload desire free of charge. When services required are not available from the launch vehicle, the payload should look first to its own design for fulfillment of the additional service requirement. . . . Caught early enough in the spacecraft design, cost to the overall space program is minimized.[37]

Bus Standardization and Off-the-Shelf Subsystems

There have been a number of initiatives in recent years within government and industry to develop standardized space vehicle "buses" to reduce the cost of satellites. (The bus is the portion of the satellite that contains the structure and systems that are generally common to all space vehicles; different satellites have unique mission payloads that mount to their respective satellite buses.) The Defense Advanced Research Projects Agency (DARPA, now the Advanced Research Projects Agency) has been a leader in developing standard bus initiatives.

The use of standard buses will almost certainly result in less than optimum solutions, in terms of weight and volume, when compared to spacecraft that are custom-designed from start to finish. However, as in the case of using off-the-shelf subsystems and components, the nonrecurring and recurring cost savings should easily outweigh the liabilities.[38] An inexpensive launch capability would make excess weight and volume margin affordable to the satellite designer; coupling this margin with the use of standard bus designs could significantly drive down spacecraft costs.

It is noteworthy that spacecraft, like launch vehicles, have generally been optimized for maximum performance and minimum weight. Although the weight and size of spacecraft can be increased (suboptimized) to reduce cost, maintaining spacecraft performance is sometimes nonnegotiable. This is particularly true of a space vehicle's unique mission payload. Therefore, designers who increase the weight and size of a mission payload package to cut costs must be careful not to also cut mission payload performance. Since bus/payload growth will likely make it easier to maintain specified payload performance levels, designers of cost-optimized satellites should have a simpler job with both the bus and mission payload than designers of minimum weight- and volume-optimized spacecraft.

Employing standard spacecraft bus designs is a variation on the concept of using standard, off-the-shelf hardware as a means to reduce spacecraft costs. Michael Callaham said of these two approaches:

> Using a standard (or previously developed) bus could reduce the cost of a spacecraft bus by about two-thirds, compared to using a customized bus. Alternatively, building a custom bus from standard subsystems might save 82 percent to 86 percent on structure and 78% to 95% on thermal control, with lower but significant savings expected on other subsystems.[39] Boeing estimated the cost of integrating off-the-shelf subsystems into a spacecraft is about three percent of the cost of designing a new subsystem.[40]

Specific Benefits of Large, Inexpensive Boosters

Due to the size and cost of the ALS booster, the Hughes ALS design guide cited a number of changes that would result in large spacecraft cost savings. According to the guide, "The real cost benefit to the payload . . . results from the judicious use of the large weight and expansive payload volume provided by the ALS."[41] Since program managers had originally targeted the ALS to reduce launch costs by an order of magnitude, the changes described in the Hughes guide would be equally applicable to payloads intended for flight on a new, low-cost, heavy booster. These types of changes would also be applicable to small satellites, although the smallsat community had previously adopted many of the ideas cited in the Hughes guide to keep satellite costs commensurate with their size.[42] What has limited the small satellite industry from exploding is the cost of small launchers, which on a dollars-per-kilogram basis is the highest in the industry.[43] Therefore, despite low-cost development tech-

162

niques, small satellites need inexpensive access to space as much as the rest of the payload community.

To clearly illustrate the cost savings that an inexpensive, large-capacity launch capability can provide to satellite designers and operators, we will consider the potential savings associated with the major subsystems common to most spacecraft: structure, propulsion, power, electronics, communications, and thermal control. We will also look at reductions in the cost of spacecraft launch and mission operations. Savings are tied to design techniques that generally increase spacecraft weight and volume. However, a simple and inexpensive booster, combined with greatly reduced spacecraft development costs, can easily overwhelm these increases and bring about a large net savings.

Benefits to Spacecraft Structural Designs

The structural materials commonly used today to minimize spacecraft weight are beryllium and high-modulus graphite, both of which have high stiffness-to-density ratios. These high-cost materials require complex structural designs, analysis, manufacturing processes, and testing. Weight minimization usually results in parts being machined from solid billets with computer-driven, numerically-controlled equipment. The joining of structural members is a very labor-intensive process. It usually requires bonding techniques or match-drilled, tight-tolerance, grip-length-type titanium fasteners.[44] Not only are these lightweight joining methods expensive but they also impose a higher failure risk than fastener methods that are not constrained by weight minimization considerations.[45]

With the introduction of low-cost space access, weldable aluminum could become the primary structural material for satellites. In fact, aluminum is the structural material used in most of the inexpensive small satellites being fabricated today. Aluminum provides a heavier structure with greater strength and more safety factors than beryllium or graphite-based structures.[46] Manufacturing processes could look to standard extrusions, welding, simple machining, and less-expensive sheet-metal fabrication. Structural components could be joined by using weld-on flanges and low-tolerance, oversized, fully-threaded bolts.[47]

Typically, space vehicle structures are subjected to very expensive and highly detailed analysis because they are designed with very narrow safety margins (as low as 1.4) to minimize weight. The detailed stress analysis often involves large finite element models for each of the hundreds of structural parts to make sure that each part is the lightest weight possible and will still not fail. New spacecraft designs require up to five coupled loads analysis cycles to derive the loads. Structural qualification is normally established by static, acoustic, and modal testing. Even spacecraft that are built to an existing design require flight acceptance testing, which involves acoustic testing and the proof testing of bonded components and beryllium structures.[48]

Designers could use high safety factors (2.0 or more), to drastically reduce, and in many cases eliminate, the requirements for analysis and testing. Much

163

of the structural qualification testing could be waived, avoiding the cost of these tests and their dedicated equipment. Engineers could delete modal testing and proof testing requirements.[49]

Today's spacecraft mechanisms are numerous, complex, subject to high failure rates, needful of extensive testing, and very expensive. The size of the payload fairings on today's boosters, along with the boosters' limited and costly lift capacity, imposes severe volume and weight constraints on spacecraft mechanical systems. These constraints force engineers to design spacecraft appendages to be deployable, thus requiring multiple mechanical joints and hinges with an accompanying reduction in structural stiffness.[50] As communication and power demands for space vehicles have steadily increased, engineers have specified more numerous and complicated deployment mechanisms to handle the increased quantities and sizes of antennas and solar arrays.[51] Lightweight deployment systems inject higher risk into the design because they use methods such as springs instead of more reliable (and heavier) techniques like actuators or cables.[52] Designers must optimize all of these mechanisms for minimum weight, which results in intricate lightweight hardware.

The FLTSATCOM spacecraft, with its deployable solar array panels and communications booms folded in a stowed position for launch.

Most spacecraft mechanisms are designed to function in the micro-gravity environment of earth orbit (and not in an aerospace factory's one-G conditions), so their structural weight and strength are limited. Since they cannot function in the earth's one-G environment, complicated and costly test setups are required to validate mechanism performance during manufacturing and testing. For example, demonstrating the deployment mechanism for a large solar array during ground tests requires a host of test equipment to negate, as much as possible, the effects of gravity.[53]

Payload fairing volume constraints engender spacecraft designs that tend to have sensor and/or antenna fields of view that congregate and overlap, creating interference with each other. This problem generates additional deployable mechanism requirements and imposes the need for extensive field-of-view analyses.[54]

A large, inexpensive launch vehicle would allow engineers to design more structurally robust mechanisms for spacecraft. Larger fairing volumes would open the door for space vehicles to have at dispersed locations fixed antennas as well as fixed solar arrays and other appendages that would have previously required multiple joints and complicated deployment schemes. The overall number of mechanism joints could be radically reduced. Fixed appendages on spacecraft would be better suited to withstand launch loads, would eliminate costly in-flight deployment failures, and would reduce the probability of thermal and vibration problems during ascent and orbital flight. All communications and power systems could be available during orbital transfer burns. By having fewer deployable elements, designers could simplify structures and eliminate load-path restrictions. Mechanisms would have higher factors of safety and would be designed for higher loads, which would simplify analysis and test requirements. Additionally, mechanism performance validation in one-G conditions would be greatly expedited, since structural components will not require gravity off-loading.[55]

Benefits to Spacecraft Propulsion System Design

Spacecraft propulsion systems are required for orbital changes and on-orbit maneuvers such as station-keeping. Orbital changes, particularly changes from low earth orbit to much higher orbits, normally require an upper stage. Upper stages typically use either solid propellant, hypergolic bipropellants, or LOX/hydrogen for propulsive power. Approximately 70 to 75 percent of the total weight of the upper stage and spacecraft combination placed in low earth orbit consists of upper stage propellant, and every kilogram of upper stage propellant that the booster must lift is one less kilogram available as usable payload. Thus, space planners have been investigating other means to accomplish orbital changes—means that would provide for a significant decrease in the upper stage propellant fraction relative to the satellite. Such a reduction would allow a corresponding increase in the weight of the spacecraft.[56]

A leading candidate for an alternative upper stage technology is electric propulsion, which is characterized by very high specific impulse but low thrust levels. The result is long transit times for orbital change maneuvers—which may be tolerable, considering the benefits electric propulsion could afford. An electric upper stage could allow space vehicles to be moved from large boosters to smaller ones.[57] The fielding of an electric propulsion upper stage, however, would require a potentially costly and risky development program.

With low-cost boosters available, the weight margin to low earth orbit would be much larger and no longer a limiting factor. Therefore, the upper stage propellant mass fraction of the upper stage/satellite combination could be 75 percent or even higher and still be acceptable. More important, the gross weight of upper stages could be allowed to increase. Engineers could call for inexpensive aluminum tanks and simple pressure-fed propulsion systems with less-than-optimum efficiencies. They could avoid the complexities and attendant high cost of LOX/hydrogen systems; and hypergolic bipropellants, or even LOX/hydrocarbon combinations, could be competitive propellant choices.[58]

Spacecraft maneuvers are normally accomplished through use of a small propulsion system that is part of the overall satellite vehicle. Although satellites have traditionally used storable (hydrazine) monopropellant systems, volume and weight constraints imposed by current launch vehicles are pushing designers more and more to systems that use either storable bipropellants (like nitrogen tetroxide and monomethylhydrazine) or monopropellants with electrically augmented thrusters. These systems have a notably higher specific impulse than simple monopropellant systems, but they are also more complicated and costly.[59]

Spacecraft propulsion systems generally use titanium propellant tanks in an effort to minimize weight. These tanks have design safety factors as low as 1.5 to 1, resulting in very thin walls that require difficult machining processes and, in some cases, chemical milling. If a spacecraft is body-stabilized, as opposed to using methods such as spin stabilization, then the tanks must have propellant management devices to positively feed propellant to the thrusters in micro gravity conditions. Monopropellant systems use elastomeric bladders for this purpose; bipropellant systems require more complicated and costly surface tension devices.[60]

Inexpensive launchers would provide sufficient weight margins to make less-efficient monopropellant propulsion an appropriate design choice. Tanks could be constructed of aluminum instead of titanium, and they could be designed for safety factors of 2 to 1 or greater. This would provide for increased reliability as well as savings in materials and manufacturing expenses that would result in tanks costing 50 percent less than current titanium versions. For spacecraft that use body stabilized designs, simple and flight-proven elastomeric bladders would suffice. Thermal control of propellant would be much simpler for the monopropellant propulsion system than for one using bipropellants. Specifying a monopropellant system and incorporating simplification steps like those described here would result in a heavier, less-efficient propulsion system that would be equal in net capability to a weight-optimized bipropellant system—at one-third the cost.[61]

Benefits to Spacecraft Power System Design

Spacecraft power system weight is typically dominated by the system's batteries and solar arrays. These power system components can have major design and operational impacts on satellites.[62]

Current satellite designs are pushing for greater power-to-weight ratios in batteries. This has led to the development of nickel hydrogen cells, which are lighter, more efficient, and much more costly than a set of nickel cadmium cells of equal capacity. Minimizing the weight of spacecraft means that designers provide little-to-no reserve battery capacity. Launch procedures usually require ground support equipment to supply a trickle charge to all spacecraft batteries until just prior to launch so that they will be at maximum charge for the mission. Many current launch windows are very short because only certain transfer orbits provide the kind of sun angles that can be tolerated by most spacecraft thermal management systems.[63]

Engineers could specify nickel cadmium batteries, which are heavier, less efficient, and much cheaper than their nickel hydrogen counterparts. Even commercial-grade (as opposed to the much more expensive space-qualified) nickel cadmium batteries could be considered for spacecraft application.[64] By including more nickel cadmium cells and/or batteries on the spacecraft, designers could compensate for the batteries' suboptimum capabilities. The generous lift margins provided by the launch vehicle make this a practical and low-cost alternative to current practices. Additionally, the satellite design could reduce battery procurement costs by expanding the acceptable limits for battery voltage, allowing acceptance of higher percentages of manufactured batteries. Once again, higher battery failure rates would be compensated for by increased numbers.[65]

By designing-in sufficient reserve on the spacecraft, engineers could eliminate on-pad charging requirements. Nickel cadmium batteries have a low self-discharge rate, compared to the more efficient nickel hydrogen batteries, making them better suited for this procedure change. Also, launch windows potentially could be expanded for many missions if there were more onboard battery capacity, allowing engineers to include additional spacecraft heaters to decrease vehicle sensitivity to sun angles. However, the advantages of expanded launch windows should be carefully weighed against the increased satellite complexity caused by additional heaters.[66]

Today's solar arrays are fragile devices that are optimized for low weight and the highest possible efficiencies. Weight and volume constraints require most arrays to have multiple folding panels and to use high-efficiency cells. Solar array manufacturers procure the highest power and lowest weight cells available in order to maximize power-to-area and power-to-weight ratios. This results in very thin, fragile cells that are both costly to make and highly susceptible to damage during manufacturing and prelaunch processing. Since solar arrays are constrained in size to minimize weight and volume, they require a highly accurate sun orientation (to ensure that they produce the maximum amount of power possible). These demanding orientation requirements cause costs to go up because of the additional sensors and mechanisms that are needed.[67]

Inexpensive launch vehicles would allow significant reductions in the cost of solar arrays and their support equipment, but these reductions would be accompanied by weight and volume penalties. Once again, however, these penalties are overcome by the liberal weight and volume margins available for very low cost from the minimum-cost booster. Designers could specify less expensive cells with lower efficiency, and then compensate for this efficiency loss with larger arrays. Larger array panels that contain some cell quantity margin would not have to be constantly maintained at precise angles with respect to the sun. This relaxation in orientation requirement would permit savings in the costly mechanisms, sensors, and telemetry systems necessary for highly accurate array alignment. Array manufacturers could use heavier and more damage-tolerant cells as well as stronger cover glass, thus reducing the amount of cell losses and rework due to processing damage. Also, additional fairing volume would make it possible to reduce or eliminate folding arrays and to use simpler and less expensive solar panel designs.[68]

Benefits to Spacecraft Electronics Design

Spacecraft electronics design and packaging technologies have traditionally been pushed by weight and volume restrictions. Systems use extremely expensive Class S parts and are densely packed in custom chassis. This causes complexity in fabrication and assembly, increased fragility and rework requirements, and thermal hot spots. Wire harness designs are optimized for low weight through the use of small gauge wire and miniature connectors, which results in complicated manufacture and fragile assemblies. Also, these harness design practices provide less shielding, thus introducing the potential for electromagnetic interference (EMI) problems.[69] The typical electronics chassis is made of magnesium, and it requires intricate machining processes to make it as light and compact as possible. This creates expensive difficulties in manufacture, inspection, and repair. Further, the inherent low design margins often result in tight thermal limits and a need for complex testing to validate the design.[70]

A low-cost launch system would offer some practical, less-expensive alternatives to current spacecraft electronics design practices. Satellite engineers could employ multiredundant electronics and use lower reliability Class B parts. Such an approach would result in electronics packages that are approximately 50 percent heavier, but the Class B parts cost only one-tenth as much as Class S parts. Since the redundant approach would provide several parallel electronic paths and only one of the paths would be required for operations, the redundant components could be left in a powered-down state unless needed. Maintaining electronics units in an inactive state would significantly reduce their failure rates.

When employing such design techniques, engineers should exercise caution. Multiredundant systems composed of Class B parts would not help if the spacecraft experienced a systemic problem such as a large radiation dose to insufficiently-hardened parts. Also, additional redundancy creates the possibility for increased complexity and testing, as discussed previously.

With a relaxation of volume constraints, electronics packaging density could be much lower, thereby easing assembly, inspection, and repair. This could permit slide-out circuit card designs, which are common in the commercial electronics industry. The chassis design could become a simple, standard aluminum housing with minimal machining requirements.[71] Wire harnesses could use heavier-gauge wire and connectors, and dispersed designs, to avoid EMI problems.[72]

Benefits to Spacecraft Communications System Design

Communications equipment represents a major subsystem on most spacecraft. It can even constitute the actual payload that the spacecraft is carrying. And since communications systems are primary users of spacecraft power, they tend to drive the sizing of the vehicle's solar arrays. To keep power requirements as small as possible, engineers usually design systems with low margins. Communications equipment typically requires high packaging densities, a large number of custom-designed components and subassemblies, and a complex and extensive testing program.[73]

Communications systems could be designed with greater performance margins, which would be accompanied by corresponding increases in power requirements and weight. Generous performance margins would permit a less intensive and less expensive test program. Lower-density packaging would permit more widespread use of commercially available components and subassemblies. These commercial products would be less compact, and would weigh more, than custom-designed communications equipment, but they would be much less costly. By relaxing spacecraft volume constraints, we would greatly simplify the layout for the many waveguides typical in communications satellites.[74]

Benefits to Spacecraft Thermal Control System Design

Spacecraft thermal control usually employs passive techniques, heat pipes, heater elements, electronic thermostats, sensor arrays, and computers to maintain tight temperature control. The high-density nature of spacecraft power systems and electronics requires a network of heat pipes for temperature dissipation.[75] Because of power and weight restrictions, designers keep the number of heaters to a minimum and control the size of doublers on high-dissipation components. The doublers are typically made of stepped beryllium plate, which requires intricate machining.[76] Weight and volume constraints limit the area of radiators, further reducing thermal margin.[77] These

169

design practices result in a spacecraft whose thermal control characteristics are highly tuned, requiring extensive thermal modeling, analysis, and testing to validate performance prior to flight. Additionally, the narrow thermal margins require a host of instrumentation to continually verify that all elements are staying within tolerable thermal limits.[78]

A large but inexpensive booster's lift margins would accommodate spacecraft using larger numbers of heaters and higher quantities of doublers with more robust designs. However, satellite engineers must carefully consider the impact of increased complexity caused by the addition of heaters. Doublers could be made from simple aluminum plate of a generous thickness.[79] Reductions in volume limitations could make the temperature dissipation problem less severe, allowing a corresponding reduction in heat pipes and other heat transfer devices.[80] Radiators could be made much larger. These changes in design approaches would likely provide a space vehicle that is more thermally forgiving and requires less extensive analysis, testing, and instrumentation.[81]

Benefits to Spacecraft Design Life Specifications

Incorporating the types of design changes described in this chapter, which would be enabled by inexpensive launch vehicles, would result in major reductions in spacecraft acquisition and operating costs. These reductions would allow space planners to make trades that were not previously practical on the design life of space vehicles. Currently, the US design approach for satellites is to make them very long-lived to minimize requirements for the costly procurement and launch of replenishment spacecraft. The potential for drastic decreases in the cost of spacecraft acquisition and launch should stimulate a review of this design philosophy.

An alternative that could be more cost effective than the current strategy would entail the more frequent acquisition and launch of less expensive and shorter-lived space vehicles.[82] Reducing design life could have a number of cost-savings benefits; for example, solar arrays that are intended for eight to 15 years of operational life require a wide range of thermal cycling tests. The solar arrays of spacecraft having shorter design lives would not require such extensive tests.[83] Also, satellite constellations made up of spacecraft with shorter design lives could have their technology and capability upgrades refreshed more often with the latest technology.

Another possibility created by the design of larger spacecraft that are less densely packaged would be to greatly expand the role of astronauts for orbital maintenance activities. Such a logistics strategy would allow the acquisition and launch of less costly satellites with shorter design lives, but at a less frequent rate than would be required if no on-orbit repair capability was available.[84]

Avoiding Misuse of Increased Launch Capacity

Some satellite managers have expressed the opinion that the added weight and volume margins provided by inexpensive launchers would not result in lower-cost spacecraft. They argue that designers would inevitably use the surplus margins to increase spacecraft capabilities and design life, rather than exploiting the extra weight and volume allocations to decrease manufacturing and operating costs through simplified designs and large safety margins.[85] This is a very real possibility, given the development history of large US space systems. However, program managers could take certain steps to ensure that satellite engineers deliver a low-cost design.

Payload fairing being lowered onto an Atlas Centaur, complex 36B, Cape Canaveral AFS.

To make sure the spacecraft design is driven by considerations that will minimize cost, and not weight and volume, managers must specify cost-saving criteria up front. For example, a design safety factor of at least two-to-one for the spacecraft structure could be established as a requirement. Managers could require the use of off-the-shelf hardware for certain components such as power supplies, communications systems, and flight computers. By exercising tight management discipline on the design, fighting to prevent any new requirements or capability enhancements from being added after the preliminary design review, and keeping cost minimization as a paramount consideration, government and industry can work together to deliver spacecraft that are significantly lower in cost than current space systems.

At least one case study indicates that additional launch capacity would be used to reduce the cost of spacecraft. In 1973, NASA restructured its High Energy Astronomy Observatory (HEAO) program to be flown on three Atlas/Centaur launch vehicles instead of two Titan III vehicles. NASA made the booster switch to lower the program budget, and the change reduced program launch costs by 28 percent.[86]

By repackaging the HEAO instruments on three space vehicles instead of two, considerable weight margin became available to the satellite designers. TRW designed the spacecraft with a three-to-one structural safety factor. Engineers used a single bus design for all three spacecraft, despite the fact the payload instruments for each vehicle were very diverse. Contingency and weight margins exceeded 25 percent at the start of the program, permitting liberal use of the margins for such problem-avoidance features as large power and thermal margins, electromagnetic interference prevention techniques, and standardized designs. Engineers were able to eliminate the requirements for structural and thermal model spacecraft, qualification spacecraft, qualification units, static load tests, and random vibration tests. TRW built one "generic" engineering model and conducted only single-axis sine vibration tests.[87] One of the keys cited for HEAO's success was the NASA program manager's determination not to change program requirements once the design had begun.[88]

Other Benefits of Low-Cost Boosters and Spacecraft

By driving down the cost of satellites through the use of inexpensive boosters, DOD and NASA will be able to afford more orbital assets, even if their space budgets stay flat or even decrease somewhat. Inexpensive launch vehicles could generate a commercial satellite boom for both large and small spacecraft, and an increase in industrial demand for spacecraft could create opportunities for significant manufacturing economies of scale.[89]

Because the launch cost is so high, today's spacecraft seek to use every kilogram and cubic centimeter that their chosen booster can carry to orbit. To the design engineer, every kilogram of lift the satellite customer purchased represents a potential kilogram of capability, reliability, and/or spacecraft life. Additionally, because most current spacecraft programs are many years in the making, payload designers may only get to work on one or two programs in their careers. Consequently, they have a tendency to pack everything they can onto one spacecraft bus. However, the large and inexpensive lift capacity and volume of frequent flying low-cost launchers will likely not be completely used up by satellite designers because dramatically lower launch costs will not demand maximum use of the available launch capacity. Thus, there will be more numerous chances for small satellites to get "piggyback" rides into orbit for little to no cost, further fueling opportunities for both government-sponsored space experiments and commercial satellite expansion.[90]

172

From a defense perspective, having military satellites available at greatly reduced cost will improve their "exchange ratio" (the cost of building satellites and getting them in orbit versus the cost to an adversary who would seek to destroy them). The reduced cost will also make satellites more amenable to orbital replenishment strategies, on-orbit sparing, and larger constellations possessing an increase in both system survivability and "graceful degradation" characteristics.[91]

Summary

There is a powerful link between the cost of boosters and the cost of their cargo. To achieve radical decreases in the cost of space exploitation and exploration, we must start with major reductions in the cost of launch. As this chapter has illustrated, making inexpensive launch capacity and volume available to satellite designers can result in dramatic drops in the cost of spacecraft. Low-cost satellites can become a reality if we: provide sufficient reductions in launch expenses; design spacecraft that are optimized for minimum cost rather than minimum weight and volume; selectively increase the redundancy of key subsystems by using simple design approaches; specify liberal contingency and weight margins for the spacecraft design early-on; use standardized and/or off-the-shelf components and busses; and design boosters with standard interfaces. The spacecraft program manager must maintain the vision for low cost throughout the life of the program. And once the design is set, the manager must steadfastly resist initiatives that would increase performance, capability, complexity, on-orbit life, and cost.

Notes

1. Hughes Aircraft Company, "Design Guide for ALS Payloads" (El Segundo, Calif.: October 1988), A-2.

2. Eric J. Hoffman, "Lightsats and Cheapsats: The Engineering Challenge of the Small Satellite," *Johns Hopkins APL Technical Digest* 9, no. 3, (1988): 294.

3. Edward L. Keith, "System Analysis and Description of an Ultra-Low Cost Ground to Low Earth Orbit Cargo Delivery System" (Paper presented at the World Space Congress, Washington, D.C., 31 August 1992), 2.

4. William H. Ganoe, "Big Questions for Small Satellites," *Ad Astra,* December 1991, 50.

5. Vincent Kiernan, "Russians Develop Big, Heavy, Cheap Communications Satellite," *Space News,* 30 November–6 December 1992, 26.

6. Eric J. Lerner, "Mission to Phobos," *Aerospace America,* September 1988, 34.

7. Office of Technology Assessment, *Affordable Spacecraft—Design and Launch Alternatives* (Washington, D.C.: Government Printing Office, January 1990), 17.

8. Ibid., 3.

9. Michael B. Callaham, "Making Spacecraft Affordable: An Assessment of Alternatives" (Paper presented at SAE Aerospace Atlantic, Dayton, Ohio, 23–26 April 1990), 3.

10. Gerard Elverum, "Scale Up to Keep Mission Costs Down" (Paper presented at the 24th International Astronautical Federation Congress, Baku, Soviet Union, October 1973), 6.

11. Sikandar Zaman, "Low-Cost Satellites and Satellite Launch Vehicles" (Paper presented at the Symposium on Space Commercialization: Roles of Developing Countries, Nashville, Tenn., 5–10 March 1989), 1, 4.

12. Elverum, "Scale Up to Keep Mission Costs Down."

13. Arthur Schnitt to Daniel S. Goldin, NASA Administrator, letter, 18 May 1992.

14. Arthur Schnitt to Richard DalBello, Office of Technology Assessment, letter, 24 October 1988.

15. Office of Technology Assessment, *Affordable Spacecraft,* 15–16.

16. Callaham.

17. Office of Technology Assessment, *Affordable Spacecraft,* 3.

18. Ibid., 17.

19. Mark Chartrand, "Spacecraftsmanship," *Ad Astra,* February 1990, 39.

20. James R. Wertz and Wiley J. Larson, eds., *Space Mission Analysis and Design* (Dordrecht/Boston/London: Kluwer Academic Publishers, 1991), 641–42.

21. Ibid.

22. Ibid.

23. Ibid., 642.

24. Paul Dergarabedian, "Research Proposal—Complexity Impact on the Cost of Space Systems," The Aerospace Corporation, El Segundo, Calif., 8 July 1992.

25. Callaham, 9.

26. G. W. Elverum, Jr., "Boosters" (Transcript of a talk presented at the Aerospace Productivity Conference, The Aerospace Corporation, El Segundo, Calif., 1987), 3.

27. Clark Kirby, TRW Spacecraft Design, briefing, subject: Weight and Volume Constraints, 16 November 1988.

28. Callaham, 10.

29. Ibid.

30. Kirby briefing.

31. Ibid.

32. M. Holguin and M. Labbee, "Launch Vehicle to Payload Interface Standardization: The Quest for a Low Cost Launch System" (Presented at the AIAA 26th Aerospace Sciences Mtg., Reno, Nev., 11–14 January 1988), 1.

33. Ibid.

34. Ibid., 2.

35. Hughes Aircraft Company, 1, 5.

36. Holguin and Labbee, 7.

37. Ibid.

38. Clark Kirby, TRW Spacecraft Design, interview with The Aerospace Corporation, 11 January 1990.

39. Callaham, 13.

40. Office of Technology Assessment, *Affordable Spacecraft,* 9.

41. Hughes Aircraft Company, 2.

42. Hoffman, 295; G. K. Pardoe and M. N. Sweeting, "Applications of Small, Cost-Effective Spacecraft" (Paper presented at the 38th International Astronautical Federation Congress, Brighton, United Kingdom, 10–17 October 1987), 3.

43. Ganoe, "Big Questions."

44. Hughes Aircraft Company, A-3.

45. Kirby briefing.

46. Hughes Aircraft Company, A-3, A-4. However, given the reliable characteristics of aluminum and the wide uncertainty band on composites, the weight difference between the two is less than many designers realize.

47. Hughes Aircraft Company.

48. Ibid., 9–10, A-4, A-5.

49. Ibid., 9–10, A-5, A-6.

50. Kirby briefing.

51. Hughes Aircraft Company, A-6.

52. Kirby briefing.

53. Hughes Aircraft Company, A-6.

54. Kirby briefing.

55. Hughes Aircraft Company, A-7.

56. Ibid., A-8.

57. Charles E. Heimach, "Low Cost Access to Space" (Paper presented at the Conference on Low-Cost Access to Space, Paris, France, 22 May 1990), 5–7.

58. Hughes Aircraft Company, A-9.

59. Ibid., A-11.

60. Ibid.

61. Ibid., A-12.

62. Ibid., A-13.

63. Ibid.

64. Zaman, 5.

65. Hughes Aircraft Company, A-14.

66. Ibid., A-15.

67. Ibid.

68. Ibid., A-16.

69. Kirby briefing.

70. Hughes Aircraft Company, A-17.

71. Ibid.

72. Kirby briefing.

73. Hughes Aircraft Company, A-19.

74. Ibid.

75. Dergarabedian.

76. Hughes Aircraft Company, A-20.

77. Kirby briefing.

78. Hughes Aircraft Company, A-20.

79. Ibid.

80. Dergarabedian.

81. Kirby briefing; Hughes Aircraft Company, A-20, A-21.

82. Hughes Aircraft Company, A-23.

83. Zaman, 4–5.

84. Jim French to John London, draft comments, June 1993.

85. Office of Technology Assessment, *Big Dumb Boosters—Low Cost Space Transportation Option?* (Washington, D.C.: Government Printing Office, February 1989), 5–6.

86. Office of Technology Assessment, *Affordable Spacecraft,* 17.

87. Kirby briefing.

88. Kirby interview.

89. William H. Ganoe, "Is Small Better?" *Ad Astra,* January 1990, 44.

90. Ibid.

91. Hoffman, 294.

Chapter 9

Minimum Cost Design Launch Vehicles

The idea of building simple and inexpensive launch vehicles is not new. The seeds were planted in the late 1950s for minimum cost launch vehicle designs. By the latter half of the 1960s, a number of aerospace companies were busily seeking a solution to the high cost of space launch by studying minimum cost boosters. All of these efforts died when the US government decided in the early 1970s that the Space Shuttle would be the long-term solution to high launch costs. Although several minimum cost booster concepts have been proposed since 1972, none have been seriously considered by DOD or NASA. However, the high and ever-increasing cost of current launch systems, combined with the failure of new initiatives like the ALS and NLS to gain continued funding, makes the idea of a launch vehicle designed for minimum cost more relevant today than it has ever been.

To appreciate the depth to which Minimum Cost Design (MCD) methodology has been investigated and how well it has been validated, one needs an understanding of the booster studies that have been accomplished over the years (see table 9). Therefore, this chapter will provide a survey of significant past studies and some current programs that employ aspects of minimum cost design methodologies to develop low cost launch systems.

Table 9

Minimum Cost Design Launch Vehicle Concepts

VEHICLE	LIFTOFF THRUST	PAYLOAD CAPACITY (LEO)	PAYLOAD LAUNCH EFFICIENCY (Cost per kg to LEO)**
Sea Dragon	356.0 MN (80.0 Mlb)	544,000 kg. (1,200,000 lb.)	N/A
Aerospace Design 3 SLV	16.671 MN (3.748 Mlb)	18,145 kg. (40,000 lb.)*	$880/kg. ($400/lb.)*
Chrysler MCD Booster	21.528 MN (4.84 Mlb)	45,360 kg. (100,000 lb.)	$752/kg. ($341/lb)
McDonnell Douglas MCD Booster	21.5 MN (4.83 Mlb)	45,360 kg (100,000 lb.)	$767/kg ($348/lb.)
Rockwell MCD Booster	20.1 MN (4.52 Mlb)	20,400 kg. (45,000 lb.)	$1,381/kg. ($626/lb.)
Martin Marietta MCD Booster	25.9 MN (5.823 Mlb)	20,400 kg. (45,000 lb.)*	$474/kg ($215/lb)*
Boeing Double Bubble Booster	12.0 MN (2.7 Mlb)	15,420 kg. (34,000 lb.)	$936/kg. ($424/lb.)
Revised Boeing MCD Booster	N/A	45,360 kg. (100,000 lb.)*	$1,437/kg. ($652/lb.)*
TRW MCD Booster	51.73 MN (11 63 Mlb)	60,000 kg. (133,000 lb.)	$1,235/kg. ($561/lb)
TRW LCSSB	30.25 MN (6 8 Mlb)	29,756 kg (65,600 lb.)	$1,989/kg ($901/lb)

* Payload capacity and launch efficiency values are for an LEO polar orbit
** Costs are in 1993 Dollars

Sea-Launched Space Booster Studies

In the late 1950s, the idea of launching rockets directly out of the ocean emerged. Ignition of the first-stage engine(s) was to take place underwater. The US Navy initiated the HYDRA program to demonstrate the feasibility of launching rockets that were partially submerged and floating vertically in sea water. The 32-meter (105-foot)-tall solid propellant HYDRA-1 was launched in March 1960, directly out of the ocean off Point Mugu, California. The Navy conducted approximately 60 launches of rocket simulators and actual rockets over the course of the project, using mostly solid propellant propulsion systems. HYDRA validated the concept of launching directly from the sea, with the rocket's initial exhaust gasses being expelled directly into water.[1]

During the same time that the Navy was conducting the HYDRA tests, Aerojet-General Corporation accomplished a series of tests to study the feasibility of sea-launched liquid propellant rockets.[2] The Aerojet effort, called the Sea Launch Program, was dubbed "SeaBee" because it used a modified Aerobee 100 sounding rocket for its test vehicle.[3] Aerojet conducted a number of demonstrations of ocean launching techniques to evaluate handling, propellant servicing, checkout, and sea launch operations. Aerojet also evaluated recovery, refurbishment, and relaunch of the test vehicle, with an eye toward future reusable launch systems.[4]

Aerojet successfully launched the SeaBee test vehicle on 24 October 1961 from a floating position off Point Mugu. It reached an altitude of 1.5 kilometers (5,000 feet), deployed a parachute, and was safely recovered after a water landing. Having sustained no damage, the SeaBee was refurbished and relaunched on 2 November 1961.[5] The success of SeaBee helped substantiate the concept of sea launch and recovery for a much larger launch vehicle proposal.

Aerojet used some independent research and development funding in the early 1960s to explore various cost aspects of space launchers. Through these studies, the corporation developed a set of five design rules for low-cost launch vehicles. The low-cost booster must be big, simple, and reusable. Also, the design must not push for the absolute maximum reliability, and it must not push the state of the technological art.[6] Aerojet combined data derived from the SeaBee program with the newly developed low-cost booster design rules to define a colossal launch vehicle. Called Sea Dragon, it was intended to support NASA's manned exploratory assault on Mars and interplanetary space (see table 9).[7]

The Sea Dragon was to be a simple, reusable launch vehicle. Like the SeaBee, it was to use a pressure-fed propulsion system; but it was scaled to represent perhaps the largest space booster ever conceived.[8] It was to have a lift-off thrust of 356 million Newtons (80 million pounds) and a lift capacity to low earth orbit of 544,000 kilograms (1,200,000 pounds).[9] The Sea Dragon was to be 168 meters (550 feet) tall and to have a diameter of 23 meters (75 feet).[10] Construction and transportation of such a booster was more amenable to a shipyard than an aerospace factory, and the vehicle's simple steel design with water launch and recovery made shipyard manufacturing appropriate and practical.[11]

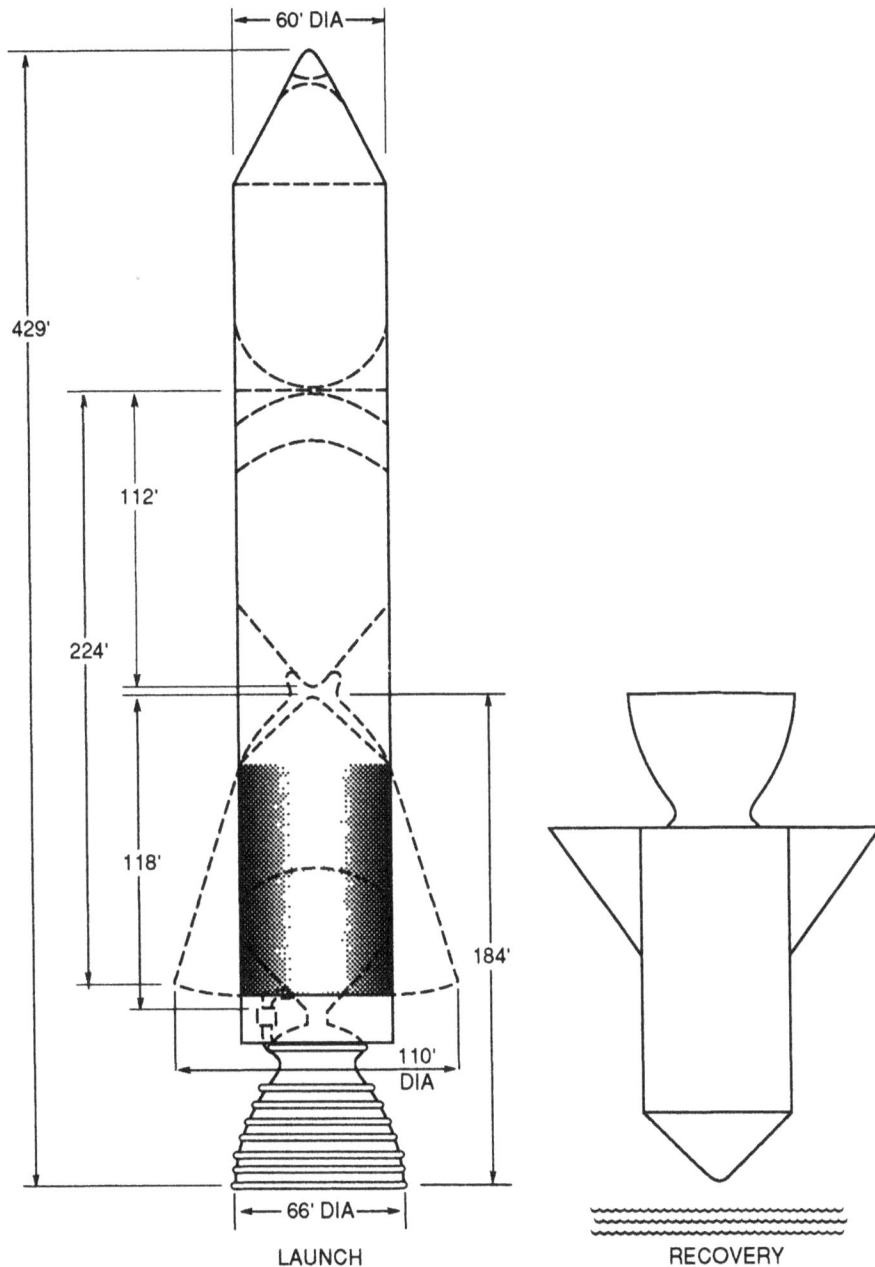

Figure 7. The Sea Dragon launch vehicle concept, illustrating the first stage recovery via water splashdown

Aerojet designed the Sea Dragon to have two stages. The first stage would use liquid oxygen and RP-1; the second stage, liquid oxygen and liquid hydrogen. Both stages would be pressure-fed, and both would use a single-engine thrust chamber. The first stage engine would be rated at 356 million Newtons (80 million pounds) of sea-level thrust—certainly the largest rocket engine ever seriously postulated.[12] Aerojet settled on single-thrust chamber stages

179

because their studies indicated it would be less expensive to develop and integrate single large engines than to develop and cluster sets of smaller engines. Also, analysis showed that even with near-exponential increases in the size of simple engines and airframes, there is only a linear increase in cost.[13] The analysis results made a strong case for the economy of very large and simple boosters with large engines, and Sea Dragon was the consummate embodiment of this design philosophy.

Sea Dragon was to be constructed—and transported to the launch location (at sea)—in a manner that was closer to a seagoing tanker than an airplane. The vehicle would have been built horizontally in a commercial shipyard, then staged out of a US coastal site. It was to be fueled with RP-1 in a dry dock, then towed horizontally to the launch point. Upon its arrival, propellant transport ships would have loaded the vehicle with cryogenic propellants, and technicians would have flooded a ballast device to position the booster vertically. The booster would jettison the ballast at lift-off.[14]

The first stage, which was to be recovered several hundred kilometers downrange, would use an inflated drag chute to decrease its water-impact velocity. The rigidity and strength of the heavy steel tankage, which was designed for the pressure-fed propulsion system, would have lent itself to surviving repeated water impacts with little damage. The second stage had an optional reusability design that would have employed retro-rockets, an ablative nosecap, and a drag-inducing device for controlled reentry to a point close to the refurbishment site.[15]

Cost estimates for using the Sea Dragon to place a payload in low earth orbit ranged from $59 per kilogram ($27 per pound) to $620 per kilogram ($282 per pound).[16] The booster researchers were able to project these low costs because the booster had the benefit of a significant economy of size, it depended on shipyard-type (as opposed to aerospace) construction techniques, and it was reusable.

The Sea Dragon was designed prior to formal codification of the classical design-for-minimum-cost (DFMC) methodology by The Aerospace Corporation. Nevertheless, its design contained the essence of the DFMC philosophy and therefore represented the first detailed launch vehicle concept that was designed for minimum cost.

After Aerojet proposed the Sea Dragon concept, NASA's Marshall Space Flight Center contracted Space Technology Laboratories, Inc. (a subsidiary of TRW) to evaluate the proposal and re-accomplish the cost estimates. Space Technology Laboratories largely confirmed Aerojet's cost data and the soundness of the design.[17] However, NASA's interest in the concept was primarily driven by the vehicle's massive lift capacity rather than its low cost. As the scope of NASA's interplanetary ambitions shrank, Sea Dragon was shelved and virtually forgotten.[18]

Early Air Force and NASA-Sponsored Studies

Studies that culminated in a formal design-for-minimum-cost criteria began in 1959 at the Space Technology Laboratories (later to be incorporated into TRW). By the fall of 1963, the Air Force and The Aerospace Corporation had initiated studies that applied the DFMC criteria to advanced ballistic missile concepts.[19] These efforts focused on the definition of a semi-mobile ICBM.[20] (Minimum cost design [MCD] ballistic missiles are still very viable weapon system concepts, particularly when considered for the delivery of conventional munitions in a limited conflict.[21]) Much of the data generated by these studies was applicable to space launch systems, and the Air Force and Aerospace gained important insights into the implications of applying the MCD methodology to launch vehicle designs.[22]

Initial MCD Booster Designs

Between 1965 and 1968, The Air Force's Space and Missile Systems Organization (SAMSO) and The Aerospace Corporation, which were collocated in El Segundo, California, began to formally apply the DFMC criteria to space launch vehicle designs. The Aerospace Corporation developed a baseline two-stage pressure-fed MCD booster concept with an 18,145-kilogram (40,000-pound) lift capacity to a polar low earth orbit (LEO). The vehicle was designed to use a hypergolic propellant combination.

The concept evolved through three major design iterations. The Design 3 space launch vehicle had a gross lift-off weight of 1,114,924 kilograms (2,458,000 pounds) and a first-stage sea-level thrust (using a single engine) of 16,671,104 Newtons (3,748,000 pounds).[23] Taking a cue from the Sea Dragon concept, Aerospace designed the MCD booster's first stage to be reusable, using an inflatable drag-inducing device and ocean splashdown for recovery.[24] The design projected a recurring launch cost of less than $880 per kilogram ($400 per pound) to polar LEO (see table 9).[25] The moniker "Big Dumb Booster" was unofficially, and sometimes irreverently, applied to this particular vehicle configuration, although it has also been used to describe some other simple, low-cost launch vehicle designs.[26]

MCD Application Studies for the Titan III. In August of 1965, the Titan III System Program Office and Aerospace, with support from the Air Force Rocket Propulsion Laboratory, began a series of studies that applied the MCD criterion to a variety of potential space booster requirements. Initial studies defined a baseline reference design for an MCD launch vehicle, considered replacing the Titan IIIC core vehicle with an MCD core vehicle, evaluated replacing the Titan IIIC solid rocket motors with MCD liquid strap-ons, compared MCD liquid strap-ons with hybrid strap-ons, and considered replacing the Titan IIIB with an MCD booster of comparable performance.[27]

Alternative MCD Titan Core Vehicle. In conjunction with a Martin Marietta study to develop a large-diameter core vehicle that would increase the capability of the Titan III vehicle family, Aerospace studied an alternative MCD core vehicle. The Aerospace design used a lower strength alloy, had simple load paths, and required no machining of vehicle skins. Compared to the Martin Marietta design, which used a minimum weight criterion, the Aerospace MCD core vehicle weighed only 7.2 percent more but had a recurring cost decrease of more than 50 percent.[28]

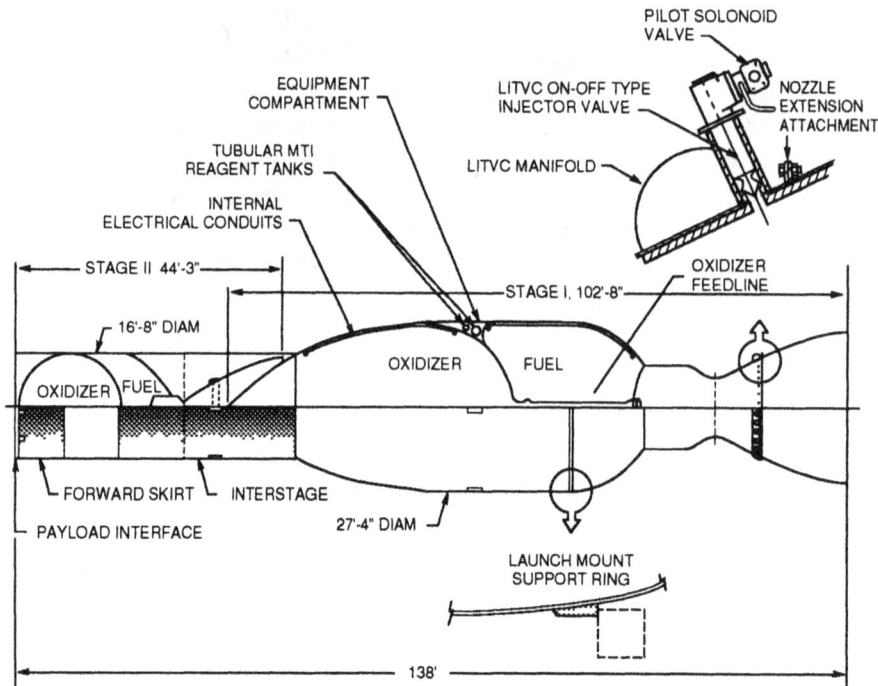

Figure 8. The Aerospace Corporation Design 3 space launch vehicle configuration

MCD Concepts for Titan SRM Replacement. Martin Marietta also studied two different solid rocket motor (SRM) growth options to increase the capability of the Titan IIIC. Aerospace considered an alternative approach, using two different liquid propellant strap-on concepts that were designed to the MCD criteria and equaled or exceeded the capabilities of the Martin SRM proposals. Projected recurring costs for both of the MCD liquid strap-on concepts that were less than half the corresponding SRM recurring costs.[29]

Comparison of MCD Liquid Strap-ons and Hybrid Strap-ons. In the latter half of 1967, Aerospace engineers compared their MCD liquid strap-on design to a United Technology hybrid booster concept that had been proposed as a strap-on for the Titan IIIC. The MCD liquid design projected recurring costs that were 25 percent less than those for the hybrid design.[30] (It should be noted that the United Technology hybrid motor design was significantly different from the current AMROC design.)

Titan IIIB Replacement Studies. In early 1968, Aerospace undertook a design study for an MCD booster to replace the Titan IIIB launch vehicle. The MCD design extrapolated Aerospace's Design 3 Space Launch Vehicle concept to approximate the performance of the Titan IIIB. The focus was on structure and propulsion; Titan IIIB systems such as guidance, telemetry, and power supply were retained in the MCD booster design. The Agena third stage and its adapter, which were also used on the Titan IIIB, were incorporated in the MCD design. Projected recurring costs for the MCD booster were significantly

182

The Titan IIIC launch vehicle.

A Titan IIIB lifts off from Vandenberg AFB.

lower than Titan IIIB recurring costs. The MCD booster's stage one and stage two tankage cost was less than $160,000 per vehicle.[31]

Collateral Developments. All of these studies indicated that application of MCD criteria would result in significant launch cost reductions.[32] During this same period, TRW was experiencing significant success with engine de-

184

velopment activities that used a simple and inexpensive pressure-fed design based on their Lunar Module Descent Engine. Also, U.S. Steel's new HY 140 alloy steel appeared to be ideal for MCD pressurized tankage applications. These positive indicators served to add momentum to the Air Force/Aerospace MCD booster initiatives.[33]

Initial Industry Studies

In May 1968, SAMSO and The Aerospace Corporation conducted briefings for industry to stimulate interest in developing MCD space launch vehicles. TRW and Boeing were the most enthusiastic about the concept.[34]

While Aerospace continued to develop MCD booster concepts, a number of aerospace contractors (including TRW and Boeing) began to conduct minimum cost design studies and to develop candidate vehicle designs (see table 9). These contractor studies, which were funded by independent research and development dollars, were not constrained by fixed requirements.[35]

Chrysler MCD Booster Concept. In February 1969, Chrysler Corporation's Space Division submitted a concept for a minimum cost design booster with a pressure-fed first stage. The design called for a two-stage launch vehicle, but the MCD focus was on the first stage. Chrysler called for the second stage to be a Saturn S-IVB (the third stage of the Saturn V launch vehicle), which was manufactured by the McDonnell Douglas Astronautics Company. The first stage design had a single engine with a thrust of 21,528,320 Newtons (4,840,000 pounds). The booster was designed for a lift capacity of 45,360 kilograms (100,000 pounds) to low earth orbit. Chrysler projected the recurring cost of the first stage to be $34.1 million per vehicle (for a 20-vehicle buy, spread over five years). The cost of the stage one tankage was estimated to be $39.70 per kilogram ($18.00 per pound).[36]

McDonnell Douglas MCD Booster Concept. A January 1968 study by McDonnell Douglas proposed an MCD launch vehicle similar to the Chrysler design. The booster was a two-stage configuration, utilizing a pressure-fed first stage and an S-IVB as the second stage. The launch vehicle was designed to lift 45,360 kilograms (100,000 pounds) to LEO. McDonnell Douglas estimated the per-vehicle cost for the first stage to be $34.8 million, assuming a 20-vehicle, five-year procurement program. The cost of the first stage structure was projected to be $89.56 per kilogram ($40.62 per pound).[37]

North American Rockwell MCD Booster Concept. North American Rockwell completed a study in October 1968 for an MCD launch vehicle. After going through several design iterations, Rockwell settled on a two-stage baseline design with a 20,400-kilogram (45,000-pound) payload capacity to low earth orbit. Both stages were pressure-fed systems using a single engine. The thrust of the first stage engine was 20.1 million Newtons (4.52 million pounds). The vehicle could be off-loaded for smaller payloads and augmented with strap-ons (extra stage ones) for larger payloads. Rockwell estimated recurring costs for the entire booster to be $28.182 million per vehicle. Cost of the structure was $44.10 per kilogram ($20.00 per pound).[38]

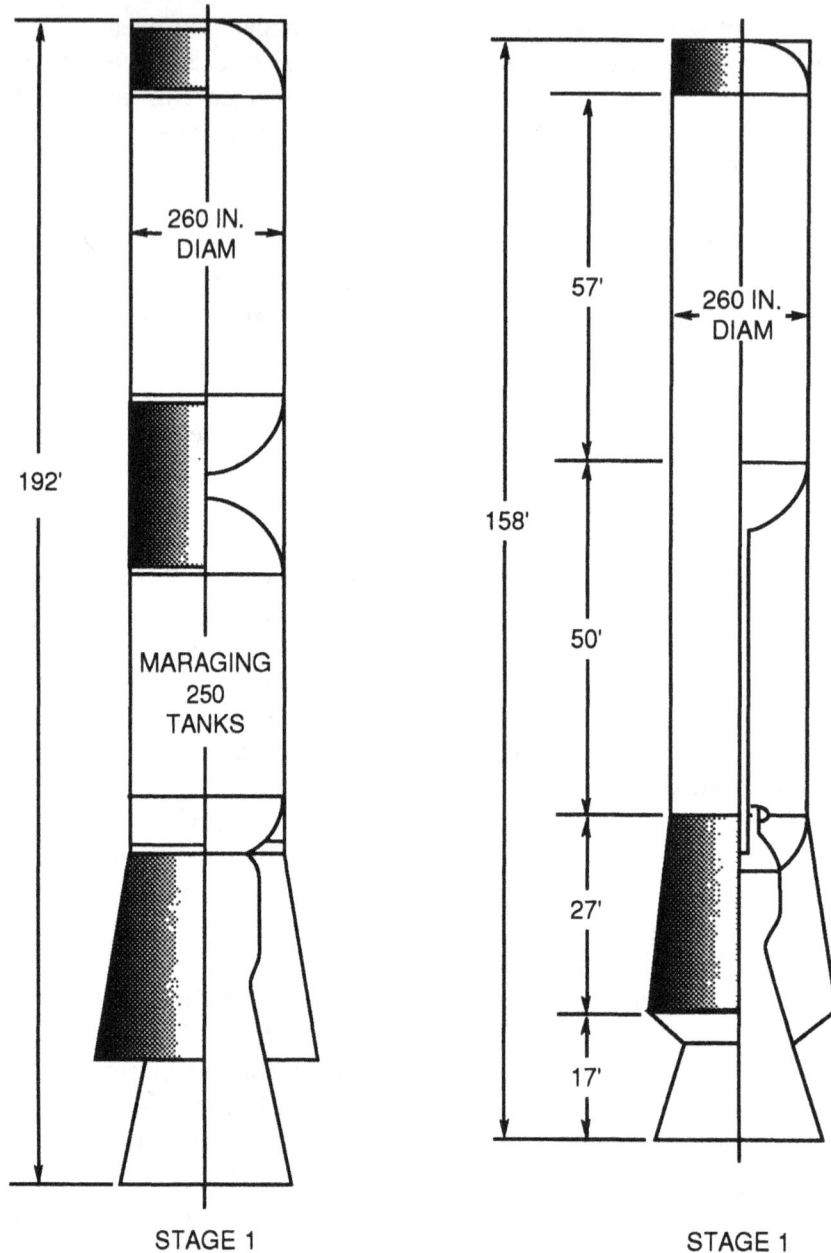

Figure 9. The Chrysler MCD booster first stage (left) and the McDonnell Douglas MCD booster first stage

Boeing MCD Booster Concept. Boeing began independent research and development studies on minimum-cost design boosters in July 1968. These efforts resulted in the development of a design called the Cost Optimized Launch Vehicle (COLV). Boeing went through three successive design iterations to arrive at the COLV III configuration. COLV III was a three-stage booster with a 15,420-kilogram (34,000-pound) lift capacity to LEO. The three

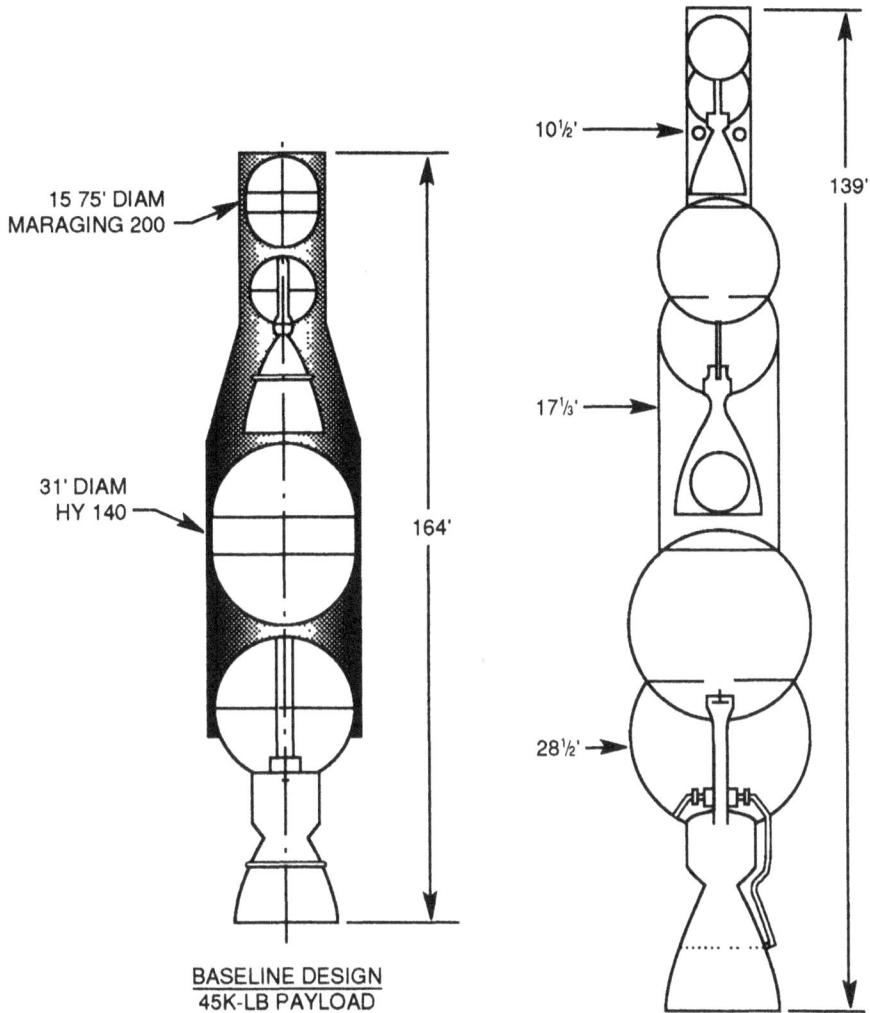

Figure 10. The two-stage Rockwell MCD booster concept (left) and the Boeing double bubble three-stage MCD booster design

stages were stacked in a tandem fashion, and a "double bubble" spherical propellant tank arrangement was used for each stage. All three stages would use TRW pressure-fed engines that were to be derived from the simple, inexpensive engines that TRW was testing at that time. The first-stage thrust was 12 million Newtons (2.7 million pounds). Total first-unit cost for the entire vehicle was $14.427 million, resulting in a launch cost per payload kilogram of $936 ($424 per pound).[39]

Martin Marietta MCD Booster Concept. Between November 1968 and January 1969, Martin Marietta developed a preliminary design for a two-stage pressure-fed MCD launch vehicle with a payload capacity of 20,400 kilograms (45,000 pounds) into a polar low earth orbit. The design employed a single engine for each stage, and the lift-off thrust was 25.9 million Newtons

187

(5.823 million pounds). Martin estimated the recurring cost per complete vehicle to be $9.661 million.[40]

Complementary Boeing Hardware Activities. During the same period that the COLV concepts were being developed, Boeing was energetically pursuing a number of complementary MCD hardware activities. The company fabricated a complete set of tanks and structure that were sized for the TRW 1.112-million-Newton (250,000-pound)-thrust MCD pressure-fed engine, which was being tested at the Air Force's Rocket Propulsion Laboratory. Using commercial fabrication techniques through the application of ASME boiler code requirements, Boeing also conducted a variety of tank fabrication and testing activities. A complete double bubble spherical tank was constructed.[41]

The Boeing MCD Booster Study Contract

The Space and Missile Systems Organization planned to release a request for proposal (RFP) in early to mid-1969 for an MCD space booster design and costing study. Prior to the RFP release, SAMSO requested that The Aerospace Corporation develop a new in-house MCD booster baseline design. This new design was to take advantage of the various MCD studies that had been completed or were on-going. The SAMSO/Aerospace configuration resulting from the study was a family of three vehicles with payload lift capabilities of 11,340, 22,680, and 40,823 kilograms (25,000, 50,000, and 90,000 pounds), respectively. The basic stage one of the smallest vehicle served as the core vehicle and as strap-ons for the larger two vehicles (two and four strap-ons, respectively). The second stage of the smallest vehicle served as the third stage for the larger two vehicles.[42]

On 7 April 1969, SAMSO issued the RFP for the MCD design and cost contract. Titled "Minimum Cost Design Launch Vehicle Design/Costing Study," the contract was for a seven-month level-of-effort study. Four contractors (Boeing-Michoud, Martin Marietta, McDonnell Douglas, and North American Rockwell) submitted proposals by the 7 May 1969 due date. SAMSO selected Boeing, and awarded a contract for $1.017 million on 25 July 1969.[43]

Using their double bubble tandem stage approach, Boeing designers initially proposed a family of three MCD boosters; but they later determined that the parallel staging concept used in the Aerospace baseline design resulted in slightly lower costs. (This was due primarily to the commonality of design and the higher production rates that the Aerospace parallel approach allowed.)

Boeing redesigned their family of three-stage vehicles to use parallel staging, resulting in a configuration that was very similar to the Aerospace baseline design. Boeing engineers used the system/subsystem cost optimization technique (SCOT), a Boeing-developed minimum-cost design methodology in their trade studies. The design called for pressure-fed TRW engines for all stages. There was a high degree of design commonality between stages (only the third stage of the smallest vehicle was unique). The three vehicle designs had payload capacities to low earth orbit of 11,340, 22,680, and 45,360 kilograms (25,000, 50,000, and 100,000 pounds), respectively. Boeing estimated that the cost of placing a kilogram into LEO using their MCD vehicle family would range from $924 to $1,437 per kilogram ($420 to $652 per pound) (see table 9). The worst cost case was for polar launches.[44]

The contract period for the Boeing study ended on 25 February 1970.[45] In an independent assessment, Aerospace calculated the launch costs to be somewhat higher than Boeing's figures. Aerospace projected the cost of placing a kilogram into LEO, using the Boeing launch system design, to be from $1,605 to $2,425 per kilogram ($728 to $1,101 per pound).[46]

In conjunction with the Boeing effort, SAMSO developed a comprehensive program management plan for the development of a minimum-cost design space launch vehicle. The plan indicated that significant total program cost savings could be realized by tailoring various management disciplines to the MCD design approach.[47]

TRW MCD Booster Concepts

TRW has proposed a number of MCD booster concepts over the years and has been a strong and consistent advocate of using simple propulsion system and vehicle designs to lower the cost of space transportation. This enthusiasm has stemmed at least partly from their remarkable success with simple and very low-cost pressure-fed rocket engine development and testing in the late 1960s. Through the Space Technology Laboratories/Aerospace studies and the Sea Dragon evaluation effort, TRW also benefited from early exposure to the concept of simple, cost-optimized boosters.

MCD Liquid Strap-on Replacement for the Titan SRMs. In October 1968, TRW proposed a low-cost, liquid strap-on design for use in place of the solid-propellant strap-ons of the Titan IIIC. The system used a single-chamber, throttleable pressure-fed engine, and had a cost of $25.95 per kilogram of structure ($11.76 per pound).[48]

A Proposal to NASA for a Family of MCD Boosters. NASA contracted with TRW, as a part of the national space booster study, to develop a concept for a low-cost launch vehicle family that would be capable of operating in the 1973 to 1985 period and placing payloads of 18,150 to 45,360 kilograms (40,000 to 100,000 pounds) into LEO. TRW used MCD design principles to propose nine different vehicle configurations that encompassed the specified lift requirements and provided an expanded LEO lift capability up to 113,400 kilograms (250,000 pounds). TRW's largest booster concept had a payload lift capability commensurate with the Saturn V. Several of the concepts depended on the Saturn S-IVB as a second or third stage. Each booster concept exhibited a high degree of commonality with the other vehicle designs.[49]

The baseline low-cost launch vehicle within the nine-vehicle family was a three-stage expendable booster with a lift capacity of 60,000 kilograms (133,000 pounds) to low earth orbit. TRW estimated the cost of placing a kilogram into LEO using the baseline vehicle to be $452 ($205 per pound), assuming recurring production costs only. After adding nonrecurring costs and launch processing and support costs, the per-kilogram price to LEO in-

189

creased to $1,235 ($561 per pound). The vehicle used a single first-stage, pressure-fed engine with a thrust of 51.73 million Newtons (11.63 million pounds), although TRW included an alternative configuration for the first stage that used four pressure-fed engines with a thrust of 13.34 million Newtons (3.0 million pounds) each (see table 9).[50]

A Lost Opportunity for MCD Booster Development

There is a significant variance in the launch cost estimates of the many different MCD vehicle concepts developed by the government and the aerospace industry in the late 1960s. However, among these concepts there was universal agreement that major launch cost reductions could be achieved through the application of a minimum-cost design methodology. There is every reason to believe that similar launch cost reduction ratios are available today if we were to apply the same cost-optimized design philosophy.

During the late 1960s, the Air Force's Space and Missile Systems Organization attempted to start a new program to design and build MCD operational boosters. However, there was stiff competition for funds from new aircraft initiatives like the F-15, F-16, and B-1, as well as from the manned orbiting laboratory. These programs received Air Force budgetary priority and, beyond the Boeing study, the MCD booster program received only a small amount of funding to pursue some pressure-fed technology studies.[51]

In March 1969 a presidential task group was formed to determine the appropriate course the US should take in space after Apollo. The task group proposed a space shuttle as the means for future space access. Preliminary design and technology studies for a shuttle were initiated in 1969, and in March 1970 President Nixon chose to pursue a manned space station and a reusable space shuttle as the next major US goals in space. The space station was soon deferred until an operational shuttle could be fielded.[52]

The shuttle concept was extolled as *the* answer to lowering launch costs, and it would use cutting-edge technology to get there. Aerospace managers and engineers were quickly enamored of the concept, as was the public. The idea of using simple unmanned boosters with steel tanks and pressure-fed engines was not technically or operationally exciting to the aerospace community at large, and it did not seem to hold the promise of billions of government dollars for development and for thousands of aerospace jobs. Further, it did not engender within the American people or their political representatives a grand vision of the future (like the Space Shuttle did), and it was far afield of NASA's charter to advance aerospace technology. Consequently, initiatives to develop a minimum-cost launch system were quietly halted.

More Recent Minimum Cost Design Initiatives

In 1980, the Air Force contracted TRW to develop a low-cost booster configuration that would have a payload lift capability equal to the maximum capacity of the Space Shuttle. TRW took the original 1969 study that had been accomplished for NASA, which proposed a family of simple pressure-fed boosters, and updated it to be consistent with 1981 technology and cost.[53] The result was an unmanned launch vehicle called the Low Cost Shuttle Surrogate Booster (LCSSB).[54]

LIFT-OFF WEIGHT	5,055,500 LB	
STAGE ONE		
ΔV	7,760 FT/SEC	
THRUST LEVEL	6.8M LB	
PROPELLENT CONSUMED	3,172,200 LB	
BURN-OUT WT (VEHICLE)	1,882,3000 LB	
STAGE TWO		
ΔV	11,400 FT/SEC	
THRUST LEVEL	1.8M LB	
PROPELLENT CONSUMED	971,200 LB	
BURN-OUT (VEHICLE)	418,100 LB	
STAGE THREE		
ΔV	11,400 FT/SEC	
THRUST LEVEL	0.3M LB	
PROPELLENT CONSUMED	190,800 LB	
BURN-OUT (VEHICLE)	95,200 LB	
PAYLOAD CAPABILITY (500 FT/SEC VEL. PAD)		
ETR	28.7° 150 n.m ORBIT	65,600 LB
WTR	90° 150 n.m ORBIT	51,100 LB
	96.6° SUNSYN ORBIT	

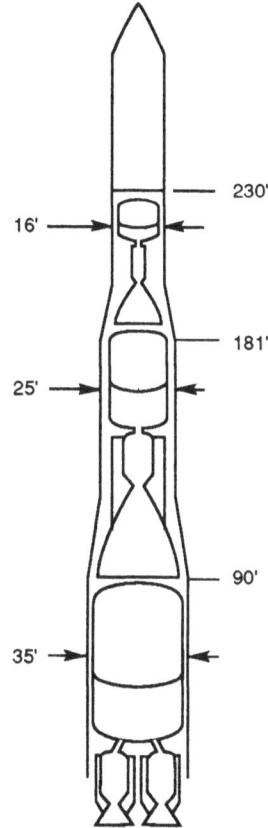

Figure 11. The TRW Low Cost Shuttle Surrogate Booster, a pressure-fed MCD launch vehicle proposed to the Air Force in 1981

The LCSSB configuration was very similar to the original baseline vehicle in the 1969 NASA study. The booster had three pressure-fed stages, with a first-stage thrust of 30.25 million Newtons (6.8 million pounds). The first stage used four engines, each with a thrust of 7.56 million Newtons (1.7 million pounds). These four engines were identical to the second-stage engine, except that the first-stage engines had a higher chamber pressure and an expansion ratio of 6:1 (for sea-level/low-altitude operations), compared with the second-stage engine expansion ratio of 31:1 (for high-altitude/vacuum operations). Keeping the designs of the first- and second-stage engines essentially the same would have kept development costs down. The booster had a payload capacity to low earth orbit of 29,756 kilograms (65,600 pounds) when launching due east from Cape Canaveral. When launching into a 90-degree polar orbit, the LCSSB had a lift capacity of 23,178 kilograms (51,100 pounds). The system had a launch cost for production vehicles of $59.2 million per launch (including all launch processing and support costs). This equated to a cost of $1,989 per kilogram ($901 per pound) to LEO, assuming an easterly launch (see table 9).[55]

Under Secretary of the Air Force Pete Aldridge encountered a storm of opposition from NASA and some members of Congress when he sought funding in the mid-1980s (pre-*Challenger*) for a small buy of Titan complementary expendable launch vehicles to augment the Shuttle fleet. It is therefore not surprising that the concept for the LCSSB, formally proposed one month after the first successful Shuttle flight, ended up going nowhere.

The SEALAR Development Effort

Truax Engineering, Inc. (TEI) has championed the original Aerojet Sea Dragon concept since the late 1960s. TEI developed a phased approach for a family of launch vehicles that led up to Sea Dragon. Starting with a small single-stage sea launch and recovery demonstrator designated the X3, TEI proposed to follow with a booster having a Shuttle-class lift capability. Called Excalibur, it was to be essentially a scaled-down version of Sea Dragon. These developmental precursors would lead ultimately to the fielding of an operational Sea Dragon launch system.[56]

In 1988, the Naval Research Laboratory's Naval Center for Space Technology (NCST) issued a broad area announcement for the SEALAR (Sea Launch and Recovery) concept, and TEI was the successful bidder.[57] NCST called for the SEALAR program to use the design-for-minimum-cost methodology as the booster's guiding design criteria. The Navy wanted a simple, two-stage, launch system that could lift 4,500 kilograms (10,000 pounds) to low earth orbit. TEI proposed a down-sized Excalibur design, appropriately named Sub-Calibur, which was one-eightieth the size of the original Sea Dragon concept.[58]

Work moved forward over the next several years. There were a number of static tests of X3 vehicle variants, as well as drop tests from a helicopter into Monterey Bay, California.[59] The X3 test articles represented near-scale demonstrators of the SubCalibur's first stage.

Progress on the SEALAR program was so encouraging that in 1990 the Senate Armed Services Committee praised the program, increased the Navy's 1991 SEALAR budget request by 900 percent, and called for a competition between SEALAR and the Air Force's Advanced Launch System (ALS) program. The Committee's report on the FY91 defense budget said that SEALAR could lower launch costs and increase operational responsiveness "for a fraction of the cost of the Air Force's advanced launch system." The report characterized the ALS development program as being "entirely unrealistic."[60]

Despite a promising start, the SEALAR program as originally envisioned did not come to fruition. An X3 test vehicle suffered a tank failure after repeated pressurization cycles, and the NCST decided to finish fabrication of a flight test demonstrator "in house." The vehicle was close to achieving its first flight when the Navy terminated funding in late 1991.

Another Lost Opportunity for MCD Booster Development

In August 1987 an article that appeared in *Newsweek* generated a renewed interest in the concept of using minimum-cost design techniques to develop low-cost launch vehicles.[61] The Office of Technology Assessment (OTA) conducted a workshop in December 1987 to allow discussion of the concept among aerospace community experts.[62] Although the OTA findings were generally favorable toward simple, low-cost booster designs, there was a prevailing perception that the Advanced Launch System program already embraced most of the principles of designing for minimum cost.[63] The opportunity to reestablish an initiative for developing simple, cost-optimized space boosters was lost.

Current Low-Cost Booster Development Efforts

There have been several recent proposals to develop new launch systems that are based, at least to some extent, on minimum-cost design principles. There are a number of motivations behind these proposals, including the continued erosion of the US launch industry's market share; the continuing need for lower launch costs (especially among the smallsat community); the failure of government and/or industry to develop a clear path to drastically reducing launch costs; and the intuitive, as well as quantifiable, benefits of simple, low-cost designs.

The McDonnell Douglas Delta Replacement

The McDonnell Douglas Space Systems Company (MDSSC), in a cooperative effort with Allied Signal and TRW Space Systems Group, is defining a family of low-cost launch vehicles. These concepts are an outgrowth of the Advanced Launch System Phase A studies. The near-term goal is to develop a commercial substitute for the Delta launch vehicle that will provide lower launch costs and ensure MDSSC a healthy niche in the future commercial launch market. A variety of growth options, with payload capacities up to 226,800 kilograms (500,000 pounds) to LEO, have been proposed.[64]

The heart of the MDSSC concept revolves around three key design features. The Delta-class vehicle is configured to use an all-welded monocoque structure, simple TRW-developed engines using ablative cooling and pintle injector technology, and low-pressure, stage-mounted, turbopump assemblies using Allied Signal-developed foil bearing technology.[65] MDSSC views the low-pressure turbopumps as an optimal compromise between complex high-pressure turbomachinery with ultra-lightweight tanks, and pressure-fed systems with heavier tanks. The TRW engines use liquid hydrogen and liquid oxygen for propellants, although RP-1 is still being studied for use as a first-stage fuel. An 88,960-Newton (20,000-pound)-thrust engine using TRW's low-cost engine design of the late 1960s has been extensively and successfully tested using LOX and hydrogen at NASA's Lewis Research Center. MDSSC projects 50 to 70 percent cost savings over current Delta prices. The Marshall Space Flight Center reviewed the initial proposals and concluded that the concept has promise but that some major technology questions must still be answered.[66]

The PacAstro Smallsat Booster

Rick Fleeter and Robert Leppo founded the PacAstro company in 1990 with the express purpose of developing and marketing a small launch vehicle that would be optimized for low cost and would meet the needs of the small satellite community. Since then, PacAstro has established a partnership with TRW for the marketing of launch services and the development and supply of the launch vehicle engines.[67] PacAstro plans to keep the launch price minimized by achieving low development costs, low hardware recurring costs, and low launch operations costs. The company believes that the key to minimizing development costs is to use simple, affordable, and off-the-shelf components as much as possible, and the PacAstro booster design reflects this philosophy.[68]

The PacAstro vehicle is an expendable two-stage pressure-fed booster with a capability for launching a payload of 250 kilograms (550 pounds) into a 750-kilometer (466-mile) altitude polar orbit.[69] The vehicle, which uses liquid oxygen and RP-1 as propellants for both stages, has a first-stage thrust of 310,000 Newtons (69,700 pounds).[70] PacAstro estimates the total launch cost to be $5 million (in FY93 costs), resulting in a per kilogram cost to orbit of $20,000 ($9,090 per pound) for a 750-kilometer polar orbit.[71] Although these costs are higher than those of existing large expendable launch vehicles, they are very competitive with existing small satellite launcher costs.

The Norwegian and Swedish space agencies have tentatively chosen PacAstro to supply boosters for polar launches from the Andoya Rocket Range in northern Norway, starting in 1996. The space agencies plan to launch up to eight small payloads annually using the PacAstro vehicle.[72]

The Microcosm Ultra-Low-Cost Booster

Microcosm, Inc. is proposing to develop an ultra-low-cost, expendable launch system that is to be optimized for the lowest possible cost. The booster's configuration bears some resemblance to the Boeing MCD launch vehicle design that was developed for the Air Force in the late 1960s. The proposed launch vehicle would have a payload capacity to low earth orbit of 6,232 kilograms (13,740 pounds). The vehicle design clusters six nearly identical strap-ons around a central core, with the payload on top. The core vehicle uses the same design as the six strap-ons, except it includes the payload and payload fairing. The core vehicle and strap-ons all employ pressure-fed propulsion systems that use liquid oxygen and RP-1 for propellants. They also each use multiple engines, and the propellant feed systems are cross-strapped so that all of the launch vehicle's engines can use propellant from only two sets of propellant tanks at a time. All engines are burning in parallel at lift-off.[73]

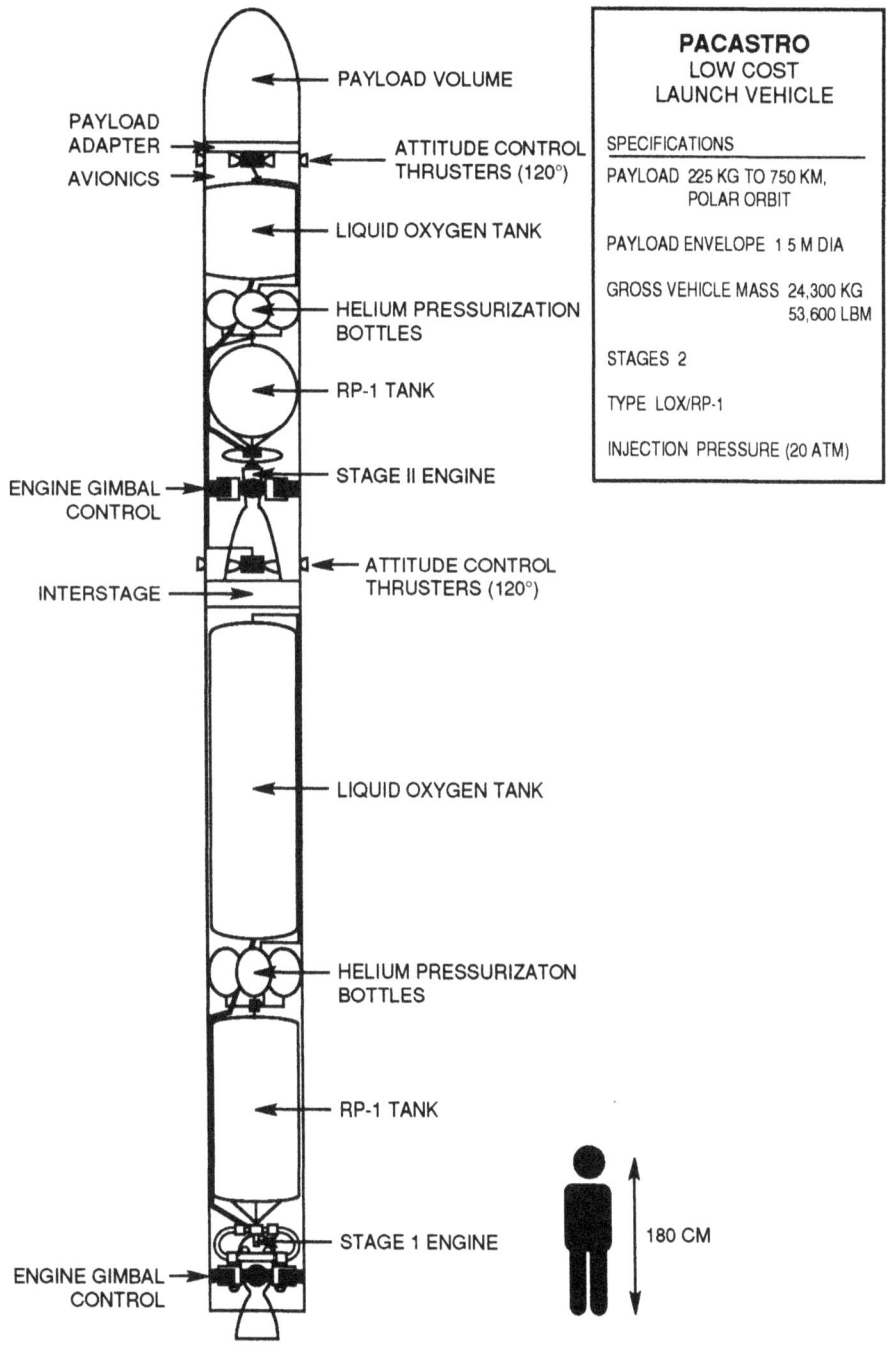

Figure 12. PacAstro low cost launch vehicle

Booster steering is accomplished through thrust magnitude control, which varies the thrust levels of appropriate engines during ascent through a network of propellant valves. This steering technique has enabled vehicle designers to

195

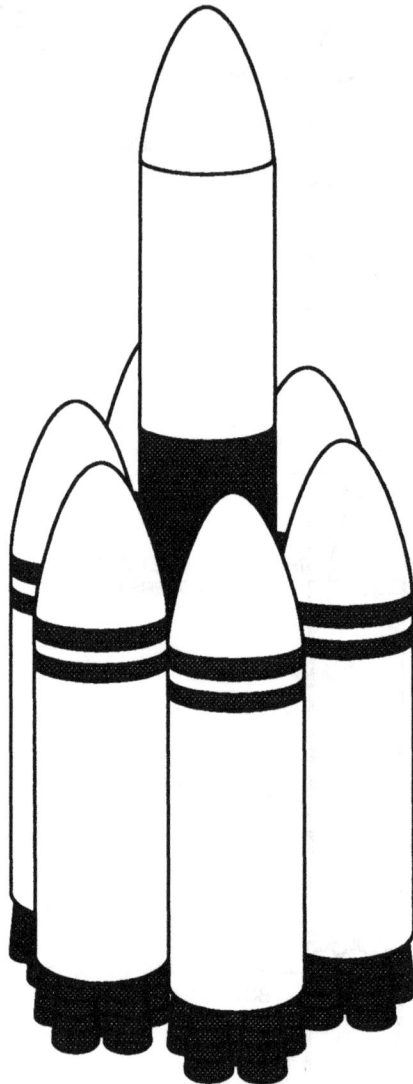

Figure 13. Microcosm's ultra-low cost launch vehicle concept, which uses pressure-fed LOX/RP-1 engines and parallel staging

avoid complex and costly thrust vector control hardware such as actuators, hydraulic systems, or liquid injection thrust vector control systems.[74]

The staging sequence results in a four-stage vehicle. At lift-off, all engines are feeding off the propellant from two opposite strap-ons. These strap-on tanks are separated when empty, constituting the end of stage one. The process is repeated for stages two and three, until only the core vehicle (and payload), containing a full load of propellant, is left to accomplish the fourth-stage burn.[75]

The booster's multiple identical engines and propellant tank sets not only keep the nonrecurring development costs low, but they also create opportunities for manufacturing economies of scale through high production rates. Mi-

196

crocosm views low development costs as key to achieving a new launch vehicle program start in today's federal and commercial budget climate.[76]

On 26 April 1993, the Air Force awarded Microcosm a Phase I small business innovative research (SBIR) contract to further refine their booster concept and study its potential application for future DOD launch requirements. Microcosm is hoping to pursue a Phase II SBIR that will lead to the development of demonstration and test hardware.[77]

Summary

There is not today a level of enthusiasm for minimum-cost launch vehicles to match the excitement within the Air Force and the aerospace industry in the late 1960s. However, the continuing burden of high launch costs is forcing government and industry to continue to seek a low-cost launch solution.

The numerous and widely varying concepts currently being proposed to achieve lower space transportation costs can be broadly allocated to two groups of supporters. One group seeks to reduce launch costs through one or more technological leaps (the futurists). This approach is characterized by generally high-risk and expensive development programs accompanied by the promise that operational costs will be so low that the development program is justified. The other group seeks to lower costs by doing what we currently do better and more efficiently (the pragmatists). This approach is characterized by more modest technological requirements and lower-risk development programs.

Designing a very simple launch vehicle with achievement of the lowest possible life cycle cost being the dominant consideration is clearly in the latter category. It represents the design philosophy that is most different from the technological leap approach. The concept of designing a launch vehicle for minimum cost has been studied by government agencies and the aerospace industry many times over the years, and the results have consistently indicated that huge reductions in launch costs are available using this technique.

Unfortunately, the arrival of the Space Shuttle concept, which was seen in the late 1960s as the answer for reducing high launch costs, combined with aerospace industry concerns about the loss of launch vehicle production profits and combined with a general inclination and desire for high technology solutions, has prevented the MCD approach from moving off the paper stage to flight hardware. It is time to seriously explore the application of minimum-cost design techniques for developing a new low-cost launch system—a system that could facilitate a broad expansion of space exploitation activities.

Notes

1. Naval Center for Space Technology, *Sea Launch and Recovery (SEALAR)—System Concept to Launch Brilliant Pebbles* (Washington, D.C.: Naval Research Laboratory, January 1992), 17.

2. R. C. Truax and J. D. Ryan, "Sea Launch of Rocket Vehicles" (SAE 433A, presented at the 1961 National Aeronautic and Space Engineering and Manufacturing Meeting, Los Angeles, Calif., 13 October 1961), 6–7.

3. Robert C. Truax, "Sea Dragon in the Manned Mars Mission," *The Journal of Practical Applications in Space,* Fall 1990, 8.

4. R. A. Raffety, "Sea Launch Flight Test Program of a Liquid-Propellant Rocket," Aerojet-General Corporation, 20 November 1961, supplement to SAE paper 433A, presented 13 October 1961, 1.

5. Ibid., 4–6.

6. R. C. Truax, "Cheap Transportation for Cheap Satellites" (Paper presented at the AIAA/DARPA Meeting on Lightweight Satellite Systems, Monterey, Calif., 4–6 August 1987), 2.

7. William H. Ganoe, "Rockets from the Sea," *Ad Astra,* July/August 1990, 71.

8. Robert C. Truax, "Thousand Tons to Orbit," *Astronautics,* January 1963, 45.

9. H. G. Campbell, *A Cost Analysis of Large Booster Systems for Planetary Exploration* (Santa Monica, Calif.: RAND Corporation, August 1963), 6.

10. Truax Engineering, Inc., Sea Dragon Launch Vehicle data sheet, Saratoga, Calif., no date.

11. Truax, "Thousand Tons to Orbit," 45–46.

12. Ibid., 45.

13. Truax, "Cheap Transportation for Cheap Satellites," 2, 4.

14. *Study of Large Sea-Launch Space Vehicle,* vol. 3, summary report, contract no. NAS8-2599 (Redondo Beach, Calif.: Space Technology Laboratories, Inc./Aerojet General Corporation, January 1963), 3–15.

15. Truax, "Sea Dragon in the Manned Mars Mission," 2.

16. "Project Private Enterprise—A Commercial Space Transport Program," Truax Engineering, Inc., Saratoga, Calif., 1984, 7; *Study of Large Sea-Launch Space Vehicle,* 1-3.

17. Truax, "Sea Dragon in the Manned Mars Mission," 8; *Study of Large Sea-Launch Space Vehicle,* 1-2, 1-3, 1-4.

18. Ganoe.

19. A. Schnitt and Colonel F. W. Kniss, "Proposed Minimum Cost Space Launch Vehicle System," TOR-0158(3415-15)-1 (El Segundo, Calif.: 1 July 1968), 1-1.

20. Walter Tydon, *Minimum Cost Design Launch Vehicle Design/Costing Study,* vol. 2, *Background Studies,* TOR-0059(6526-01)-2 (El Segundo, Calif.: The Aerospace Corporation, 31 July 1970), 1-2.

21. John R. London III, "The Ultimate Standoff Weapon," *Airpower Journal,* Summer 1993, 67.

22. Tydon.

23. Ibid., 4–6.

24. Schnitt and Kniss, 3–17.

25. Tydon.

26. Gregg Easterbrook, "Big Dumb Rockets," *Newsweek,* 17 August 1987, 46.

27. Tydon, 1-3.

28. Ibid., 4-7.

29. Ibid., 4-8, 4-9.

30. Ibid., 4-10.

31. Ibid., 4-11.

32. Schnitt and Kniss, 1-1, 1-2.

33. Tydon, 1-2, 1-3.

34. R. M. Allman, "Minimum-Cost-Design Space Launch Vehicle," briefing to The Aerospace Corporation Board of Trustees ad hoc committee on space systems costs, El Segundo, Calif., 25 September 1987.

35. Tydon, 4-1, 4-13.

36. Ibid., 4-13, 4-17.

37. Ibid., 4-13, 4-18.

38. Ibid., 4-13, 4-19, 4-20, 4-21.

39. Ibid., 4-22.

40. Ibid., 4-24, 4-25.

41. Ibid., 4-23.

42. Ibid., 5-1.

43. Walter Tydon, *Minimum Cost Design Launch Vehicle Design/Costing Study,* vol. 1, *Summary,* TOR-0059(6526-01)-2 (El Segundo, Calif.: The Aerospace Corporation, 31 July 1970), 11.

44. Ibid., 11–15.

45. Walter Tydon, *Minimum Cost Design Launch Vehicle Design/Costing Study,* vol. 3, *Critique of Boeing MCD Study,* TOR-0059(6526-01)-2 (El Segundo, Calif.: The Aerospace Corporation, 31 July 1970), 3-2.

46. Tydon, vol. 1, 17.

47. David J. Teal, "Minimum Cost Design Space Launch Vehicle Management Plan," SAMSO-TR-70-185, Space and Missile Systems Organization, Los Angeles AFS, Calif., 1970, iii/iv, I-1.

48. Tydon, vol. 2, 4-13, 4-14.

49. TRW Systems Group, "Low Cost Launch Vehicle Study," final briefing, NASA contract no. NASw-1792, Redondo Beach, Calif., 23 June 1969, 1.6–1.9.

50. Ibid.

51. Allman.

52. Walter A. McDougall, *The Heavens and the Earth* (New York: Basic Books, Inc., 1985), 421.

53. D. E. Fritz and R. L. Sackheim, "Study of a Cost Optimized Pressure Fed Liquid Rocket Launch Vehicle" (Paper presented at the AIAA/SAE/ASME 18th Joint Propulsion Conference, Cleveland, Ohio, 21–23 June 1982), 1.

54. TRW, Inc., "Low Cost Shuttle Surrogate Booster (LCSSB)," final report (Redondo Beach, Calif., 15 May 1981), 1.

55. Ibid., 35, 46, 47, 109.

56. "Project Private Enterprise—A Commercial Space Transport Program," 10.

57. Ganoe.

58. Proposal for SEALAR Program, Truax Engineering, Inc., Saratoga, Calif., 1988, A-2.

59. "Test Successful on Scale Model SEALAR Vehicle," *Sea Technology,* July 1990, 66.

60. "Panel Seeks Competition of Navy, USAF Launchers," *Aviation Week & Space Technology,* 30 July 1990, 28.

61. Easterbrook, 46–60.

62. Office of Technology Assessment, *Big Dumb Boosters - A Low Cost Space Transportation Option?* (Washington, D.C.: Government Printing Office, February 1989), 1.

63. Allman.

64. J. P. Henneberry et al., "Low-Cost Expendable Launch Vehicles" (Paper presented at the AIAA/SAE/ASME/ASEE 28th Joint Propulsion Conference and Exhibit, Nashville, Tenn., 6–8 July 1992), 1, 14.

65. Ibid., 2, 4, 14.

66. Marshall Space Flight Center, Heavy Lift Launch Vehicle Definition Office, An Assessment of the McDonnell Douglas Space Systems Company Low Cost Vehicle Family, NASA Report, Huntsville, Ala., 27 July 1992.

67. PacAstro Summary data sheet, PacAstro, Herndon, Virginia, 1992.

68. Rick Fleeter to John London, letter, 28 September 1992.

69. Ibid.

70. PacAstro, "A Low Cost Expendable Launch Vehicle for 500-Pound Class Satellites," submitted to the Strategic Defense Initiative Organization (Herndon, Va., 26 May 1992).

71. Fleeter to London, letter.

72. Peter B. de Selding, "U.S. Firm Enlisted for Small Satellite Launches," *Space News,* 22–28 February 1993, 8.

73. Edward L. Keith, "System Analysis and Description of an Ultra-Low Cost Ground to Low Earth Orbit Cargo Delivery System" (Paper presented at the World Space Congress, Washington, D.C., 31 August 1992), 4, 5, 9.

74. Ibid., 7.
75. Ibid., 5.
76. Ibid.
77. Bob Conger, Microcosm, Inc., telephone conversation with author, 9 June 1993

Chapter 10

Conclusions and Recommendations

To achieve drastic reductions in the cost of space transportation, the US must take a number of specific steps. The US commercial launch industry is currently at great risk of being increasingly diminished or even eliminated by foreign competition. Without an injection of cost-cutting leadership by the US government in this area, future low-cost boosters may be made only in other countries. US spacecraft builders seeking inexpensive space access could be held hostage to foreign launch suppliers. Additionally, the failure of the US commercial launch industry would represent the loss of a national technical and defense treasure, billions of dollars in commercial revenue, and numerous jobs. It is therefore critically important that the US government invest in the country's future by immediately initiating efforts to radically drive down space launch costs.

This study has sought to identify the nature of high launch costs and reasons for them, and to offer some practical ways to reduce these costs. In this chapter, we will first provide overall conclusions of the study. We then will make specific recommendations on actions that the US government, in partnership with US industry, should take to finally achieve the kind of launch cost reductions that will enable an explosion of space exploitation. We will cover recommendations for making a national commitment to develop a low-cost booster, for specific design characteristics of an inexpensive launch system designed for minimum cost, and for some changes in space launch policy—including a recommended future path for the Space Shuttle and manned space flight.

Conclusions

The United States needs a means of space access that costs much less than current launch systems. The drawdown in defense spending is causing tremendous turbulence and large cutbacks in the US aerospace industry. It is also having a negative effect on the lives of many of America's skilled aerospace workers. A shrinking US military is becoming increasingly dependent on the force-multiplying characteristics of space systems to compensate for the loss of force structure. Foreign competition continues to chip away at the US commercial launch industry. A dramatic expansion in military, civil, and commercial space initiatives could help fuel a technology-based economic revitalization in the United States, but this expansion will not come about unless drastic reductions in space launch costs are achieved.

Faced with the threat of low-cost foreign launch competition, the US should not continue to pursue protectionist methods to preserve the existing US launch vehicle industry. The issue should not be how to protect the US industry status quo—the issue should be how can the US launch industry develop vehicles with low enough launch costs to cause commercial space business to take off. If this occurs, the US launch industry will be able to take care of itself.

A simple expendable launch vehicle that is designed for minimum cost holds the promise of achieving long-sought order-of-magnitude reductions in space launch cost. Although such a vehicle has been proposed a number of times since the 1960s, there has never been a serious government-sponsored effort to put hardware on the launch pad. There needs to be a serious effort now.

The argument that a simple MCD booster using a suboptimized propulsion system would cost too much because of its weight simply does not hold water. MCD booster proponents ought to have a chance to prove what they believe—and the cost to do so is not prohibitive.

Because of the low development costs for an MCD booster, the development could be affordably accomplished in parallel with one or more competing development efforts for completely different launch systems. For the cost of many aerospace system paper studies, an MCD booster could be developed and launched. The simple nature of an MCD vehicle design, using existing technology and hardware, would accommodate reliable program cost estimates that would instill Congressional and public confidence in the program's ultimate success. If the Ballistic Missile Defense Organization and McDonnell Douglas can design, manufacture, and launch a fairly sophisticated aerospace vehicle like the DC-X for less than $70 million and in under two years, a very simple MCD booster prototype should be able to be built and flown to low earth orbit with a similar budget and schedule. Because of the extremely wide diversity of opinions about which design approach is best for a future US launch system, and because of the bad experience of "stove-piping" our national resources onto one launch system that did not live up to its advanced billing (the Space Shuttle), it makes good sense to pursue several launch vehicle concept alternatives. A booster designed for minimum cost should be one of them.

An ultra-low-cost launch system cannot be developed using traditional government acquisition practices. A large number of personnel, heavy documentation requirements, complicated and time-consuming procedural compliance, and an almost inevitable complexity in design are all associated with the typical acquisition of an aerospace system. These traditional acquisition characteristics will drive the cost of the launch system well above what anyone would consider low. Therefore, the program for developing a low-cost launch system must be accomplished in a highly streamlined manner. This doesn't mean that the system should be developed without proper oversight, but the program should be afforded a high enough priority that the oversight can be both limited and conducted at a very high level. And a high program priority should not imply large funding levels.

The development of a launch system designed for minimum cost may not be possible using traditional aerospace industry design and manufacturing methods. Robert Truax said: "I sometimes doubt whether an industry that designs $250 toilet seats is organically capable of producing a low-cost launch vehicle. Big, complex organizations tend to produce big, complex solutions, even to simple problems."[1] The aerospace industry must take a revolutionary approach to addressing the problem of high launch costs, and the government must be innovative in seeking industrial sources to design and build low-cost boosters.

Proponents of advanced technology solutions to reduce launch costs often characterize existing expendable launch vehicles as "boosters that are using decades-old technology." The problem with these boosters, however, is not that their *technology* is decades old; the problem is that their *designs* are decades wrong.

A simple, staged, expendable launch system designed with existing technology is not very exciting technically. It will probably not capture the imagination of the majority of technically oriented people in government and industry. Similarly, an eighteen-wheel truck does not evoke a lot of technical excitement, but it is vital to our economy. Gerard Elverum of TRW commented about the bias against a launch vehicle program that does not use cutting-edge technology: "It's really frustrating to be told, 'Yes, this is a great idea, but it doesn't advance the technology'."[2] A lack of technical sophistication should not be allowed to stand in the way of moving the program forward. It will take leadership and a zeal for cutting launch costs to shepherd this concept through the approval process. People must take hold of the idea that the low-cost booster is a means to achieve some highly desirable ends; and they should focus on these ends when considering the merits of the launch system.

Recommendations

1. Make a national commitment to develop a designed-for-minimum-cost (DFMC) launch system that will meet both military and civil space launch needs *and* compete commercially against all foreign boosters and surplus strategic missiles. DOD and NASA sorely need a low-cost launch capability to reduce space system life-cycle costs—and a domestically available inexpensive booster would be an important national security asset. Additionally, the survival of the US commercial launch industry will likely depend on the development of a launch capability that is priced lower than the foreign competition. The Spacelifter concept proposed in November 1992 by Pete Aldridge's National Space Council working group took a step in the right direction by moving away from the National Launch System's "family of vehicles" ap-

proach. If the November 1992 Spacelifter concept were to be designed under a DFMC criteria like the Aerospace or Boeing methodologies of the 1960s, an even simpler, less-expensive configuration than the current concept could emerge.

2. Do not plan for the minimum cost design (MCD) booster to rally political support because numerous congressional districts have a piece of the program. A launch system that is designed for minimum cost must not consume large amounts of federal funding for development or operations. Geographically spreading pieces of the program would ensure a complicated integration task, large manpower requirements, and high costs. The MCD booster will not be a jobs program, although the long-term impact of such a launch capability will create many new jobs through the development of a large agenda of affordable space exploitation. To keep costs minimized, the vehicle must be developed by a small, tightly integrated government/industry team. The program must garner political support based on merit.

3. Impart a vision to government, industry, and the American people that the MCD launch system is the cornerstone for greatly expanded space exploitation. Some launch industry executives have been understandably apprehensive about the development of a new low-cost launch system. They feel it represents the threat of one contractor (the MCD launch vehicle competition winner) cornering the market on launch vehicles, with no customers available to buy any of the current fleet of expensive (but profitable) launch vehicles. However, a drastic reduction in space launch costs will likely create a huge increase in space initiatives and a corresponding demand for industry to develop a host of new space systems to support these initiatives. In the long term, the aerospace industry stands to make big gains through the availability of inexpensive space access.

Keeping the cost of expendable launch vehicles in the $50 million to $200 million range and garnering a profit from the sale of a few of them is analogous to the automobile industry keeping car prices at $1 million a copy and selling 500 cars annually. Automobile manufacturers have found it much more profitable to mass produce and sell millions of cars at much lower prices.

Another analogy is the development of new commercial transport aircraft. The US aircraft industry doesn't wait for the government to fund the development of new and improved aircraft. Because the commercial transportation market is so large and well established, companies invest their own money to develop more competitive designs.

Once an MCD booster is operational and the demand for space launch begins to increase due to the low launch costs, there will be nothing to prevent private companies from using their own capital to develop competing boosters built to the DFMC criteria. The increased market demand for launchers, coupled with the intrinsically low development costs of DFMC designs, should make commercial development efforts profitable. Also, the development of competing MCD boosters will provide multiple sources of launchers to the US government. And since more than one MCD booster will be operational, the

204

government can safely and confidently move away from existing expendable boosters without placing all of its launch eggs in one MCD booster basket.

4. Approach the application of MCD principles to space boosters from the standpoint of "How can we make this work?" as opposed to "What's wrong with this idea?"

5. Establish a policy that says the government-sponsored MCD booster will provide only a standard interface and limited services to satellite customers. Although satellite builders will initially complain about this policy, the market forces created by the greatly reduced launch costs of the MCD booster will ultimately drive commercial spacecraft manufacturers to comply. This policy will benefit the satellite community in the long run because it will enable manufacturers to develop inexpensive launchers, and less-expensive spacecraft designs, which will encourage expanded demand.

6. Embrace a management philosophy that says it is appropriate to take well-considered risks and that it is acceptable to occasionally fail. View failure as an important learning tool in the development of aerospace systems. Be willing to conduct a developmental flight test, even if there is an above-average risk of failure, when the flight test is less expensive and more comprehensive than a complicated series of ground simulations.

MCD Booster Specifics

7. Establish a small but highly empowered program office to develop, with a clean-sheet approach, a new launch vehicle that is designed for minimum cost. The program office should have fewer than 10 people, be organizationally "flat," and have a drastically truncated chain-of-command.

8. Give the program office a small budget. A very inexpensive booster must necessarily be inexpensive to develop because a launch system designed for minimum cost will depend on existing hardware and technologies, simple design and manufacturing techniques, and commercial (versus government/aerospace) standards and practices. If the program has a large budget, it will likely have large development and recurring costs. Also, large budgets attract large numbers of government and contractor personnel, which compounds program costs and complexity. Finally, a small budget will help to minimize the number of costly and time-consuming oversight and review boards the program is subjected to since it should stay below the large program budget threshold.

9. Establish a tight schedule for the program to ensure that it either comes to fruition quickly or fails quickly. This country's need for a low-cost launcher is so acute that solutions must be found in a hurry. A compressed schedule will keep the program, its management team, and its contractors highly focused. Additionally, a tight schedule will serve as a forcing function to ensure that the system design stays simple and inexpensive.

BMDO's Single Stage Rocket Technology (SSRT) program is a good example of a development effort that has made extraordinary strides despite a small budget and a compressed schedule. Given the relative complexity of the

DC-X vehicle, it is reasonable to expect that a simple MCD booster could be developed with similar budget and schedule limitations.

10. Develop an acquisition strategy that provides strong contractual incentives for developing very low-cost vehicles, encourages nontraditional thinking and creativity, and carries at least three competing contractors to the point of flying prototype launchers. The overriding bottom line of the program must be minimum cost within a specified launch capacity range and an acceptable reliability level. Prospective contractors should challenge the traditional high-cost methods of government-sponsored aerospace development. Make it clear to contractors that current methods of aerospace system acquisition are not sacrosanct.

The development budget should be big enough to allow the government to carry multiple competing contractors through the development process. This should be acceptable, since the overall program budget (relative to other proposed new launch system development budgets) would still be small. Colonel Ralph Gajewski, program manager for the Brilliant Eyes satellite system, extolled the virtues of having competing contractors when he said, "You can have one contractor for the price of two, or you can have two contractors for the price of two."[3] Competition can be a powerful influence in motivating contractor efficiency and performance, especially when billions of dollars of potential follow-on production work hangs in the balance.

11. Look both inside and outside traditional aerospace launch industry circles for prospective contractors. The offering should be crafted to encourage small, burgeoning launch companies and appropriate nonaerospace companies to compete. The simple nature of the MCD booster ought to lengthen the list of commercial firms that could realistically compete and deliver a workable solution.

12. Establish the requirement (mandatory) that the MCD booster reduce launch costs by at least two-thirds, with a cost reduction goal (highly desirable) of an order of magnitude. Evaluate competing contractors against their accomplishment of the requirement and the goal.

13. Keep development costs sufficiently low to avoid the need for long-term amortization strategies. Do not depend on high flight rates or large mission models to amortize development costs.

14. Use only those technologies that are necessary to achieve minimum cost designs. Make it clear from the outset, to both government and industry, that the development of an MCD booster will not serve as a mechanism to push any technologies or to advance the state-of-the-art.

15. Design the launch vehicle to be unmanned and expendable. This will allow simple designs and large production runs. The government should establish a strategy for appropriate vehicle hardware and stages to become reusable eventually, but this strategy must not impose any design penalties on the initial expendable system that would increase its development or operating costs. The reusability strategies should emphasize water recovery, with parachutes or other simple drag-inducing devices used for booster components.

16. Consider using interfaces minimization and the total vehicle part count as contractor measures of merit. Such criteria would force simple designs and low-cost development and operations.

17. Ensure that contractors maximize the use of off-the-shelf hardware and off-the-shelf technology. Using existing hardware and technology will turn the vehicle development process into largely an integration exercise. Development costs and risks will be very low. Off-the-shelf hardware components that have maximum performance/minimum weight cost and complexity liabilities should not be used.

18. Design the MCD launch vehicle to be optimized for minimum cost and suboptimized with regard to performance and weight.

19. Make the documentation system paperless and extremely limited in quantity. Desktop computers and local area networks have already made paperless documentation systems practical. The inherent simplicity of the DFMC vehicle should allow significant reductions compared to traditional aerospace system documentation. The government can further decrease documentation by drastically reducing, or eliminating altogether, requirements for documentation such as contractor data requirements lists and military standards and specifications compliance. Reducing documentation, of course, will also reduce manpower requirements and budgets in all phases of the launch system's life cycle. The Strategic Defense Initiative Organization (now BMDO) was very successful in cutting costs and compressing schedules on a number of programs by specifying that the contractor should "use best engineering judgment" instead of trying to legislate performance and quality by requiring contractual compliance to a mountain of government regulations and specifications.

20. Design the MCD booster with robust and forgiving design margins. This will provide for easier and less expensive manufacturing, allow a decrease in testing and inspection requirements, accommodate reductions in redundant system requirements, and result in a more reliable system.

21. Design the launch vehicle to minimize requirements for redundant systems. The booster's large design margins and simple design should allow engineers to reduce the number of redundant systems and still have a vehicle that is more reliable than current launch systems.

22. Design the booster to use only one liquid propellant combination. Specifying a single propellant combination creates opportunities for common propulsion component designs between stages. The use of liquid propellants simplifies manufacturing and operating practices. Propellant design choices should focus on liquid oxygen/hydrocarbon combinations because they are inexpensive, simple to design to, and relatively easy to handle. Also, they have been widely used for many years. Liquid hydrogen should be avoided despite being very energetic as a fuel, because its extremely low boiling temperature, high volume requirements, and propensity for leaking through most seals render it not amenable to simple MCD designs.

23. Focus on engine, propellant tankage, and pressurization systems that use pressure-fed designs or very simple pump designs. Turbomachinery is a

major contributor to engine complexity and cost. DFMC boosters that are suboptimized for performance and weight should not require the types of complex turbomachinery that are typical today.

24. Incorporate features of parallel staging and modularity, and design the vehicle with high production rates in mind. Such an approach will accommodate common designs and manufacturing economies of scale.

25. Minimize vehicle instrumentation requirements. The simple and robust nature of the vehicle design should make significant reductions in instrumentation achievable and appropriate. Instrumentation reductions will not only reduce booster complexity and cost, but will also reduce the requirements for remote monitoring collection and display systems as well as for manpower to interpret the data.

26. Design the launch control system to be small and to require very few personnel to operate. One van of equipment and people should be the upper limit. BMDO's SSRT program is a good example of the minimal launch control that is a fundamental requirement for low-cost launch operations.

27. Accomplish tracking and telemetry collection by using methods that do not require the use of costly terrestrial-based range support. Examples of space-based systems that could provide the needed support are NASA's Tracking and Data Relay Satellite System (TDRSS) and DOD's Global Positioning System (GPS). Elimination of dependence on existing range support infrastructure will not only save operational costs—it will also free launch systems to operate from many geographic locations.

Policy Changes and Initiatives

28. Investigate different launch basing strategies for future launch vehicles. Candidate strategies should include sea launch, air launch, and transportable launch. These different launch strategies could be particularly applicable to small boosters developed to the DFMC criteria. The benefits of such strategies include the ability to select the optimum launch points for a particular mission's requirements (not being tied to an existing launch base infrastructure), as well as the ability to minimize the launch system's support personnel. The late Thomas O. Paine, NASA Administrator during the Apollo Program, once said the reason the Pegasus booster needed to be launched from a B-52 was to limit the number of launch support participants.[4]

29. Investigate the use of additional booster capability (made affordable by the DFMC design) as a means of compensating for less-than-optimum launch site locations. This would be an alternative to the launch strategies that optimize launch points through mobility.

30. Completely scrub, from top to bottom, the way the US conducts launch operations. A large number of functions and organizations have become institutionalized and bureaucratically entrenched. These programs continue to expand in manpower, equipment, and cost. Each program should justify its activities—item by item, requirement by requirement. Analogous functions in aircraft operations should be considered for comparison. If the responsible

organizations for each of these launch operations functions cannot make a strong case to continue into the 1990s and beyond, they should be pared back or eliminated.

31. Find the right programmatic home for the DFMC booster and for the SSRT-derived SSTO programs. If they are allocated to a traditional program office environment, these programs will probably fail to achieve their promise of low launch cost.

32. Pursue the NASP concept at a relatively low—but steady—funding level and treat it strictly as a long-term hypersonics technology program. Do not plan for it to ultimately become a carrier of payloads to low earth orbit.

33. Define a joint program for MCD satellites to be developed in conjunction with the development of MCD boosters. Such an arrangement will "build-in" synergism between the MCD launch system and satellites designed to take advantage of the booster's large, low-cost capacity.

34. Develop plans for phasing out the Space Shuttle by the end of the 1990s—sooner if possible. The oppressive weight of the Shuttle's annual operating budget is hamstringing NASA's ability to prosecute other important projects. The deployment of a US space station will diminish the Shuttle's utility to almost zero unless it is the only launch system available for ferrying crews to and from the station.

35. Optimize unmanned launch systems for minimum cost and manned launch systems for maximum safety. Never again design a launch system to carry both personnel and payloads; do not design new unmanned systems to have a "man-rateable" option.

36. Develop an interim capability for carrying astronauts into low earth orbit and returning them to earth. Developing this interim capability would allow phaseout of the Shuttle without creating a US manned launch capability gap. Options for such an interim human spaceflight capability should center on the simplest and least expensive designs possible so that they will be affordable in the current budget environment and be fully operational before the end of the decade. One possibility is to develop a low lift-to-drag manned capsule similar to those used for the Mercury, Gemini, and Apollo Programs. To minimize recovery expenses and crew risk, the capsule should be recovered on land, probably at some appropriate site in the southwest US; for example, White Sands Missile Range. Although returning people from space in a capsule and landing them in the desert by parachute may be viewed by some as "inelegant," it is likely to be the least expensive and most expedient method to develop.[5]

Another possibility for an interim astronaut transport capability would be to exploit the existing Russian Soyuz manned spacecraft and recover it on land. Whether a new US-developed capsule or the Soyuz is selected, it should be launched on an existing US expendable booster that has been "man-rated" for this purpose. After the US establishes a long-term solution for manned space access, the interim capsule capability could be retained as a complementary or backup manned space transportation system.

37. Develop a long-term capability for carrying astronauts into low earth orbit and returning them to earth. For a long-term solution to providing a US manned space access capability, the NASA Langley HL-20 Personnel Launch System is one possibility. It is designed to carry only astronauts, which represents a dramatic improvement over the manned Space Shuttle concept. However, many of the liabilities associated with the Shuttle Orbiter's runway recovery mode would also be present in the HL-20 design.

Another, and perhaps superior, alternative for a long-term solution would be to derive a piloted vertical takeoff/vertical landing single-stage-to-orbit (SSTO) transporter from the technologies being developed by the Ballistic Missile Defense Organization's (BMDO) Single Stage Rocket Technology program. The SSTO astronaut transporter would be totally dedicated to carrying personnel and the equipment specifically required by the crew during the flight, with no requirement to carry any additional payload or cargo. Designed to carry crews to and from space only, it would have little orbital loitering capability. Limiting the SSTO vehicle's lift requirement to short personnel transport trips would greatly reduce the technical challenges of the vehicle's inherently low structural fraction and high performance demands. The SSTO personnel transporter should be designed to be piloted, in a manner similar to the way large transport aircraft are designed (where constant human operator presence is assumed). By developing an operational SSTO system for astronaut transport, the US would be laying a strong technical foundation for follow-on SSTO cargo carriers that could someday operate with airline-like efficiencies and economies.

38. If the Space Shuttle is retained into the next century, cancel the Advanced Solid Rocket Motor (ASRM) program and replace it with a pressure-fed liquid booster strap-on for the Shuttle. It is worth remembering that the late Wernher von Braun once said "Solids are not safe for manned flight because they cannot be throttled or shutdown."[6] NASA should develop a simple, expendable, pressure-fed booster using liquid oxygen and RP-1 that would replace the Shuttle's existing Redesigned Solid Rocket Motor. To blunt political protests about the cancellation of the ASRM, consideration should be given to developing the new liquid strap-on at the ASRM site in northern Mississippi. The new liquid booster should be configured so that many of its elements could be applied to developing the first stage of an unmanned, expendable, pressure-fed launch vehicle. The liquid strap-on should be flight-tested as an unmanned stand-alone vehicle before being used on a Shuttle mission. The launch pad developed for the liquid strap-on flight tests should be designed to also accommodate (with minimum modifications) the liquid strap-on-derived unmanned expendable booster.

39. Develop and deploy a space station that will be fully operational before the end of the 1990s. An operational space station is key to allowing the US to continue a robust human space effort without depending on the Space Shuttle. If the US does not deploy a space station, NASA will be forced to continue depending on the Shuttle for manned orbital operations. The sooner the station is deployed, the sooner the US can start to use less expensive crew

launchers that are designed for transportation of people only. The Shuttle system can then be retired and its budget eliminated, since its capabilities as a payload and personnel launcher or as a manned orbital research facility will no longer be required.

40. Develop a long-range strategy for astronauts to provide maintenance, servicing, and enhancements for future earth-orbiting satellites. Satellites should be designed to accommodate orbital repair and modification, and with the assumption that an astronaut repair capability will be routinely available. Building satellites with modular remove-and-replace components will be made easier, since these space systems will be designed for inexpensive boosters with excess lift capacity and will, therefore, not be densely packaged.

To give astronauts access to the majority of its orbiting assets, the US must develop a manned orbital transfer and satellite repair vehicle. The space station would serve as an excellent basing and servicing node for such a vehicle. Using astronauts to routinely service spacecraft will take advantage of America's decades-long investment in human space flight technologies, and will provide a practical capability with a quantifiable benefit.

Keys to establishing this capability and making it cost-effective are:
- routine and inexpensive earth-to-orbit human transport;
- inexpensive unmanned MCD boosters that carry large, modular-designed spacecraft;
- an operational space station; and
- a simple and reliable manned orbital transfer vehicle.

Summary

Developing a launch system that is designed for minimum cost could reduce launch costs by an order of magnitude. Without major reductions in the cost of space access, the US faces the prospect of losing the commercial race for space and missing the opportunity to increase military and civil space exploitation. With major reductions, the US can lead an economic revolution that will dwarf the one created by the passenger jet. Joseph Shea, an MIT professor and NASA veteran, said, "I submit the aerospace industry does not know how to design to cost."[7] By designing and successfully operating a launch system for minimum cost, the US government and US industry can prove to the American people, and to the world, that it *can* be done.

Notes

1. R. C. Truax, "Cheap Transportation for Cheap Satellites" (Paper presented at the AIAA/DARPA Meeting on Lightweight Satellite Systems, Monterey, Calif., 4–6 August 1987), 6.
2. Gregg Easterbrook, "Big Dumb Rockets," *Newsweek,* 17 August 1987, 52.
3. Col Ralph Gajewski, comments at a Brilliant Eyes acquisition planning meeting, Space Systems Division, Los Angeles AFB, Calif., October 1991.

4. E. Keith, "Low Cost Space Transportation: Hurdles of Implementation" (Paper presented at the AIAA/SAE/ASME/ASEE 27th Joint Propulsion Conference, Sacramento, Calif., 24–26 June 1991), 10.

5. Robert C. Truax, "Shuttles - What Price Elegance?" *Astronautics and Aeronautics,* June 1970, 22–23.

6. Charles P. Vick, "Liquid Rocket Boosters: The Soviet Lesson," *Aerospace America,* February 1989, B68.

7. James R. Asker, "Station Redesign Team Gropes for Solutions," *Aviation Week & Space Technology,* 3 May 1993, 18.

Afterword

The concept of using minimum cost design (MCD) principles to develop low-cost space boosters is equally applicable to the development of low-cost ballistic missiles. In fact, since the ballistic missile is not required to place its payload into orbit, its performance requirements are generally less stressing than those of a launch vehicle. Consequently, a ballistic missile designed for minimum cost could be a very affordable and highly capable weapon system.

Given the military force structure implications of the post–cold war era, many would likely question the wisdom of developing a new ballistic missile, even if it could be done inexpensively. It is the very nature of the post–cold war era, however, that makes the idea of a low-cost ballistic missile attractive.

A low-cost, conventionally-armed, ballistic missile with intercontinental range would provide an extremely rapid, secure, and potent force projection capability. It could strike any potential adversary with virtual impunity.[1] Using current high-cost intercontinental ballistic missiles to carry conventional warheads would be impractical (unless they were surplus assets), but simple and inexpensive ICBMs could provide a powerful new military capability that would have profound doctrinal implications.[2]

On a darker note, the adversaries we might target with a conventional ICBM could also use simple design practices to build affordable and capable ballistic missiles. Even without nuclear, biological, or chemical warheads, an enemy that has a stockpile of conventionally-armed ICBMs could pose a very troubling military challenge. If, in December 1990, Iraq had possessed just one well-hidden ICBM armed with a conventional high explosive and had targeted it at New York City, the political support for, and the military planning and execution of, Operation Desert Storm would likely have been radically altered. The predicted accuracy of such a weapon would have been inconsequential.[3]

Ballistic missiles are easier to build than our aerospace heritage allows us to recognize—a reality that ought to provide a strong warning about the nature of future conflicts. A small country or group possessing a very limited ballistic missile capability could potentially hold the US hostage, both politically and militarily. This fact should be a compelling motivation for the United States to develop a capable ballistic missile defense for the 1990s and beyond.

Notes

1. Captain R. C. Truax, "The Global Ballistic Missile—A Weapon System for the Post Cold-War Era" (Paper presented at the US Naval Postgraduate School, Monterey, California, 12 March 1991), 1–3.

2. John R. London III, "The Ultimate Standoff Weapon," *Airpower Journal,* Summer 1993, 58–68.

3. Ibid, 67.